AF553883

HISTORY OF LITERATURE IN ENGLISH

P. K. Sinha
Jagdish K. Ghosh

History of Literature in English

Edition : 2025

ISBN 978-81-311-0325-8

Published by **:**
COMMONWEALTH PUBLISHERS (P) LTD.
4831/24, Govind Lane,
Ansari Road, Darya Ganj,
New Delhi - 110002
Ph. : 23272541, 23242541
e-mail : commonwealthpublishers2016@gmail.com

Distributed by :
ARJUN PUBLISHING HOUSE
4831/24, Govind Lane,
Ansari Road, Darya Ganj,
New Delhi - 110002
Ph. : 23272541, 23242541
e-mail : arjunbooks2001@gmail.com

Laser Typesetting by :
Dimple Computers
Delhi

Printed at :
Milan Enterprises
Delhi

Preface

English descends from the language spoken by the north Germanic tribes who settled in England from the 5th century A.D. onwards. They had no writing until they learned the Latin alphabet from Roman missionaries. The earliest written works in Old English were probably composed orally at first, and may have been passed on from speaker to speaker before being written. Old English literature is mostly chronicle and poetry—lyric, descriptive but chiefly narrative or epic. The English language and literature widespread gradually and English has become the universal language.

This book presents the whole splendid history of English literature from Anglo-Saxon times to the Postmodern Era. It aims to create or to encourage in every student the desire to read the best books, and to know literature itself rather than what has been written about literature. It interprets literature both personally and historically to show how a great book generally reflects not only the author's life and thought but also the spirit of the age and the ideals of the nation's history. By through study of each successive period, the book show how English literature has steadily developed from its first simple songs and stories to its present complexity in prose and poetry.

Authors

Contents

1

Introduction to English Literature.

English literature is the literature written in the English language, including literature composed in English by writers not necessarily from England; Joseph Conrad was born in Poland, Robert Burns was Scottish, James Joyce was Irish, Dylan Thomas was Welsh, Edgar Allan Poe was American, V.S. Naipaul was born in Trinidad, Vladimir Nabokov was Russian. In other words, English literature is as diverse as the varieties and dialects of English spoken around the world. In academia, the term often labels departments and programmes practising *English studies* in secondary and tertiary educational systems. Despite the variety of authors of English literature, works of William Shakespeare remain paramount throughout the English-speaking world.

Old English

The first works in English, written in Old English, appeared in the early Middle Ages (the oldest surviving text is Cædmon's *Hymn*). The oral tradition was very strong in the early English culture and most literary works were written to be performed. Epic poems were thus very popular and many, including

Beowulf, have survived to the present day in the rich corpus of Anglo-Saxon literature that closely resemble today's Icelandic, Norwegian, North Frisian and the Northumbrian and Scots English dialects of modern English. Much Old English verse in the extant manuscripts is probably a "milder" adaptation of the earlier Germanic war poems from the continent. When such poetry was brought to England it was still being handed down orally from one generation to another, and the constant presence of alliterative verse, or consonant rhyme helped the Anglo-Saxon peoples remember it. Such rhyme is a feature of Germanic languages and is opposed to vocalic or end-rhyme of Romance languages. But the first written literature dates to the early Christian monasteries founded by St. Augustine of Canterbury and his disciples and it is reasonable to believe that it was somehow adapted to suit to needs of Christian readers. Even without their crudest lines, the Old English war poems, and to a larger extent all Germanic war poems, still smell of blood feuds and their consonant rhymes sound like the smashing of swords under the gloomy northern sky: there is always a sense of imminent danger in the narratives. Sooner or later, all things must come to an end, as Beowulf eventually dies at the hands of the monsters he spends the tale fighting. The feelings of Beowulf that nothing lasts, that youth and joy will turn to death and sorrow entered Christianity and were to dominate the future landscape of English fiction.

Renaissance Literature

Following the introduction of a printing press into England by William Caxton in 1476, vernacular literature flourished. The Reformation inspired the production of vernacular liturgy which led to the Book of Common Prayer, a lasting influence on literary English language. The poetry, drama, and prose produced under both Queen Elizabeth I and King James I constitute what is today labelled as Early modern.

Early Modern Period

Elizabethan Era

The Elizabethan era saw a great flourishing of literature, especially in the field of drama. The Italian Renaissance had rediscovered the ancient Greek and Roman theatre, and this was instrumental in the development of the new drama, which was then beginning to evolve apart from the old mystery and miracle plays of the Middle Ages. The Italians were particularly inspired by Seneca (a major tragic playwright and philosopher, the tutor of Nero) and Plautus (its comic clichés, especially that of the boasting soldier had a powerful influence on the Renaissance and after). However, the Italian tragedies embraced a principle contrary to Seneca's ethics: showing blood and violence on the stage. In Seneca's plays such scenes were only acted by the characters. But the English playwrights were intrigued by Italian model: a conspicuous community of Italian actors had settled in London and Giovanni Florio had brought much of the Italian language and culture to England. It is also true that the Elizabethan Era was a very violent age and that the high incidence of political assassinations in Renaissance Italy (embodied by Niccolò Machiavelli's *The Prince*) did little to calm fears of popish plots. As a result, representing that kind of violence on the stage was probably more cathartic for the Elizabethan spectator. Following earlier

Elizabethan plays such as *Gorboduc* by Sackville & Norton and *The Spanish Tragedy* by Kyd that was to provide much material for *Hamlet*, William Shakespeare stands out in this period as a poet and playwright as yet unsurpassed. Shakespeare was not a man of letters by profession, and probably had only some grammar school education. He was neither a lawyer, nor an aristocrat as the "university wits" that had monopolised the English stage when he started writing. But he was very gifted and incredibly versatile, and he surpassed "professionals" as Robert Greene who mocked this "shake-scene" of low origins. Though most dramas met with great success, it is in his later years (marked by the early reign of James I) that he wrote what have been considered his greatest plays: *Hamlet, Romeo and Juliet, Othello, King Lear, Macbeth, Antony and Cleopatra*, and *The Tempest*, a tragicomedy that inscribes within the main drama a brilliant pageant to the new king. Shakespeare also popularized the English sonnet which made significant changes to Petrarch's model.

The sonnet was introduced into English by Thomas Wyatt in the early 16th century. Poems intended to be set to music as songs, such as by Thomas Campion, became popular as printed literature was disseminated more widely in households. Other important figures in Elizabethan theatre include Christopher Marlowe, Thomas Dekker, John Fletcher and Francis Beaumont. Had Marlowe (1564-1593) not been stabbed at twenty-nine in a tavern brawl, says Anthony Burgess, he might have rivalled, if not equalled Shakespeare himself for his poetic gifts. Remarkably, he was born only a few weeks before Shakespeare and must have known him well. Marlowe's subject matter, though, is different: it focuses more on the moral drama of the renaissance man than any other thing. Marlowe was fascinated and terrified by the new frontiers opened by modern science. Drawing on German lore, he introduced Dr. Faustus to England, a scientist and magician who is obsessed by the thirst of knowledge and the desire to push man's technological power to its limits. He acquires supernatural gifts that even allow him to go back in time and wed Helen of Troy, but at the end of his twenty-four years' covenant with the devil he has to surrender his soul to him. His dark heroes may have something of Marlowe himself, whose death remains a mystery. He was known for being an atheist, leading a lawless life, keeping many mistresses, consorting with ruffians: living the 'high life' of London's underworld. But many suspect that this might have been a cover-up for his activities as a secret agent for Elizabeth I, hinting that the 'accidental stabbing' might have been a premeditated assassination by the enemies of The Crown. Beaumont and Fletcher are less-known, but it is almost sure that they helped Shakespeare write some of his best dramas, and were quite popular at the time. It is also at this time that the city comedy genre develops. In the later 16th century English poetry was characterised by elaboration of language and extensive allusion to classical myths. The most important poets of this era include Edmund Spenser and Sir Philip Sidney. Elizabeth herself, a product of Renaissance humanism, produced occasional poems such as *On Monsieur's Departure.*

Jacobean Literature

After Shakespeare's death, the poet and dramatist Ben Jonson was the leading literary figure of the Jacobean era (The reign of James I). However, Jonson's aesthetics hark back to the Middle Ages rather than to the Tudor Era: his characters embody the theory of humours. According to this contemporary medical theory, behavioral differences result from a prevalence of one of the body's four "humours" (blood, phlegm, black bile, and yellow bile) over the other three; these humours correspond with the four elements of the universe: air, water, fire, and earth. This leads Jonson to exemplify such differences to the point of creating types, or clichés.

Jonson is a master of style, and a brilliant satirist. His *Volpone* shows how a group of scammers are fooled by a top con-artist, vice being punished by vice, virtue meting out its reward.

Others who followed Jonson's style include Beaumont and Fletcher, who wrote the brilliant comedy, *The Knight of the Burning Pestle,* a mockery of the rising middle class and especially of those nouveaux riches who pretend to dictate literary taste without knowing much literature at all. In the story, a couple of grocers wrangle with professional actors to have their illiterate son play a leading role in a drama. He becomes a knight-errant wearing, appropriately, a burning pestle on his shield. Seeking to win a princess' heart, the young man is ridiculed much in the way Don Quixote was. One of Beaumont and Fletcher's chief merits was that of realising how feudalism and chivalry had turned into snobbery and make-believe and that new social classes were on the rise.

Another popular style of theatre during Jacobean times was the revenge play, popularized by John Webster and Thomas Kyd. George Chapman wrote a couple of subtle revenge tragedies, but must be remembered chiefly on account of his famous translation of Homer, one that had a profound influence on all future English literature, even inspiring John Keats to write one of his best sonnets.

The King James Bible, one of the most massive translation projects in the history of English up to this time, was started in 1604 and completed in 1611. It represents the culmination of a tradition of Bible translation into English that began with the work of William Tyndale. It became the standard Bible of the Church of England, and some consider it one of the greatest literary works of all time. This project was headed by James I himself, who supervised the work of forty-seven scholars. Although many other translations into English have been made, some of which are widely considered more accurate, many aesthetically prefer the King James Bible, whose meter is made to mimic the original Hebrew verse.

Besides Shakespeare, whose figure towers over the early 1600s, the major poets of the early 17th century included John Donne and the other Metaphysical poets. Influenced by continental Baroque, and taking as his subject matter both Christian mysticism and eroticism, metaphysical poetry uses unconventional or "unpoetic" figures, such as a compass or a mosquito, to reach surprise effects. For example, in "A Valediction: Forbidding Mourning", one of Donne's Songs and Sonnets, the points of a compass represent two lovers, the woman who is home, waiting, being the centre, the farther point being her lover sailing away from her. But the larger the distance, the more the hands of the compass lean to each other: separation makes love grow fonder. The paradox or the oxymoron is a constant in this poetry whose fears and anxieties also speak of a world of spiritual certainties shaken by the modern discoveries of geography and science, one that is no longer the centre of the universe. Apart from the metaphysical poetry of Donne, the 17th century is also celebrated for its Baroque poetry. Baroque poetry served the same ends as the art of the period; the Baroque style is lofty, sweeping, epic, and religious. Many of these poets have an overtly Catholic sensibility (namely Richard Crashaw) and wrote poetry for the Catholic counter-Reformation in order to establish a feeling of supremacy and mysticism that would ideally persuade newly emerging Protestant groups back toward Catholicism.

Caroline and Cromwellian Literature

The turbulent years of the mid-17th century, during the reign of Charles I and the subsequent Commonwealth and Protectorate, saw a flourishing of political literature in English. Pamphlets written by sympathisers of every faction in the English civil war ran from vicious personal attacks and polemics, through many forms of propaganda, to high-minded schemes to reform the nation. Of the latter type, *Leviathan* by Thomas Hobbes would prove to be one of the most important works of British political philosophy. Hobbes's writings are some of the few political works from the era which are still regularly published while John Bramhall, who was Hobbes's chief critic, is largely forgotten. The period also saw a flourishing of news books, the precursors to the British newspaper, with journalists such as Henry Muddiman, Marchamont Needham, and John Birkenhead representing the views and activities of the contending parties. The frequent arrests of authors and the suppression of their works, with the consequence of foreign or underground printing, led to the proposal of a licensing system. The *Areopagitica*, a political pamphlet by John Milton, was written in opposition to licensing and is regarded as one of the most eloquent defenses of press freedom ever written.

Specifically in the reign of Charles I (1625-42), English Renaissance theatre experienced its concluding efflorescence. The last works of Ben Jonson appeared on stage and in print, along with the final generation of major voices in the drama of the age: John Ford, Philip Massinger, James Shirley, and Richard Brome. With the closure of the theatres at the start of the English Civil War in 1642, drama was suppressed for a generation, to resume only in the altered society of the English Restoration in 1660.

Other forms of literature written during this period are usually ascribed political subtexts, or their authors are grouped along political lines. The cavalier poets, active mainly before the civil war, owed much to the earlier school of metaphysical poets. The forced retirement of royalist officials after the execution of Charles I was a good thing in the case of Izaak Walton, as it gave him time to work on his book *The Compleat Angler*. Published in 1653, the book, ostensibly a guide to fishing, is much more: a meditation on life, leisure, and contentment. The two most important poets of Oliver Cromwell's England were Andrew Marvell and John Milton, with both producing works praising the new government; such as Marvell's *An Horatian Ode upon Cromwell's Return from Ireland*. Despite their republican beliefs they escaped punishment upon the Restoration of Charles II, after which Milton wrote some of his greatest poetical works (with any possible political message hidden under allegory). Thomas Browne was another writer of the period; a learned man with an extensive library, he wrote prolifically on science, religion, medicine and the esoteric.

Restoration Literature

Restoration literature includes both *Paradise Lost* and the Earl of Rochester's *Sodom,* the high spirited sexual comedy of *The Country Wife* and the moral wisdom of *Pilgrim's Progress.* It saw Locke's *Two Treatises on Government,* the founding of the Royal Society., the experiments of Robert Boyle and the holy meditations of Boyle, the hysterical attacks on theatres from Jeremy Collier, the pioneering of literary criticism from Dryden, and the first newspapers. The official break in literary culture caused by censorship and radically moralist standards under Cromwell's Puritan regime created a gap in literary tradition, allowing a seemingly fresh start for all forms of literature after the Restoration. During the Interregnum, the royalist forces attached to the court of Charles I went into exile with the twenty-year old Charles II. The nobility who travelled with Charles II were therefore lodged for over a decade in the midst of the continent's literary scene. Charles spent his time attending plays in France, and he developed a taste for Spanish plays. Those nobles living in Holland began to learn about mercantile exchange as well as the tolerant, rationalist prose debates that circulated in that officially tolerant nation.

The largest and most important poetic form of the era was satire. In general, publication of satire was done anonymously. There were great dangers in being associated with a satire. On the one hand, defamation law was a wide net, and it was difficult for a satirist to avoid prosecution if he were proven to have written a piece that seemed to criticize a noble. On the other hand, wealthy individuals would respond to satire as often as not by having the suspected poet physically attacked by ruffians. John Dryden was set upon for being merely *suspected* of having written the *Satire on Mankind*. A consequence of this anonymity is that a great many poems, some of them of merit, are unpublished and largely unknown.

Prose in the Restoration period is dominated by Christian religious writing, but the Restoration also saw the beginnings of two genres that would dominate later periods: fiction and journalism. Religious writing often strayed into political and economic writing, just as political and economic writing implied or directly addressed religion. The Restoration was also the time when John Locke wrote many of his philosophical works. Locke's empiricism was an attempt at understanding the basis of human understanding itself and thereby devising a proper manner for making sound decisions. These same scientific methods led Locke to his three *Treatises on Government*, which later inspired the thinkers in the American Revolution.

As with his work on understanding, Locke moves from the most basic units of society toward the more elaborate, and, like Thomas Hobbes, he emphasizes the plastic nature of the social contract. For an age that had seen absolute monarchy overthrown, democracy attempted, democracy corrupted, and limited monarchy restored, only a flexible basis for government could be satisfying. The Restoration moderated most of the more strident sectarian writing, but radicalism persisted after the Restoration. Puritan authors such as John Milton were forced to retire from public life or adapt, and those Digger, Fifth Monarchist, Leveller, Quaker, and Anabaptist authors who had preached against monarchy and who had participated directly in the regicide of Charles I were partially suppressed. Consequently, violent writings were forced underground, and many of those who had served in the Interregnum attenuated their positions in the Restoration. John Bunyan stands out beyond other religious authors of the period.

Bunyan's *The Pilgrim's Progress* is an allegory of personal salvation and a guide to the Christian life. Instead of any focus on eschatology or divine retribution, Bunyan instead writes about how the individual saint can prevail against the temptations of mind and body that threaten damnation. The book is written in a straightforward narrative and shows influence from both drama and biography, and yet it also shows an awareness of the grand allegorical tradition found in Edmund Spenser. During the Restoration period, the most common manner of getting news would have been a broadsheet publication. A single, large sheet of paper might have a written, usually partisan, account of an event. However, the period saw the beginnings of the first professional and periodical journalism in England. Journalism develops late, generally around the time of William of Orange's claiming the throne in 1689. Coincidentally or by design, England began to have newspapers just when William came to court from Amsterdam, where there were already newspapers being published.

It is impossible to satisfactorily date the beginning of the novel in English. However, long fiction and fictional biographies began to distinguish themselves from other forms in England during the Restoration period. An existing tradition of *Romance* fiction in France and Spain was popular in England. The "Romance" was considered a feminine form, and women were taxed with reading "novels" as a vice. One of the most significant figures in the rise of the novel in the Restoration period is Aphra Behn. She was not only the first professional female novelist, but she may be among the first professional novelists of either sex in England. Behn's most famous novel was *Oroonoko* in 1688. This was a biography of an entirely fictional African king who had been enslaved in Suriname. Behn's novels show the influence of tragedy and her experiences as a dramatist.

As soon as the previous Puritan regime's ban on public stage representations was lifted, the drama recreated itself quickly and abundantly. The most famous plays of the early Restoration period are the unsentimental or "hard" comedies of John Dryden, William Wycherley, and George Etherege, which reflect the atmosphere at Court, and celebrate an aristocratic macho lifestyle of unremitting sexual intrigue and conquest. After a sharp drop in both quality and quantity in the 1680s, the mid-90s saw a brief second flowering of the drama, especially comedy.

Comedies like William Congreve's *Love For Love* (1695) and *The Way of the World* (1700), and John Vanbrugh's *The Relapse* (1696) and *The Provoked Wife* (1697) were "softer" and more middle-class in ethos, very different from the aristocratic extravaganza twenty years earlier, and aimed at a wider audience. The playwrights of the 1690s set out to appeal to more socially mixed audiences with a strong middle-class element, and to female spectators, for instance by moving the war between the sexes from the arena of intrigue into that of marriage. The focus in comedy is less on young lovers outwitting the older generation, more on marital relations after the wedding bells.

Augustan Literature

The term Augustan literature derives from authors of the 1720s and 1730's themselves, who responded to a term that George I of England preferred for himself. While George I meant the title to reflect his might, they instead saw in it a reflection of Ancient Rome's transition from rough and ready literature to highly political and highly polished literature. Because of the aptness of the metaphor, the period from 1689 - 1750 was called "the Augustan Age" by critics throughout the 18th century (including Voltaire and Oliver Goldsmith). The literature of the period is overtly political and thoroughly aware of critical dictates for literature. It is an age of exuberance and scandal, of enormous energy and inventiveness and outrage, that reflected an era when English, Scottish, and Irish people found themselves in the midst of an expanding economy, lowering barriers to education, and the stirrings of the Industrial Revolution.

The most outstanding poet of the age is Alexander Pope, but Pope's excellence is partially in his constant battle with other poets, and his serene, seemingly neo-Classical approach to poetry is in competition with highly idiosyncratic verse and strong competition from such poets as Ambrose Philips. It was during this time that James Thomson produced his melancholy *The Seasons* and Edward Young wrote *Night Thoughts.* It is also the era that saw a serious competition over the proper model for the pastoral. In criticism, poets struggled with a doctrine of *decorum,* of matching proper words with proper sense and of achieving a diction that matched the gravity of a subject. At the same time, the mock-heroic was at its zenith. Pope's *Rape of the Lock* and *The Dunciad* are still the greatest mock-heroic poems ever written.

In prose, the earlier part of the period was overshadowed by the development of the English essay. Joseph Addison and Richard Steele's *The Spectator* established the form of the British periodical essay, inventing the pose of the detached observer of human life who can meditate upon the world without advocating any specific changes in it. However, this was also the time when the English novel, first emerging in the Restoration, developed into a major artform. Daniel Defoe turned from journalism and writing criminal lives for the press to writing fictional criminal lives with *Roxana* and *Moll Flanders.* He also wrote a fictional treatment of the travels of Alexander Selkirk called *Robinson Crusoe* (1719). The novel would benefit indirectly from a tragedy of the stage, and in mid-century many more authors would begin to write novels.

If Addison and Steele overawed one type of prose, then Jonathan Swift did another. Swift's prose style is unmannered and direct, with a clarity that few contemporaries matched. He was a profound skeptic about the modern world, but he was similarly profoundly distrustful of nostalgia. He saw in history a record of lies and vanity, and he saw in the present a madness of vanity and lies. Core Christian values were essential, but these values had to be muscular and assertive and developed by constant rejection of the games of confidence men and their gullies. Swift's *A Tale of a Tub* announced his skeptical analysis of the claims of the modern world, and his later prose works, such as his war with Patridge the astrologer, and most of all his derision of pride in *Gulliver's Travels* left only the individual in constant fear and humility safe. After his "exile" to Ireland, Swift reluctantly began defending the Irish people from the predations of colonialism. His *A Modest Proposal* and the Drapier Letters provoked riots and arrests, but Swift, who had no love of Irish Roman Catholics, was outraged by the abuses and barbarity he saw around him.

Drama in the early part of the period featured the last plays of John Vanbrugh and William Congreve, both of whom carried on the Restoration comedy with some alterations. However, the majority of stagings were of lower farces and much more serious and domestic tragedies. George Lillo and Richard Steele both produced highly moral forms of tragedy, where the characters and the concerns of the characters were wholly middle class or working class. This reflected a marked change in the audience for plays, as royal patronage was no longer the important part of theatrical success.

Additionally, Colley Cibber and John Rich began to battle each other for greater and greater spectacles to present on stage. The figure of Harlequin was introduced, and pantomime theatre began to be staged. This "low" comedy was quite popular, and the plays became tertiary to the staging. Opera also began to be popular in London, and there was significant literary resistance to this Italian incursion. This trend was broken only by a few attempts at a new type of comedy. Pope and John Arbuthnot and John Gay attempted a play entitled *Three Hours After Marriage* that failed. In 1728, however, John Gay returned to the playhouse with *The Beggar's Opera.* Gay's opera was in English and retold the story of Jack Sheppard and Jonathan Wild. However, it seemed to be an allegory for Robert Walpole and the directors of the South Sea Company, and so Gay's follow up opera was banned without performance. The Licensing Act 1737 brought an abrupt halt to much of the period's drama, as the theatres were once again brought under state control.

An effect of the Licensing Act was to cause more than one aspiring playwright to switch over to writing novels. Henry Fielding began to write prose satire and novels after his plays could not pass the censors. Henry Brooke also turned to novels. In the interim, Samuel Richardson had produced a novel intended to counter the deleterious effects of novels in *Pamela, or Virtue Rewarded* (1749). Henry Fielding attacked the absurdity of this novel with two of his own works, *Joseph Andrews* and *Shamela,* and then countered Richardson's *Clarissa* with *Tom Jones.*

Henry Mackenzie wrote *The Man of Feeling* and indirectly began the sentimental novel. Laurence Sterne attempted a Swiftian novel with a unique perspective on the impossibility of biography (the model for most novels up to that point) and understanding with *Tristram Shandy,* even as his detractor Tobias Smollett elevated the picaresque novel with his works. Each of these novels represents a formal and thematic divergence from the others. Each novelist was in dialogue and competition with the others, and, in a sense, the novel established itself as a diverse and open-formed genre in this explosion of creativity. The most lasting effects of the experimentation would be the psychological realism of Richardson, the bemused narrative voice of Fielding, and the sentimentality of Brooke.

18th Century Literature

During the Age of Sensibility, literature reflected the worldview of the Age of Enlightenment (or Age of Reason)–a rational and scientific approach to religious, social, political, and economic issues that promoted a secular view of the world and a general sense of progress and perfectibility. Led by the philosophers who were inspired by the discoveries of the previous century and the writings of Descartes, Locke and Bacon.

They sought to discover and to act upon universally valid principles governing humanity, nature, and society. They variously attacked spiritual and scientific authority, dogmatism, intolerance, censorship, and economic and social restraints. They considered the state the proper and rational instrument of progress. The extreme rationalism and skepticism of the age led naturally to deism; the same qualities played a part in bringing the later reaction of romanticism. The Encyclopédie of Denis Diderot epitomized the spirit of the age.

During the end of the 19th century Ann Radcliffe would be the pioneer of the Gothic Novel. Her novel, The Castles of Athlin and Dunbayne in 1789, sets the tone for the majority of her work, which tended to involve innocent, but heroic young women who find themselves in gloomy, mysterious castles ruled by even more mysterious barons with dark pasts. The Romance of the Forest would follow and her most famous novel, The Mysteries of Udolpho, is considered the ultimate Gothic Novel of the late 18th century. Increased emphasis on instinct and feeling, rather than judgment and restraint. A growing sympathy for the Middle Ages during the Age of Sensibility sparked an interest in medieval ballads and folk literature. Ann Radcliffe's novel would embody all of this in The Mysteries of Udolpho.

Romanticism

The changing landscape of Britain brought about by the steam engine has two major outcomes: the boom of industrialism with the expansion of the city, and the consequent depopulation of the countryside as a result of the enclosures, or privatisation of pastures. Most peasants poured into the city to work in the new factories.

This abrupt change is revealed by the change of meaning in five key words: industry (once meaning "creativity"), democracy (once disparagingly used as "mob rule"), class (from now also used with a social connotation), art (once just meaning "craft"), culture (once only belonging to farming).

But the poor condition of workers, the new class-conflicts and the pollution of the environment causes a reaction to urbanism and industrialisation prompting poets to rediscover the beauty and value of nature. Mother earth is seen as the only source of wisdom, the only solution to the ugliness caused by machines.

The superiority of nature and instinct over civilisation had been preached by Jean Jacques Rousseau and his message was picked by almost all European poets. The first in England were the Lake Poets, a small group of friends including William Wordsworth and Samuel Taylor Coleridge. These early

Romantic Poets brought a new emotionalism and introspection, and their emergence is marked by the first romantic Manifesto in English literature, the "Preface to the Lyrical Ballads". This collection was mostly contributed by Wordsworth, although Coleridge must be credited for his long and impressive *Rime of the Ancient Mariner,* a tragic ballad about the survival of one sailor through a series of supernatural events on his voyage through the south seas which involves the slaying of an albatross, the death of the rest of the crew, a visit from Death and his mate, Life-in-Death, and the eventual redemption of the Mariner.

Coleridge and Wordsworth, however, understood romanticism in two entirely different ways: while Coleridge sought to make the supernatural "real" (much like sci-fi movies use special effects to make unlikely plots believable), Wordsworth sought to stir the imagination of readers through his down-to-earth characters taken from real life (for eg. in "The Idiot Boy"), or the beauty of the Lake District that largely inspired his production (as in "Lines Composed a Few Miles Above Tintern Abbey").

The "Second generation" of Romantic poets includes Lord Byron, Percy Bysshe Shelley, Mary Shelley and John Keats. Byron, however, was still influenced by 18th-century satirists and was, perhaps the least 'romantic' of the three. His amours with a number of prominent but married ladies was also a way to voice his dissent on the hypocrisy of a high society that was only apparently religious but in fact largely libertine, the same that had derided him for being physically impaired. His first trip to Europe resulted in the first two cantos of Childe Harold's

Pilgrimage, a mock-heroic epic of a young man's adventures in Europe but also a sharp satire against London society. Despite *Childe Harold*'s success on his return to England, accompanied by the publication of *The Giaour* and *The Corsair* his alleged incestuous affair with his half-sister Augusta Leigh in 1816 actually forced him to leave England for good and seek asylum on the continent. Here he joined Percy Bysshe Shelley, his wife Mary, with his secretary Dr. John Polidori on the shores of Lake Geneva during the 'year without a summer' of 1816.

Although his is just a short story, Polidori must be credited for introducing The Vampyre, conceived from the same competition which spawned Mary Shelley's *Frankenstein,* to English literature. Percy, like Mary, had much in common with Byron; he was an aristocrat from a famous and ancient family, had embraced atheism and free-thinking and, like him, was fleeing from scandal in England.

Shelley had been expelled from college for openly declaring his atheism. He had married a 16-year-old girl, Harriet Westbrook whom he had abandoned soon after for Mary (Harriet took her own life after that). Harriet did not embrace his ideals of free love and anarchism, and was not as educated as to contribute to literary debate. Mary was different: the daughter of philosopher and revolutionary William Godwin, she was intellectually more of an equal, shared some of his ideals and was a feminist like her late mother, Mary Wollstonecraft, author of *Vindication of the Rights of Women.*

One of Percy Shelley's most prominent works is the *Ode to the West Wind.* Despite his apparent refusal to believe in God, this poem is considered a homage to pantheism, the recognition of a spiritual presence in nature.

Mary Shelley did not go down in history for her poetry, but for giving birth to science fiction: the plot for the novel is said to have come from a nightmare during stormy nights on Lake Geneva in the company of Percy Shelley, Lord Byron, and John Polidori. Her idea of making a body with human parts stolen from different corpses and then animating it with electricity was perhaps influenced by Alessandro Volta's invention and Luigi Galvani's experiments with dead frogs. Frankenstein's chilling tale also suggests modern organ transplants, tissue regeneration, reminding us of the moral issues raised by today's medicine. But the creature of Frankenstein is incredibly romantic as well. Although "the monster" is intelligent, good and loving, he is shunned by everyone because of his ugliness and deformity, and the desperation and envy that result from social exclusion turn him against the very man who created him.

John Keats did not share Byron's and Shelley's extremely revolutionary ideals, but his cult of pantheism is as important as Shelley's. Keats was in love with the ancient stones of the Parthenon that Lord Elgin had brought to England from Greece, also known as the Elgin Marbles). He celebrates ancient Greece: the beauty of free, youthful love couples here with that of classical art. Keats's great attention to art, especially in his *Ode on a Grecian Urn* is quite new in romanticism, and it will inspire Walter Pater's and then Oscar Wilde's belief in the absolute value of art as independent from aesthetics.

Some rightly think that the most popular novelist of the era was Sir Walter Scott, whose grand historical romances inspired a generation of painters, composers, and writers throughout Europe. His most remembered work, Ivanhoe, continues to be studied to this day.

In retrospect, we now look back to Jane Austen, who wrote novels about the life of the landed gentry, seen from a woman's point of view, and wryly focused on practical social issues, especially marriage and choosing the right partner in life, with love being above all else. Her most important and popular novel, Pride and Prejudice, would set the model for all Romance Novels to follow. Jane Austen created the ultimate hero and heroine in Darcy and Elizabeth, who must overcome their own stubborn pride and the prejudices they have toward each other, in order to come to a middle ground, where they finally realize their love for one another. In her novels, Jane Austen brings to light the hardships women faced, who usually did not inherit money, could not work and where their only chance in life depended on the man they married. She brought to light not only the difficulties women faced in her day, but also what was expected of men and of the careers they had to follow. This she does with wit and humour and with endings where all characters, good or bad, receive exactly what they deserve.

Poet, painter and printmaker William Blake is usually included among the English Romanticists, though his visionary work is much different from that of the others discussed in this section.

Victorian Literature

It was in the Victorian era (1837-1901) that the novel became the leading form of literature in English. Most writers were now more concerned to meet the tastes of a large middle class reading public than to please aristocratic patrons. The best known works of the era include the emotionally powerful works of the Brontë sisters; the satire *Vanity Fair* by William Makepeace Thackeray; the realist novels of George Eliot; and Anthony Trollope's insightful portrayals of the lives of the landowning and professional classes.

Charles Dickens emerged on the literary scene in the 1830s, confirming the trend for serial publication. Dickens wrote vividly about London life and the struggles of the poor, but in a good-humoured fashion which was acceptable to readers of all classes. His early works such as the *Pickwick Papers* are masterpieces of comedy. Later his works became darker, without losing his genius for caricature.

The Bronte sisters were English writers of the 1840s and 1850s. Their novels caused a sensation when they were first published and were subsequently accepted into the canon of great English literature. They had written compulsively from early childhood and were first published, at their own expense, in 1846 as poets under the pseudonyms Currer, Ellis and Acton Bell. The book attracted little attention, selling only two copies. The sisters returned to prose, producing a novel each in the following year. Charlotte's Jane Eyre, Emily's Wuthering Heights and Anne's Agnes Grey were released in 1847 after their long search to secure publishers.

An interest in rural matters and the changing social and economic situation of the countryside may be seen in the novels of Thomas Hardy, Elizabeth Cleghorn Gaskell, and others. Leading poetic figures included Alfred Tennyson, Robert Browning, Elizabeth Barrett Browning, Matthew Arnold, Dante Gabriel Rossetti, and Christina Rossetti.

Modernist Literature

The movement known as English literary modernism grew out of a general sense of disillusionment with Victorian era attitudes of certainty, conservatism, and objective truth. The movement was greatly influenced by the ideas of Romanticism, Karl Marx's political writings, and the psychoanalytic theories of subconscious Sigmund Freud. The continental art movements of Impressionism, and later Cubism, were also important inspirations for modernist writers.

Although literary modernism reached its peak between the First and Second World Wars, the earliest examples of the movement's attitudes appeared in the mid to late nineteenth century. Gerard Manley Hopkins, A. E. Housman, and the poet and novelist Thomas Hardy represented a few of the major early modernists writing in England during the Victorian period.The first decades of the twentieth century saw several major works of modernism published, including the seminal short story collection *Dubliners* by James Joyce, Joseph Conrad's *Heart of Darkness,* and the poetry and drama of William Butler Yeats.

Important novelists between the World Wars included Virginia Woolf, E. M. Forster, Evelyn Waugh, P.G. Wodehouse and D. H. Lawrence. T. S. Eliot was the preeminent English poet of the period. Across the Atlantic writers like William Faulkner, Ernest Hemingway, and the poets Wallace Stevens and Robert Frost developed a more American take on the modernist aesthetic in their work.Perhaps the most contentiously important figure in the development of the modernist movement was the American poet Ezra Pound. Credited with "discovering" both T. S. Eliot and James Joyce, whose stream of consciousness novel

Ulysses is considered to be one of the century's greatest literary achievements, Pound also advanced the cause of imagism and free verse, forms which would dominate English poetry into the twenty-first century.

Gertrude Stein, an American expat, was also an enormous literary force during this time period, famous for her line "Rose is a rose is a rose is a rose."Other notable writers of this period included H.D., Marianne Moore, Elizabeth Bishop, W. H. Auden, Vladimir Nabokov, William Carlos Williams, Ralph Ellison, Dylan Thomas, R.S. Thomas and Graham Greene. However, some of these writers are more closely associated with what has become known as post-modernism, a term often used to encompass the diverse range of writers who succeeded the modernists.

Post-modern Literature

The term Postmodern literature is used to describe certain tendencies in post-World War II literature. It is both a continuation of the experimentation championed by writers of the modernist period (relying heavily, for example, on fragmentation, paradox, questionable narrators, etc.) and a reaction against Enlightenment ideas implicit in Modernist literature. Postmodern literature, like postmodernism as a whole, is difficult to define and there is little agreement on the exact characteristics, scope, and importance of postmodern literature.

2

Old English Literature

Old English literature encompasses literature written in Old English (also called Anglo-Saxon), during the 600-year Anglo-Saxon period of England, from the mid-5th century to the Norman Conquest of 1066. These works include genres such as epic poetry, hagiography, sermons, Bible translations, legal works, chronicles, riddles, and others. In all there are about 400 surviving manuscripts from the period, a significant corpus of both popular interest and specialist research.

Among the most important works of this period is the poem *Beowulf,* which has achieved national epic status in Britain. The *Anglo-Saxon Chronicle* otherwise proves significant to study of the era, preserving a chronology of early English history, while the poem *Cædmon's Hymn* from the 7th century survives as the oldest extant work of literature in English.

Anglo-Saxon literature has gone through different periods of research—in the 19th and early 20th centuries the focus was on the Germanic roots of English, later the literary merits were emphasized, and today the focus is upon paleography and the physical manuscripts themselves more generally: scholars debate such issues as dating, place of origin, authorship, and the connections between Anglo-Saxon culture and the rest of Europe in the Middle Ages

A large number of manuscripts remain from the 600-year Anglo-Saxon period, with most written during the last 300 years (9th–11th century), in both Latin and the vernacular. Old English literature is among the oldest vernacular languages to be written down. Old English began, in written form, as a practical necessity in the aftermath of the Danish invasions—church officials were concerned that because of the drop in Latin literacy no one could read their work. Likewise King Alfred the Great (849–899), wanting to restore English culture, lamented the poor state of Latin education:

> *"So general was [educational] decay in England that there were very few on this side of the Humber who could...translate a letter from Latin into English; and I believe there were not many beyond the Humber"*
>
> (Pastoral Care, introduction).

King Alfred proposed that students be educated in Old English, and those who excelled would go on to learn Latin. In this way many of the texts that have survived are typical teaching and student-oriented texts.

Extant Manuscripts

In total thère are about 400 surviving manuscripts containing Old English text, 189 of them considered major. These manuscripts have been highly prized by collectors since the 16th century, both for their historic value and for their aesthetic beauty of uniformly spaced letters and decorative elements.

There are four major manuscripts:

— The *Junius manuscript*, also known as the *Caedmon manuscript*, which is an illustrated poetic anthology.

— The *Exeter Book*, also an anthology, located in the Exeter Cathedral since it was donated there in the 11th century.

— The *Vercelli Book*, a mix of poetry and prose; how it came to be in Vercelli, Italy, no one knows, and is a matter of debate.

— The *Nowell Codex*, also a mixture of poetry and prose. This is the manuscript that contains Beowulf.

Research in the 20th century has focused on dating the manuscripts (19th-century scholars tended to date them older than modern scholarship has found); locating where the manuscripts were created—there were seven major scriptoria from which they originate: Winchester, Exeter, Worcester, Abingdon, Durham, and two Canterbury houses Christ Church and St. Augustine; and identifying the regional dialects used: Northumbrian, Mercian, Kentish, West Saxon.

Not all of the texts can be fairly called literature; some are merely lists of names or aborted pen trials. However those that can present a sizable body of work, listed here in descending order of quantity: sermons and saints' lives (the most numerous), biblical translations; translated Latin works of the early Church Fathers; Anglo-Saxon chronicles and narrative history works; laws, wills and other legal works; practical works on grammar, medicine, geography; lastly, but not least important, poetry.

Nearly all Anglo-Saxon authors are anonymous, with some exceptions.

Old English Poetry

Old English poetry is of two types, the heroic Germanic pre-Christian and the Christian. It has survived for the most part in the four major manuscripts.

The Anglo-Saxons left behind no poetic rules or explicit system; everything we know about the poetry of the period is based on modern analysis. The first widely accepted theory was constructed by Eduard Sievers (1885). He distinguished five distinct alliterative patterns. The theory of John C. Pope (1942), which uses musical notation to track the verse patterns, has been accepted in some quarters;to be hotly debated.

The most popular and well-known understanding of Old English poetry continues to be Sievers' alliterative verse. The system is based upon accent, alliteration, the quantity of vowels, and patterns of syllabic accentuation. It consists of five permutations on a base verse scheme; any one of the five types can be used in any verse. The system was inherited from and exists in one form or another in all of the older Germanic languages. Two poetic figures commonly found in Old English poetry are the kenning, an often formulaic phrase that describes one thing in terms of another (e.g. in Beowulf, the sea is called the *whale's road*) and litotes, a dramatic understatement employed by the author for ironic effect.

Roughly, Old English verse lines are divided in half by a pause; this pause is termed a "caesura." Each half-line has two stressed syllables. The first stressed syllable of the second half-line should alliterate with one or both of the stressed syllables of the first half-line (meaning, of course, that the stressed syllables in the first half-line could alliterate with each other). The second stressed syllable of the second half-line should not alliterate with either of the stressed syllables of the first half.

Old English poetry was an oral craft, and our understanding of it in written form is incomplete; for example, we know that the poet (referred to as the *Scop*) could be accompanied by a harp, and there may be other aural traditions of which we are not aware.

Poetry represents the smallest amount of the surviving Old English text, but Anglo-Saxon culture had a rich tradition of oral storytelling, of which little has survived in written form.

The Poets

Most Old English poets are anonymous; twelve are known by name from Medieval sources, but only four of those are known by their vernacular works to us today with any certainty: Caedmon, Bede, Alfred, and Cynewulf. Of these, only Caedmon, Bede, and Alfred have known biographies.

Caedmon is the best-known and considered the father of Old English poetry. He lived at the abbey of Whitby in Northumbria in the 7th century. Only a single nine line poem remains, called *Hymn*, which is also the oldest surviving text in English:

Aldhelm, bishop of Sherborne (d. 709), is known through William of Malmesbury who said he performed secular songs while accompanied by a harp. Much of his Latin prose has survived, but none of his Old English remains.

Cynewulf has proven to be a difficult figure to identify, but recent research suggests he was from the early part of the 9th century to which a number of poems are attributed including *The Fates of the Apostles* and *Elene* (both found in the Vercelli Book), and *Christ II* and *Juliana* (both found in the Exeter Book).

Heroic Poems

The Old English poetry which has received the most attention deals with the Germanic heroic past. The longest (3,182 lines), and most important, is *Beowulf,* which appears in the damaged Nowell Codex. The poem tells the story of the legendary Geatish hero Beowulf who is the title character. The story is set in Scandinavia, in Sweden and Denmark, and the tale likewise probably is of Scandinavian origin. The story is biographical and sets the tone for much of the rest of Old English poetry. It has achieved national epic status, on the same level as the Iliad, and is of interest to historians, anthropologists, literary critics, and students the world over.

Beyond *Beowulf,* other heroic poems exist. Two heroic poems have survived in fragments: *The Fight at Finnsburh,* a retelling of one of the battle scenes in *Beowulf* (although this relation to *Beowulf* is much debated), and *Waldere,* a version of the events of the life of Walter of Aquitaine.

Two other poems mention heroic figures: *Widsith* is believed to be very old in parts, dating back to events in the 4th century concerning Eormanric and the Goths, and contains a catalogue of names and places associated with valiant deeds. *Deor* is a lyric, in the style of *Consolation of Philosophy,* applying examples of famous heroes, including Weland and Eormanric, to the narrator's own case.

The *Anglo-Saxon Chronicle* contains various heroic poems inserted throughout. The earliest from 937 is called *The Battle of Brunanburh,* which celebrates the victory of King Athelstan over the Scots and Norse. There are five shorter poems: capture of the Five Boroughs (942); coronation of King Edgar (973); death of King Edgar (975); death of Prince Alfred (1036); and death of King Edward the Confessor (1065).

The 325 line poem *The Battle of Maldon* celebrates Earl Byrhtnoth and his men who fell in battle against the Vikings in 991. It is considered one of the finest, but both the beginning and end are missing and the only manuscript was destroyed in a fire in 1731. A well-known speech is near the end of the poem:

> Old English heroic poetry was handed down orally from generation to generation. As Christianity began to appear, retellers often recast the tales of Christianity into the older heroic stories.

Elegiac Poetry

Related to the heroic tales are a number of short poems from the Exeter Book which have come to be described as "elegies" or "wisdom poetry". They are lyrical and Boethian in their description of the up and down fortunes of life. Gloomy in mood is *The Ruin,* which tells of the decay of a once glorious city of Roman Britain (cities in Britain fell into decline after the Romans departed in the early 5th c., as the early English continued to live their rural life), and *The Wanderer,* in which an older man talks about an attack that happened in his youth, where his close friends and kin were all killed; memories of the slaughter have remained with him all his life. He questions the wisdom of the impetuous decision to engage a possibly superior fighting force: the wise man engages in warfare to *preserve* civil society, and must not rush into battle but seek out allies when the odds may be against him. This poet finds little glory in bravery for bravery's sake. *The Seafarer* is the story of a somber exile from home on the sea, from which the only hope of redemption is the joy of heaven. Other wisdom poems include *Wulf and Eadwacer, The Wife's Lament,* and *The Husband's Message.* King Alfred the Great wrote a wisdom poem over the course of his reign based loosely on the neoplatonic philosophy of Boethius called the *Lays of Boethius.*

Classical and Latin Poetry

Several Old English poems are adaptations of late classical philosophical texts. The longest is a 10th century translation of Boethius' *Consolation of Philosophy* contained in the Cotton manuscript. Another is *The Phoenix* in the Exeter Book, an allegorization of the *De ave phoenice* by Lactantius.

Christian Poetry

Saints' Lives

The Vercelli Book and Exeter Book contain four long narrative poems of saints' lives, or hagiography. In Vercelli are *Andreas* and *Elene* and in Exeter are *Guthlac* and *Juliana.*

Andreas is 1,722 lines long and is the closest of the surviving Old English poems to *Beowulf* in style and tone. It is the story of Saint Andrew and his journey to rescue Saint Matthew from the Mermedonians. *Elene* is the story of Saint Helena (mother of Constantine) and her discovery of the True Cross. The cult of the True Cross was popular in Anglo-Saxon England and this poem was instrumental. *Guthlac* is actually two poems about English Saint Guthlac (7th century). *Juliana* is the story of the virgin martyr Juliana of Nicomedia.

Biblical Paraphrases

The Junius manuscript contains three paraphrases of Old Testament texts. These were re-wordings of Biblical passages in Old English, not exact translations, but paraphrasing, sometimes into beautiful poetry in its own right. The first and longest is of *Genesis,* the second is of *Exodus* and the third is *Daniel.* The fourth and last poem, *Christ and Satan,* which is contained in the second part of the Junius manuscript, does not paraphrase any particular biblical book, but retells a number of episodes from both the Old and New Testament.

The Nowell Codex contains a Biblical poetic paraphrase, which appears right after *Beowulf,* called *Judith,* a retelling of the story of Judith. This is not to be confused with Ælfric's homily *Judith,* which retells the same Biblical story in alliterative prose.

Old English translations of Psalms 51-150 have been preserved, following a prose version of the first 50 Psalms. It is believed there was once a complete psalter based on evidence, but only the first 150 have survived. There are a number of verse translations of the Gloria in Excelsis, the Lord's Prayer, and the Apostles' Creed, as well as a number of hymns and proverbs.

Christian Poems

In addition to Biblical paraphrases are a number of original religious poems, mostly lyrical (non-narrative). The Exeter Book contains a series of poems entitled

Christ, sectioned into *Christ I, Christ II* and *Christ III*. Considered one of the most beautiful of all Old English poems is *Dream of the Rood*, contained in the Vercelli Book. It is a dream vision of Christ on the cross, with the cross personified, speaking thus: The dreamer resolves to trust in the cross, and the dream ends with a vision of heaven.

There are a number of religious debate poems. The longest is *Christ and Satan* in the Junius manuscript, it deals with the conflict between Christ and Satan during the forty days in the desert. Another debate poem is *Solomon and Saturn*, surviving in a number of textual fragments, Saturn is portrayed as a magician debating with the wise king Solomon.

Other Poems

Other poetic forms exist in Old English including riddles, short verses, gnomes, and mnemonic poems for remembering long lists of names.

The Exeter Book has a collection of ninety-five riddles. Some of them play on obscene interpretations of the object described. The answers are not supplied, a number of them to this day remain a puzzle.There are short verses found in the margins of manuscripts which offer practical advice There are remedies against the loss of cattle, how to deal with a delayed birth, swarms of bees, etc.. the longest is called *Nine Herbs Charm* and is probably of pagan origin.

There are a group of mnemonic poems designed to help memorise lists and sequences of names and to keep objects in order. These poems are named *Menologium, The Fates of the Apostles, The Rune Poem, The Seasons for Fasting*, and the *Instructions for Christians*.

Simile and Metaphor

Anglo-Saxon poetry is marked by the comparative rarity of similes. This is a particular feature of Anglo-Saxon verse style, and is a consequence of both its structure and the rapidity with which images are deployed, to be unable to effectively support the expanded simile. As an example of this, the epic Beowulf contains at best five similes, and these are of the short variety. This can be contrasted sharply with the strong and extensive dependence that Anglo-Saxon poetry has upon metaphor, particularly that afforded by the use of kennings. The most prominent example of this in The Wanderer is the reference to battle as a "storm of spears". This reference to battle gives us an opportunity to see how Anglo-Saxons viewed battle:

> As unpredictable, chaotic, violent, and perhaps even a function of nature. It is with these stylistic and thematic elements in mind, that one should first approach Anglo-Saxon poetry.

Caesura

Old English poetry is also commonly marked by the German caesura or pause. In addition to setting pace for the line the caesura also grouped each line into two couplets.

Old English Poetry and Oral Tradition

The hypotheses of Milman Parry and Albert Lord on the Homeric Question came to be applied (by Parry and Lord, but also by Francis Magoun) to verse written in Old English. That is, the theory proposes that certain features of at least some of the poetry may be explained by positing Oral-Formulaic Composition. While Anglo-Saxon (Old English) epic poetry may bear some resemblance to Ancient Greek epics such as the *Iliad* and *Odyssey*, the question of if and how Anglo-Saxon poetry was passed down through an oral tradition remains a subject of debate, and the question for any particular poem unlikely to be answered with perfect certainty.

Parry and Lord had already demonstrated the density of metrical formulas in Ancient Greek, and observed that the same phenomenon was apparent in the Old English alliterative line:

> In addition to verbal formulas, many themes have been shown to appear among the various works of Anglo-Saxon literature. The theory proposes to explain this fact by suggesting that the poetry was composed of formulae and themes from a stock common to the poetic profession, as well as literary passages composed by individual artists in a more modern sense. Larry Benson introduced the concept of "written-formulaic" to describe the status of some Anglo-Saxon poetry which, while demonstrably written, contains evidence of oral influences, including heavy reliance on formulas and themes Frequent oral-formulaic themes in Old English poetry include "Beasts of Battle" and the "Cliff of Death". The former, for example, is characterized by the mention of ravens, eagles, and wolves preceding particularly violent depictions of battle.

Crowne drew on examples of the theme's appearance in twelve Anglo-Saxon texts, including one occurrence in Beowulf. It was also observed in other works of Germanic origin, Middle English poetry, and even an Icelandic prose saga. John Richardson held that the schema was so general as to apply to virtually any character at some point in the narrative, and thought it an instance of the "threshhold" feature of Joseph

Campbell's Hero's Journey monomyth. J.A. Dane, in an article characterized as "polemics without rigor" claimed that the appearance of the theme in Ancient Greek poetry, a tradition without known connection to the Germanic, invalidated the notion of "an autonomous theme in the baggage of an oral poet." Foley's response was that Dane misunderstood the nature of oral tradition, and that in fact the appearance of the theme in other cultures evidenced its traditionality.

Old English Prose

The amount of surviving Old English prose is much greater than the amount of poetry. Of the surviving prose, sermons and Latin translations of religious works are the majority. Old English prose first appears in the 9th century, and continues to be recorded through the 12th century as the last generation of scribes, trained as boys in the standardized West Saxon before the Conquest, died as old men.

Christian Prose

The most widely known author of Old English was King Alfred, who translated many books from Latin into Old English. These translations include: Gregory the Great's *The Pastoral Care,* a manual for priests on how to conduct their duties; *The Consolation of Philosophy* by Boethius; and *The Soliloquies* of Saint Augustine. Alfred was also responsible for a translation of the fifty Psalms into Old English. Other important Old English translations completed by associates of Alfred include: *The History of the World* by Orosius, a companion piece for Augustine of Hippo's *The City of God;* the Dialogues of Gregory the Great;

and the *Ecclesiastical History of the English People* by Bede.

Elfric of Eynsham, wrote in the late 10th and early 11th century. He was the greatest and most prolific writer of Anglo-Saxon sermons, which were copied and adapted for use well into the 13th century. He also wrote a number of saints lives, an Old English work on time-reckoning, pastoral letters, translations of the first six books of the Bible, glosses and translations of other parts of the Bible including Proverbs, Wisdom and Ecclesiasticus.

In the same category as Aelfric, and a contemporary, was Wulfstan II, archbishop of York. His sermons were highly stylistic. His best known work is *Sermo Lupi ad Anglos* in which he blames the sins of the British for the Viking invasions. He wrote a number of clerical legal texts *Institutes of Polity* and *Canons of Edgar*.

One of the earliest Old English texts in prose is the *Martyrology*, information about saints and martyrs according to their anniversaries and feasts in the church calendar. It has survived in six fragments. It is believed to date from the 9th century by an anonymous Mercian author.

The oldest collection of church sermons are the *Blickling homilies* in the Vercelli Book and dates from the 10th century.

There are a number of saint's lives prose works. Beyond those written by Ælfric are the prose life of Saint Guthlac (Vercelli Book), the life of Saint Margaret and the life of Saint Chad. There are four lives in the Julius manuscript: Seven Sleepers of Ephesus, Saint Mary of Egypt, Saint Eustace and Saint Euphrosyne.

There are many Old English translations of many parts of the Bible. Ælfric made a number of Old Testament translations, which were later used and supplemented by another author for a lavishly illustrated copy of the Old English Hexateuch. There is a translation of the Gospels. The most popular was the *Gospel of Nicodemus,* others included "..the *Gospel of Pseudo-Matthew, Vindicta salvatoris, Vision of Saint Paul* and the *Apocalypse of Thomas*".

One of the largest bodies of Old English text is found in the legal texts collected and saved by the religious houses. These include many kinds of texts: records of donations by nobles; wills; documents of emancipation; lists of books and relics; court cases; guild rules. All of these texts provide valuable insights into the social history of Anglo-Saxon times, but are also of literary value. For example, some of the court case narratives are interesting for their use of rhetoric.

Secular Prose

The *Anglo-Saxon Chronicle* was probably started in the time of King Alfred and continued for over 300 years as a historical record of Anglo-Saxon history.

A single example of a Classical romance has survived, it is a fragment of the story of *Apollonius of Tyre,* from the 11th century.

A monk who was writing in Old English at the same time as Aelfric and Wulfstan was Byrhtferth of Ramsey, whose books *Handboc* and *Manual* were studies of mathematics and rhetoric.

Aelfric wrote two neo-scientific works, *Hexameron* and *Interrogationes Sigewulfi,* dealing with the stories of Creation. He also wrote a grammar and glossary in Old English called *Latin,* later used by students interested in learning Old French because it had been glossed in Old French.

There are many surviving rules and calculations for finding feast days, and tables on calculating the tides and the season of the moon.

In the Nowell Codex is the text of *The Wonders of the East* which includes a remarkable map of the world, and other illustrations. Also contained in Nowell is *Alexander's Letter to Aristotle.* Because this is the same manuscript that contains *Beowulf,* some scholars speculate it may have been a collection of materials on exotic places and creatures.

There are a number of interesting medical works. There is a translation of Apuleius's *Herbarium* with striking illustrations, found together with *Medicina de Quadrupedibus.* A second collection of texts is *Bald's Leechbook,* a 10th century book containing herbal and even some surgical cures. A third collection, known as the *Lacnunga,* includes many charms and incantations.

Anglo-Saxon legal texts are a large and important part of the overall corpus. By the 12th century they had been arranged into two large collections. They include laws of the kings, beginning with those of Aethelbert of Kent, and texts dealing with specific cases and places in the country. An interesting example is *Gerefa* which outlines the duties of a reeve on a large manor estate. There is also a large volume of legal documents related to religious houses.

Historiography

Old English literature did not disappear in 1066 with the Norman Conquest. Many sermons and works continued to be read and used in part or whole up through the 14th century, and were further catalogued and organised. During the Reformation, when monastic libraries were dispersed, the manuscripts were collected by antiquarians and scholars. These included Laurence Nowell, Matthew Parker, Robert Bruce Cotton and Humfrey Wanley. In the 17th century begun a tradition of Old English literature dictionaries and references. The first was William Somner's *Dictionarium Saxonico-Latino-Anglicum* (1659). Lexicographer Joseph Bosworth began a dictionary in the 19th century which was completed by Thomas Northcote Toller in 1898 called *An Anglo-Saxon Dictionary*, which was updated by Alistair Campbell in 1972.

Because Old English was one of the first vernacular languages to be written down, nineteenth century scholars searching for the roots of European "national culture" took special interest in studying Anglo-Saxon literature, and Old English became a regular part of university curriculum. Since WWII there has been increasing interest in the manuscripts themselves—Neil Ker, a paleographer, published the groundbreaking *Catalogue of Manuscripts Containing Anglo-Saxon* in 1957, and by 1980 nearly all Anglo-Saxon manuscript texts were in print. J.R.R. Tolkien is credited with creating a movement to look at Old English as a subject of literary theory in his seminal lecture *Beowulf: The Monsters and the Critics* (1936).

Old English literature has had an influence on modern literature. Some of the best-known translations include William Morris' translation of *Beowulf* and Ezra Pound's translation of *The Seafarer*. The influence of the poetry can be seen in modern poets T. S. Eliot, Ezra Pound and W. H. Auden. Tolkien adapted the subject matter and terminology of heroic poetry for works like *The Hobbit* and *The Lord of the Rings*.

3

Middle English Literature

The term Middle English literature refers to the literature written in the form of the English language known as Middle English, from the 12th century until the 1470s, when the Chancery Standard, a form of London-based English, became widespread and the printing press regularized the language. Between the 1470s and the middle of the following century there is a transition to early Modern English though in literary terms the characteristics of the literary works written does not change radically until the effects of the Renaissance and Reformed Christianity become more apparent in the reign of King Henry VIII. There are three main categories of Middle English Literature: Religious, Courtly love, and Arthurian, though much of Chaucer's work stands outside these. Among the many religious works are those in the Katherine Group and the writings of Julian of Norwich and Richard Rolle.

Early Period

After the Norman conquest of England, the written form of the Anglo-Saxon language continued in some monasteries but few literary works are known from this period. The new aristocracy spoke French, and this became the standard language of courts, parliament, and polite society. As the invaders integrated, their language and literature mingled with that of the natives: the Norman French dialect of the upper classes became Anglo-Norman, and Anglo-Saxon underwent a gradual transition into Middle English. Since the political power was no longer in English hands the West Saxon literary language had no more influence than any other dialect so Middle English literature is written in many dialects depending on the situation of the writers.

While Anglo-Norman or Latin was preferred for high culture and administration, English literature by no means died out, and a number of important works illustrate the development of the language. Around the turn of the thirteenth century, Layamon wrote his *Brut,* based on Wace's twelfth century Anglo-Norman epic of the same name; Layamon's language is recognisably Middle English, though his prosody shows a strong Anglo-Saxon influence remaining. Other transitional works were preserved as popular entertainment, including a variety of romances and lyrics. With time, the English language regained prestige, and in 1362 it replaced French and Latin in Parliament and courts of law. Early examples of Middle English literature are the Ormulum and Havelock the Dane.

Late Period

It was with the fourteenth century that major works of English literature began once again to appear; these include the so-called Pearl Poet's *Pearl, Patience, Cleanness,* and *Sir Gawain and the Green Knight;* Langland's political and religious allegory *Piers*

Plowman; Gower's *Confessio Amantis*; and, of course, the works of Chaucer, the most highly regarded English poet of the Middle Ages, who was seen by his contemporaries as a successor to the great tradition of Virgil and Dante.

The latter portion of the 14th century also saw not only the consolidation of English as a written language, taking over from French or Latin in certain areas, but a large shift from primarily theological or religious subject matter to that of a more secular nature. Literature during this period also saw a growth in the amount of (secular) books being copied in English. Thus, the latter portion of the 14th century can be seen as the most significant period in the history of the English language.

The reputation of Chaucer's successors in the 15th century has suffered in comparison with him, though Lydgate and Skelton are widely studied. However, the century really belongs to a group of remarkable Scottish writers. The rise of Scottish poetry began with the writing of *The Kingis Quair* by James I of Scotland. The main poets of this Scottish group were Robert Henryson, William Dunbar and Gavin Douglas. Henryson and Douglas introduced a note of almost savage satire, which may have owed something to the Gaelic bards, while Douglas's version of Virgil's *Aeneid* is one of the early monuments of Renaissance literary humanism in English.

Caxton and English Literature

William Caxton printed four-fifths of his works in English. He translated a large number of works into English; Caxton translated 26 of the titles himself. Caxton is credited with printing as many as 108 books,

87 of which were different titles. However, the English language was changing rapidly in Caxton's time and the works he was given to print were in a variety of styles and dialects. Caxton was a technician rather than a writer and he often faced dilemmas concerning language standardisation in the books he printed. (He wrote about this subject in the preface to his *Eneydos*.) His successor Wynkyn de Worde faced similar problems.

Caxton is credited with standardising the English language (that is, homogenising regional dialects) through printing. This facilitated the expansion of English vocabulary, the development of inflection and syntax and the ever-widening gap between the spoken and the written word. However, Richard Pynson, a Frenchman who started printing in London in 1491 or 1492 and who favoured Chancery Standard, was a more accomplished stylist and consequently pushed the English language further toward standardisation.

4

Renaissance English Literature

The English Renaissance was a cultural and artistic movement in England dating from the early 16th century to the early 17th century. It is associated with the pan-European Renaissance that many cultural historians believe originated in Tuscany in the 14th century. This era in English cultural history is sometimes referred to as "the age of Shakespeare" or "the Elizabethan era", the first period in English and British history to be named after a reigning monarch.

Poets such as Edmund Spenser and John Milton produced works that demonstrated an increased interest in understanding English Christian beliefs, such as the allegorical representation of the Tudor Dynasty in The Faerie Queen and the retelling of mankind's fall from paradise in Paradise Lost; playwrights, such as Christopher Marlowe and William Shakespeare, composed theatrical representations of the English take on life, death, and history.

Nearing the end of the Tudor Dynasty, philosophers like Sir Thomas More and Sir Francis Bacon published their own ideas about humanity and the aspects of a perfect society, pushing the limits of metacognition at that time. England came closer to reaching modern science with the Baconian Method, a forerunner of the Scientific Method.

Slow Transition and Mixture

The steadfast English mind clung to the old order of things, and relinquished with reluctance the last relics of a style that had been for centuries a part of its life. If it must have the Egg-and-dart, it would keep the Tudor rose too.

Thus all the Renaissance that came into England, after the bloody Wars of the Roses made it possible to think of art and luxury, paid toll to the Gothic on the way, and the result was a singular miscellany, for its Gothic had now forgotten, and its Renaissance had never known why it had existed. It is rather the talent with which the medley of material was handled, the broad masses, yet curious elaboration, and the scale of magnificence, that give the style its charm rather than anything in its original and bastard composition.

Something of this same charm is to be found in most of the literature of the era, in accordance with that subtle relationship existing between the literature and the art of any period. It is in the lawless mixture of Gothic and Grecian characterizing the Elizabethan that Shakespeare peoples his *A Midsummer Night's Dream* with Gothic fairies reveling in the Athenian forest, and poet Edmund Spenser fills his pages with a pageantry of medieval monsters and classic masks. Shakespeare is a peculiar product of the Renaissance.

English and Italian Renaissances

The English Renaissance is different from the Italian Renaissance in several ways. The dominant art forms of the English Renaissance were literature and music. Visual arts in the English Renaissance were much less significant than in the Italian Renaissance. The English period began far later than the Italian, which is usually considered to begin with Dante, Petrarch and Giotto in the early 1300s, and was moving into Mannerism and the Baroque by the 1550s or earlier. In contrast, the English Renaissance can only be said to begin, shakily, in the 1520s, and continued until perhaps 1620.

The Italian and English Renaissances were similar in sharing a specific musical aesthetic. In the late 16th century Italy was the musical center of Europe, and one of the principal forms which emerged from that singular explosion of musical creativity was the madrigal. In 1588, Nicholas Yonge published in England the *Musica transalpina*—a collection of Italian madrigals that had been Anglicized — an event which began a vogue of madrigal in England which was almost unmatched in the Renaissance in being an instantaneous adoption of an idea, from another country, adapted to local aesthetics. (In a delicious irony of history, a military invasion from a Catholic country - Spain - failed in that year, but a cultural invasion from another Catholic county, Italy, succeeded).

English poetry was exactly at the right stage of development for this transplantation to occur, since forms such as the sonnet were uniquely adapted to setting as madrigals: indeed, the sonnet was already well-developed in Italy. Composers such as Thomas Morley, the only contemporary composer to set Shakespeare, and whose work survives, published collections of their own, roughly in the Italian manner but yet with a unique Englishness; many of the compositions of the English Madrigal School remain in the standard repertory in the 21st century.

The colossal polychoral productions of the Venetian School had been anticipated in the works of Thomas Tallis, and the Palestrina style from the Roman School had already been absorbed prior to the publication of *Musical transalpina*, in the music of masters such as William Byrd.

While the Classical revival led to a flourishing of Italian Renaissance architecture, architecture in Britain took a more eclectic approach. Elizabethan architecture retained many features of the Gothic, even while the occasional building such as the tomb in the Henry VII Lady Chapel at Westminster Abbey, or the French-influenced architecture of Scotland showed interest in the new style.

Ideas of English Renaissance

The notion of calling this period "The Renaissance" is a modern invention, having been popularized by the historian Jacob Burckhardt in the nineteenth century. The idea of the Renaissance has come under increased criticism by many cultural historians, and some have contended that the "English Renaissance" has no real tie with the artistic achievements and aims of the northern Italian artists (Leonardo, Michelangelo, Donatello) who are closely identified with the Renaissance. Indeed, England had already experienced a flourishing of literature over 200 years before the time of Shakespeare when Geoffrey Chaucer was working. Chaucer's popularizing of English as a medium of literary composition rather than Latin was only 50 years after Dante had started using Italian for serious poetry. At the same time William Langland, author of *Piers Plowman,* and John Gower were also writing in English. The Hundred Years' War and the subsequent civil war in England known as the Wars of the Roses probably hampered artistic endeavor until the relatively peaceful and stable reign of Elizabeth I allowed drama in particular to develop. Even during these war years, though, Thomas Malory, author of *Le Morte D'Arthur,* was a notable figure. For this reason, scholars find the singularity of the period called the English Renaissance questionable; C. S. Lewis, a professor of Medieval and Renaissance literature at Oxford and Cambridge, famously remarked to a colleague that he had "discovered" that there was no English Renaissance, and that if there had been one, it had "no effect whatsoever"

Historians have also begun to consider the word "Renaissance" as an unnecessarily loaded word that implies an unambiguously positive "rebirth" from the supposedly more primitive Middle Ages. Some historians have asked the question "a renaissance for whom?," pointing out, for example, that the status of women in society arguably declined during the Renaissance. Many historians and cultural historians now prefer to use the term "early modern" for this period, a neutral term that highlights the period as a transitional one that led to the modern world, but does not have any positive or negative connotations.

Major Renaissance Figures

William Shakespeare, chief figure of the English Renaissance, as portrayed in the Chandos portrait. The major literary figures in the English Renaissance include:

— Francis Bacon

- Thomas Dekker
- John Donne
- John Fletcher
- John Ford
- Ben Jonson
- Thomas Kyd
- Christopher Marlowe
- Phillip Massinger
- Thomas Middleton
- John Milton
- Sir Thomas More
- Thomas Nashe
- William Rowley
- William Shakespeare
- James Shirley
- Sir Philip Sidney
- Edmund Spenser
- John Webster
- Sir Thomas Wyatt

Thomas Tallis, Thomas Morley, and William Byrd were the most notable English musicians of the time, and are often seen as being a part of the same artistic movement that inspired the above authors. Elizabeth herself, a product of Renaissance humanism trained by Roger Ascham, wrote occasional poems such as *On Monsieur's Departure* at critical moments of her life.

5

Early Modern English

Early Modern English is the stage of the English language used from about the end of the Middle English period (the latter half of the 15th century) to 1650. Thus, the first edition of the King James Bible and the works of William Shakespeare both belong to the late phase of Early Modern English, although the King James Bible intentionally keeps some archaisms that were not common even when it was published. Prior to and following the accession of James I to the English throne the emerging English standard began to influence the spoken and written Middle Scots of Scotland.

Current readers of English are generally able to understand Early Modern English, though occasionally with difficulties arising from grammar changes, changes in the meanings of some words, and spelling differences. The standardization of English spelling falls within the Early Modern English period and is influenced by conventions predating the Great Vowel Shift, explaining much of the non-phonetic spelling of contemporary Modern English.

In Early Modern English, there were two second person personal pronouns: *thou,* the informal singular pronoun, and *ye*, which was both the plural pronoun and the formal singular pronoun, (like modern French *tu* and *vous*). (*Thou* was already falling out of use in the Early Modern English period, but remained customary for addressing God and certain other solemn occasions and sometimes for addressing inferiors.)

Like other personal pronouns, *thou* and *ye* had different forms depending on their grammatical case; specifically, the objective form of *thou* was *thee*, its possessive forms were *thy* and *thine*, and its reflexive or emphatic form was *thyself*, while the objective form of *ye* was *you*, its possessive forms were *your* and *yours*, and its reflexive or emphatic forms were *yourself* and *yourselves*.

In other respects, the pronouns were much the same as today. One difference is that, much as *a* becomes *an* before a vowel, *my* and *thy* became *mine* and *thine* before vowels as well; thus, *mine eyes*, *thine uncle*, and so on.

Orthographic Conventions

The orthography in Early Modern English was fairly similar to that of today, but spelling was unphonetic and unstable; for example, the word *acuity* could be spelled either <acuity> or <acuitie>. Further, there were a number of features of spelling that have not been retained:

— The letter <S> had two distinct lowercase forms: <s> as today, and <n> (*long s*). The former was used at the end of a word, and the latter everywhere else, except that double-lowercase-*S* was variously written <nn> or <ns>.

- <u> and <v> were not yet considered two distinct letters, but different forms of the same letter. Typographically, <v> was used at the start of a word and <u> elsewhere; hence *vnmoued* (for modern *unmoved*) and *loue* (for *love*).
- <i> and <j> were also not yet considered two distinct letters, but different forms of the same letter, hence "ioy" for "joy" and "iust" for "just".
- A silent <e> was often appended to words. The last consonant sometimes was doubled when adding this <e>; hence *npeake, cowarde, manne* (for *man*), *runne* (for *run*).
- The sound /Œ/ was often written <o> (as in *son*); hence *nommer, plombe* (for modern *summer, plumb*).

Nothing was standard, however. For example, "Julius Caesar" could be spelled "Julius Cænar", "Ivlivs Cænar", "Jvlivs Cænar", or "Iulius Cænar" and the word "he" could be found being spelled "he" or "hee" in the same sentence in Shakespeare's plays.

Verbs

Verb conjugations in the "thou" form (second person informal singular) end in -(e)st (e.g. "thou takest"). In Early Modern English, third person singular conjugations end in -(e)th instead of -s (e.g. "he taketh"). Both the second person informal singular and third person singular lost their endings in the subjunctive, which uses the bare stem of the verb.

The perfect tenses of the verbs had not yet been standardized to all use the auxiliary verb "to have". Some took as their auxiliary verb "to be", as in this example from the King James Bible, "But which of you ... will say unto him ... when he is come from the field,

Go and sit down...". The rules that were followed as to which verbs took which auxiliaries were similar to those still used in German and French.

Vocabulary

Although the language is otherwise very similar to that current, there have in time developed a few "false friends" within the English language itself, rendering difficulty in understanding even the still-prestigious phrasing of the King James Bible. The most glaring is that the passage "Suffer the little children" meant, "Permit..." (this usage of the word "suffer" is still sometimes used in some dialects in formal circumstances).

The change from Middle English to Early Modern English was not just a matter of vocabulary or pronunciation changing: it was the beginning of a new era in the history of English.

An era of linguistic change in a language with large variations in dialect was replaced by a new era of a more standardized language with a richer lexicon and an established (and lasting) literature. Shakespeare's plays are familiar and comprehensible today, 400 years after they were written, but the works of Geoffrey Chaucer and William Langland, written only 200 years earlier, are considerably more difficult for the average reader.

Timeline

- 1476—William Caxton starts printing in Westminster, but the language he uses reflects the variety of styles and dialects used by the authors whose work he prints.

- 1485 – Tudor dynasty established; start of period of (relative) political and social stability.
- 1491 or 1492 – Richard Pynson starts printing in London; his style tends to prefer Chancery Standard, the form of English used by government.
- c. 1509 – Pynson becomes the king's official printer.
- From 1525 – Publication of William Tyndale's Bible translation (which was initially banned).
- 1539 – Publication of the *Great Bible,* the first officially authorised Bible in English, edited by Myles Coverdale, largely from the work of Tyndale. This Bible is read to congregations regularly in churches, familiarising much of the population of England with a standard form of the language.
- 1549 – Publication of the first *Book of Common Prayer* in English, under the supervision of Thomas Cranmer. This book standardises much of the wording of church services. Since attendance at prayer book services was required by law for many years some have argued that the repetitive use of the language of the prayer book helped to standardize modern English.
- 1557 – Publication of *Tottel's Miscellany.*
- c. 1590 to c. 1612 – William Shakespeare's plays written; they are still widely read and familiar in the 21st century.
- 1607 – The first successful permanent English colony in the New World, Jamestown, is established in Virginia. The beginnings of American English.

— 1611 – The *King James Bible* is published, largely based on Tyndale's translation. It remains the standard Bible in the Church of England for many years.

— c. 1640–1660 – Period of social upheaval in England (the English Civil War and the era of Oliver Cromwell).

— 1651 – Publication of *Leviathan* by Thomas Hobbes.

— 1662 – New edition of the *Book of Common Prayer*, largely based on the 1549 and subsequent editions. This also long remains a standard work in English.

— 1667 – Publication of *Paradise Lost*, by John Milton.

Development to Modern English

The 17th century was a time of political and social upheaval in England, particularly the period from about 1640 to 1660. The increase in trade around the world meant that the English port towns (and their forms of speech) would have gained in influence over the old county towns. England experienced a new period of internal peace and relative stability, encouraging the arts including literature, from around the 1690s onwards. Another important episode in the development of the English language started around 1607: the British settlement of America. By 1750 a distinct American dialect of English had developed.

Cultural Context of Early Modern England

Early Modern Britain is the history of Great Britain, roughly corresponding to the 16th, 17th, and 18th centuries. Major historical events in Early Modern British history include the English Renaissance, the English Reformation and Scottish Reformation, the

English Civil War, the Restoration of Charles II, the Glorious Revolution, the Treaty of Union, the Scottish Enlightenment and the formation of the First British Empire.

The term "English Renaissance" is used by many historians to refer to a cultural movement in England in the 1500s and 1600s that was heavily influenced by the Italian Renaissance. This movement is characterized by the flowering of English music (particularly the English adoption and development of the madrigal), notable achievements in drama (by William Shakespeare, Christopher Marlowe, and Ben Jonson), and the development of English epic poetry (most famously Edmund Spenser's The Faerie Queene and John Milton's Paradise Lost).

The idea of the Renaissance has come under increased criticism by many cultural historians, and some have contended that the "English Renaissance" has no real tie with the artistic achievements and aims of the northern Italian artists who are closely identified with the Renaissance.Other cultural historians have countered that, regardless of whether the name "renaissance" is apt, there was undeniably an artistic flowering in England under the Tudor monarchs, culminating in Shakespeare and his contemporaries.

Rise of the Tudors

Some scholars date the beginning of Early Modern Britain to the end of the Wars of the Roses and the crowning of Henry Tudor in 1485 after his victory at the battle of Bosworth Field. Henry VII's largely peaceful reign ended decades of civil war and brought the peace and stability to England that art and commerce need to thrive. A major war on English soil would not occur again until the English Civil War of the seventeenth century.

During this period Henry VII and his son Henry VIII greatly increased the power of the English monarch. A similar pattern was unfolding on the continent as new technologies, such as gunpowder, and social and ideological changes undermined the power of the feudal nobility and enhanced that of the sovereign. Henry VIII also made use of the Protestant Reformation to seize the power of the Roman Catholic Church, confiscating the property of the monasteries and declaring himself the head of the new Anglican Church. Under the Tudors the English state was centralized and rationalized as a bureaucracy built up and the government became run and managed by educated functionaries. The most notable new institution was the Star Chamber.

The new power of the monarch was given a basis by the notion of the divine right of kings to rule over their subjects. James I was a major proponent of this idea and wrote extensively on it.

The same forces that had reduced the power of the traditional aristocracy also served to increase the power of the commercial classes. The rise of trade and the central importance of money to the operation of the government gave this new class great power, but power that was not reflected in the government structure. This would lead to a long contest during the seventeenth century between the forces of the monarch and parliament.

Reign of Queen Elizabeth

The Elizabethan Era is the reign of Queen Elizabeth I (1558–1603) and is known to be a golden age in

English history. It was the height of the English Renaissance and saw the flowering of English literature and poetry. This was also the time during which Elizabethan theatre was famous and William Shakespeare, among others, composed plays that broke away from England's past style of plays and theatre. It was an age of expansion and exploration abroad, while at home the Protestant Reformation became entrenched in the national mindset.

The Elizabethan Age is viewed so highly because of the contrasts with the periods before and after. It was a brief period of largely internal peace between the English Reformation and the battles between Protestants and Catholics and the battles between parliament and the monarchy that engulfed the seventeenth century. The Protestant/Catholic divide was settled, for a time, by the Elizabethan Religious Settlement, and parliament was not yet strong enough to challenge royal absolutism. England was also well-off compared to the other nations of Europe. The Italian Renaissance had come to an end under the weight of foreign domination of the peninsula. France was embroiled in its own religious battles that would only be settled in 1598 with the Edict of Nantes. In part because of this, but also because the English had been expelled from their last outposts on the continent, the centuries long conflict between France and England was largely suspended for most of Elizabeth's reign.

The one great rival was Spain, with which England conflicted both in Europe and the Americas in skirmishes that exploded into the Anglo-Spanish War of 1585–1604. An attempt by Philip II of Spain to invade England with the Spanish Armada in 1588 was famously defeated, but the tide of war turned against

England with a disastrously unsuccessful attack upon Spain, the Drake-Norris Expedition of 1589. Thereafter Spain provided some support for Irish Catholics in a draining guerilla war against England, and Spanish naval and land forces inflicted a series of defeats upon English forces. This badly damaged both the English Exchequer and economy that had been so carefully restored under Elizabeth's prudent guidance. English colonisation and trade would be frustrated until the signing of the Treaty of London the year following Elizabeth's death.

England during this period had a centralised, well-organised, and effective government, largely a result of the reforms of Henry VII and Henry VIII. Economically, the country began to benefit greatly from the new era of trans-Atlantic trade.

Scotland from 15th century to 1603

Scotland advanced markedly in educational terms during the fifteenth century with the founding of the University of St Andrews in 1413, the University of Glasgow in 1450 and the University of Aberdeen in 1495, and with the passing of the Education Act 1496.

In 1468 the last great acquisition of Scottish territory occurred when James III married Margaret of Denmark, receiving the Orkney Islands and the Shetland Islands in payment of her dowry.

After the death of James III in 1488, during or after the Battle of Sauchieburn, his successor James IV successfully ended the quasi-independent rule of the Lord of the Isles, bringing the Western Isles under effective Royal control for the first time. In 1503, he married Henry VII's daughter, Margaret Tudor, thus laying the foundation for the 17th century Union of the

Crowns. James IV's reign is often considered to be a period of cultural flourishing, and it was around this period that the European Renaissance began to infiltrate Scotland. James IV was the last known Scottish king known to speak Gaelic, although some suggest his son could also.

In 1512, under a treaty extending the Auld Alliance, all nationals of Scotland and France also became nationals of each other's countries, a status not repealed in France until 1903 and which may never have been repealed in Scotland. However a year later, the Auld Alliance had more disastrous effects when James IV was required to launch an invasion of England to support the French when they were attacked by the English under Henry VIII. The invasion was stopped decisively at the battle of Flodden Field during which the King, many of his nobles, and over 10,000 troops — *The Flowers of the Forest* — were killed. The extent of the disaster impacted throughout Scotland because of the large numbers killed, and once again Scotland's government lay in the hands of regents. The song *The Flooers o' the Forest* commemorated this, an echo of the poem *Y Gododdin* on a similar tragedy in about 600.

When James V finally managed to escape from the custody of the regents with the aid of his redoubtable mother in 1528, he once again set about subduing the rebellious Highlands, Western and Northern isles, as his father had had to do. He married the French noblewoman Marie de Guise. His reign was fairly successful, until another disastrous campaign against England led to defeat at the battle of Solway Moss (1542). James died a short time later. The day before his death, he was brought news of the birth of an heir:

a daughter, who became Mary I of Scotland (or 'Mary, Queen of Scots'). James is supposed to have remarked in Scots that *"it cam wi a lass, it will gang wi a lass"* - referring to the House of Stewart which began with Walter Stewart's marriage to the daughter of Robert the Bruce. Once again, Scotland was in the hands of a regent, James Hamilton, Earl of Arran.

Within two years, the Rough Wooing, Henry VIII's military attempt to force a marriage between Mary and his son, Edward, had begun. This took the form of border skirmishing. To avoid the "rough wooing", Mary was sent to France at the age of five, as the intended bride of the heir to the French throne. Her mother stayed in Scotland to look after the interests of Mary — and of France — although the Earl of Arran acted officially as regent. In 1547, after the death of Henry VIII, forces under the English regent Edward Seymour, 1st Duke of Somerset were victorious at the Battle of Pinkie Cleugh, the climax of the *Rough Wooing* and followed up by occupying Edinburgh.

Protestant Reformation

During the 16th century, Scotland underwent a Protestant Reformation. In the earlier part of the century, the teachings of first Martin Luther and then John Calvin began to influence Scotland. the execution of a number of Protestant preachers, most notably the Lutheran influenced Patrick Hamilton in 1528 and later the proto-Calvinist George Wishart in 1546 who was burnt at the stake in St. Andrews by Cardinal Beaton for heresy, did nothing to stem the growth of these ideas. Beaton was assassinated shortly after the execution of George Wishart.

The eventual Reformation of the Scottish Church followed a brief civil war in 1559-60, in which English intervention on the Protestant side was decisive. A Reformed confession of faith was adopted by Parliament in 1560, while the young Mary Queen of Scots was still in France.

The Reformation remained somewhat precarious through the reign of Queen Mary, who remained Roman Catholic but tolerated Protestantism. Following her deposition in 1567, her infant son James VI was raised as a Protestant. In 1603, following the death of the childless Queen Elizabeth I, the crown of England passed to James. He took the tle James I of England and James VI of Scotland, thus unifying these two countries under his personal rule. For a time, this remained the only political connection between two independent nations, but it foreshadowed the eventual 1707 union of Scotland and England under the banner of the Great Britain.

Jacobite Risings

major Jacobite Risings were called the Jacobite Rebellions by the ruling governments. The "First Jacobite Rebellion" and "Second Jacobite Rebellion" were known respectively as "The Fifteen" and "The Forty-Five", after the years in which they occurred.

Although each Jacobite Rising has unique features, they all formed part of a larger series of military campaigns by Jacobites attempting to restore the Stuart kings to the thrones of Scotland and England (and after 1707, Great Britain) after James VII of Scotland and II of England was deposed in 1688 and the thrones claimed by his daughter Mary II jointly with her husband, the Dutch born William of Orange. The risings continued, and even intensified, after the House of Hanover succeeded to the British Throne in 1714. They continued until the last Jacobite Rebellion ("the Forty-Five"), led by Charles Edward Stuart (the Young Pretender), was soundly defeated at the Battle of Culloden in 1746, ending any realistic hope of a Stuart restoration.

British Empire

The Seven Years' War, which began in 1756, was the first war waged on a global scale, fought in Europe, India, North America, the Caribbean, the Philippines and coastal Africa. The signing of the Treaty of Paris (1763) had important consequences for Britain and its empire. In North America, France's future as a colonial power there was effectively ended with the ceding of New France to Britain and Louisiana to Spain. Spain ceded Florida to Britain. In India, the Carnatic War had left France still in control of its enclaves but with military restrictions and an obligation to support British client states, effectively leaving the future of India to Britain. The British victory over France in the Seven Years War therefore left Britain as the world's dominant colonial power.

During the 1760s and 1770s, relations between the Thirteen Colonies and Britain became increasingly strained, primarily because of resentment of the British Parliament's ability to tax American colonists without their consent. Disagreement turned to violence and in 1775 the American War of Independence began. The following year, the colonists declared the independence of the United States and with economical and naval assistance from France, would go on to win the war in 1783.

The loss of the United States, at the time Britain's most populous colony, is seen by historians as the event defining the transition between the "first" and "second" empires, in which Britain shifted its attention away from the Americas to Asia, the Pacific and later Africa. During its first century of operation, the focus of the British East India Company had been trade, not the building of an empire in India. Company interests turned from trade to territory during the 18th century as the Mughal Empire declined in power and the British East India Company struggled with its French counterpart, the *La Compagnie française des Indes orientales,* during the Carnatic Wars of the 1740s and 1750s. The Battle of Plassey, which saw the British, led by Robert Clive, defeat the French and their Indian allies, left the Company in control of Bengal and a major military and political power in India.

In 1770, James Cook had discovered the eastern coast of Australia whilst on a scientific voyage to the South Pacific. In 1778, Joseph Banks, Cook's botanist on the voyage, presented evidence to the government on the suitability of Botany Bay for the establishment of a penal settlement, and in 1787 the first shipment of convicts set sail, arriving in 1788.

At the threshold to the 19th century, Britain was challenged again by France under Napoleon, in a struggle that, unlike previous wars, represented a contest of ideologies between the two nations. It was not only Britain's position on the world stage that was threatened: Napoleon threatened invasion of Britain itself, and with it, a fate similar to the countries of continental Europe that his armies had overrun. The Napoleonic Wars were therefore ones that Britain invested large amounts of capital and resources to win.

6

Elizabethan Literature

The Elizabethan era saw a great flourishing of literature, especially in the field of drama. The Italian Renaissance had rediscovered the ancient Greek and Roman theatre, and this was instrumental in the development of the new drama, which was then beginning to evolve apart from the old mystery and miracle plays of the Middle Ages. The Italians were particularly inspired by Seneca (a major tragic playwright and philosopher, the tutor of Nero) and Plautus (its comic clichés, especially that of the boasting soldier had a powerful influence on the Renaissance and after). However, the Italian tragedies embraced a principle contrary to Seneca's ethics: showing blood and violence on the stage. In Seneca's plays such scenes were only acted by the characters. But the English playwrights were intrigued by Italian model: a conspicuous community of Italian actors had settled in London and Giovanni Florio had brought much of the Italian language and culture to England.

Following earlier Elizabethan plays such as *Gorboduc* by Sackville & Norton and *The Spanish Tragedy* by Kyd that was to provide much material for *Hamlet*, William Shakespeare stands out in this period as a poet and playwright as yet unsurpassed. Shakespeare was very gifted and incredibly versatile, and he surpassed "professionals" as Robert Greene who mocked this "shake-scene" of low origins. Though most dramas met with great success, it is in his later years (marked by the early reign of James I) that he wrote what have been considered his greatest plays: *Hamlet, Romeo and Juliet, Othello, King Lear, Macbeth, Antony and Cleopatra,* and *The Tempest,* a tragicomedy that inscribes within the main drama a brilliant pageant to the new king.

William Shakespeare

William Shakespeare (baptised 26 April 1564; died 23 April 1616) was an English poet and playwright, widely regarded as the greatest writer in the English language and the world's preeminent dramatist. He is often called England's national poet and the "Bard of Avon". His surviving works, including some collaborations, consist of 38 plays, 154 sonnets, two long narrative poems, and several other poems. His plays have been translated into every major living language and are performed more often than those of any other playwright.

Shakespeare was born and raised in Stratford-upon-Avon. At the age of 18, he married Anne Hathaway, who bore him three children: Susanna, and twins Hamnet and Judith. Between 1585 and 1592, he began a successful career in London as an actor, writer, and part owner of a playing company called the Lord Chamberlain's Men, later known as the King's Men. He appears to have retired to Stratford around 1613, where he died three years later. Few records of Shakespeare's private life survive, and there has been considerable speculation about such matters as his physical appearance, sexuality, religious beliefs, and whether the works attributed to him were written by others.

Shakespeare produced most of his known work between 1589 and 1613. His early plays were mainly comedies and histories, genres he raised to the peak of sophistication and artistry by the end of the sixteenth century. He then wrote mainly tragedies until about 1608, including *Hamlet, King Lear,* and *Macbeth,* considered some of the finest works in the English language. In his last phase, he wrote tragicomedies, also known as romances, and collaborated with other playwrights.

Many of his plays were published in editions of varying quality and accuracy during his lifetime. In 1623, two of his former theatrical colleagues published the First Folio, a collected edition of his dramatic works that included all but two of the plays now recognised as Shakespeare's. Shakespeare was a respected poet and playwright in his own day, but his reputation did not rise to its present heights until the nineteenth century. The Romantics, in particular, acclaimed Shakespeare's genius, and the Victorians worshipped Shakespeare with a reverence that George Bernard Shaw called "bardolatry". In the twentieth century, his work was repeatedly adopted and rediscovered by new movements in scholarship and performance.

Early Life

William Shakespeare was the son of John Shakespeare, a successful glover and alderman originally from Snitterfield, and Mary Arden, the daughter of an affluent landowning farmer. He was born in Stratford-upon-Avon and baptised on 26 April 1564. His actual birthdate is unknown, but is traditionally observed on 23 April, St George's Day. This date, which can be traced back to an eighteenth-century scholar's mistake, has proved appealing because Shakespeare died on 23 April 1616. He was the third child of eight and the eldest surviving son.

Although no attendance records for the period survive, most biographers agree that Shakespeare was educated at the King's New School in Stratford, a free school chartered in 1553, about a quarter of a mile from his home. Grammar schools varied in quality during the Elizabethan era, but the curriculum was dictated by law throughout England, and the school would have provided an intensive education in Latin grammar and the classics.

At the age of 18, Shakespeare married the 26-year-old Anne Hathaway. The consistory court of the Diocese of Worcester issued a marriage licence on 27 November 1582. Two of Hathaway's neighbours posted bonds the next day as surety that there were no impediments to the marriage. The couple may have arranged the ceremony in some haste, since the Worcester chancellor allowed the marriage banns to be read once instead of the usual three times. Anne's pregnancy could have been the reason for this. Six months after the marriage, she gave birth to a daughter, Susanna, who was baptised on 26 May 1583. Twins, son Hamnet and daughter Judith, followed almost two years later and were baptised on 2 February 1585. Hamnet died of unknown causes at the age of 11 and was buried on 11 August 1596.After the birth of the twins, there are few historical traces of

Shakespeare until he is mentioned as part of the London theatre scene in 1592. Because of this gap, scholars refer to the years between 1585 and 1592 as Shakespeare's "lost years". Biographers attempting to account for this period have reported many apocryphal stories. Nicholas Rowe, Shakespeare's first biographer, recounted a Stratford legend that Shakespeare fled the town for London to escape prosecution for deer poaching. Another eighteenth-century story has Shakespeare starting his theatrical career minding the horses of theatre patrons in London. John Aubrey reported that Shakespeare had been a country schoolmaster. Some twentieth-century scholars have suggested that Shakespeare may have been employed as a schoolmaster by Alexander Hoghton of Lancashire, a Catholic landowner who named a certain "William Shakeshafte" in his will. No evidence substantiates such stories other than hearsay collected after his death.

London and Theatrical Career

It is not known exactly when Shakespeare began writing, but contemporary allusions and records of performances show that several of his plays were on the London stage by 1592. He was well enough known in London by then to be attacked in print by the playwright Robert Greene:

> ...there is an upstart Crow, beautified with our feathers, that with his *Tiger's heart wrapped in a Player's hide,* supposes he is as well able to bombast out a blank verse as the best of you: and being an absolute *Johannes factotum,* is in his own conceit the only Shake-scene in a country.

Scholars differ on the exact meaning of these words, but most agree that Greene is accusing Shakespeare of reaching above his rank in trying to match university-educated writers, such as Christopher Marlowe, Thomas Nashe and Greene himself. The italicised phrase parodying the line "Oh, tiger's heart wrapped in a woman's hide" from Shakespeare's *Henry VI, part 3*, along with the pun "Shake-scene", identifies Shakespeare as Greene's target.

Greene's attack is the first recorded mention of Shakespeare's career in the theatre. Biographers suggest that his career may have begun any time from the mid-1580s to just before Greene's remarks. From 1594, Shakespeare's plays were performed only by the Lord Chamberlain's Men, a company owned by a group of players, including Shakespeare, that soon became the leading playing company in London. After the death of Queen Elizabeth in 1603, the company was awarded a royal patent by the new king, James I, and changed its name to the King's Men.

In 1599, a partnership of company members built their own theatre on the south bank of the Thames, which they called the Globe. In 1608, the partnership also took over the Blackfriars indoor theatre. Records of Shakespeare's property purchases and investments indicate that the company made him a wealthy man. In 1597, he bought the second-largest house in Stratford, New Place, and in 1605, he invested in a share of the parish tithes in Stratford.

Some of Shakespeare's plays were published in quarto editions from 1594. By 1598, his name had become a selling point and began to appear on the title pages. Shakespeare continued to act in his own and other plays after his success as a playwright. The 1616 edition of Ben Jonson's *Works* names him on the cast lists for *Every Man in His Humour* (1598) and *Sejanus,*

His Fall (1603). The absence of his name from the 1605 cast list for Jonson's *Volpone* is taken by some scholars as a sign that his acting career was nearing its end. The First Folio of 1623, however, lists Shakespeare as one of "the Principal Actors in all these Plays", some of which were first staged after *Volpone,* although we cannot know for certain what roles he played. In 1610, John Davies of Hereford wrote that "good Will" played "kingly" roles. In 1709, Rowe passed down a tradition that Shakespeare played the ghost of Hamlet's father. Later traditions maintain that he also played Adam in *As You Like It* and the Chorus in *Henry V,* though scholars doubt the sources of the information.

Shakespeare divided his time between London and Stratford during his career. In 1596, the year before he bought New Place as his family home in Stratford, Shakespeare was living in the parish of St. Helen's, Bishopsgate, north of the River Thames. He moved across the river to Southwark by 1599, the year his company constructed the Globe Theatre there. By 1604, he had moved north of the river again, to an area north of St Paul's Cathedral with many fine houses. There he rented rooms from a French Huguenot called Christopher Mountjoy, a maker of ladies' wigs and other headgear.

Later Years and Death

Rowe was the first biographer to pass down the tradition that Shakespeare retired to Stratford some years before his death; but retirement from all work was uncommon at that time, and Shakespeare continued to visit London.[1] In 1612 he was called as a witness in a court case concerning the marriage settlement of Mountjoy's daughter, Mary. In March

1613 he bought a gatehouse in the former Blackfriars priory; and from November 1614 he was in London for several weeks with his son-in-law, John Hall.

After 1606–1607, Shakespeare wrote fewer plays, and none are attributed to him after 1613. His last three plays were collaborations, probably with John Fletcher, who succeeded him as the house playwright for the King's Men.

Shakespeare died on 23 April 1616 and was survived by his wife and two daughters. Susanna had married a physician, John Hall, in 1607, and Judith had married Thomas Quiney, a vintner, two months before Shakespeare's death.

In his will, Shakespeare left the bulk of his large estate to his elder daughter Susanna. The terms instructed that she pass it down intact to "the first son of her body". The Quineys had three children, all of whom died without marrying. The Halls had one child, Elizabeth, who married twice but died without children in 1670, ending Shakespeare's direct line. Shakespeare's will scarcely mentions his wife, Anne, who was probably entitled to one third of his estate automatically. He did make a point, however, of leaving her "my second best bed", a bequest that has led to much speculation. Some scholars see the bequest as an insult to Anne, whereas others believe that the second-best bed would have been the matrimonial bed and therefore rich in significance.

Shakespeare was buried in the chancel of the Holy Trinity Church two days after his death. The stone slab covering his grave is inscribed with a curse against moving his bones:

> in his memory on the north wall, with a half-effigy of him in the act of writing. Its plaque compares him to

> Nestor, Socrates, and Virgil. In 1623, in conjunction with the publication of the First Folio, the Droeshout engraving was published.

Shakespeare has been commemorated in many statues and memorials around the world, including funeral monuments in Southwark Cathedral and Poet's Corner in Westminster Abbey.

Plays

Most playwrights of the period typically collaborated with others at some point, and critics agree that Shakespeare did the same, mostly early and late in his career. Some attributions, such as *Titus Andronicus* and the early history plays, remain controversial, while *The Two Noble Kinsmen* and the lost *Cardenio* have well-attested contemporary documentation. Textual evidence also supports the view that several of the plays were revised by other writers after their original composition.

The first recorded works of Shakespeare are *Richard III* and the three parts of *Henry VI*, written in the early 1590s during a vogue for historical drama. Shakespeare's plays are difficult to date, however, and studies of the texts suggest that *Titus Andronicus, The Comedy of Errors, The Taming of the Shrew* and *The Two Gentlemen of Verona* may also belong to Shakespeare's earliest period. His first histories, which draw heavily on the 1587 edition of Raphael Holinshed's *Chronicles of England, Scotland, and Ireland,* dramatise the destructive results of weak or corrupt rule and have been interpreted as a justification for the origins of the Tudor dynasty. The early plays were influenced by the works of other Elizabethan dramatists, especially Thomas Kyd and Christopher Marlowe, by the traditions of medieval drama, and by the plays of

Seneca. *The Comedy of Errors* was also based on classical models, but no source for the *The Taming of the Shrew* has been found, though it is related to a separate play of the same name and may have derived from a folk story. Like *The Two Gentlemen of Verona,* in which two friends appear to approve of rape, the *Shrew's* story of the taming of a woman's independent spirit by a man sometimes troubles modern critics and directors.

Shakespeare's early classical and Italianate comedies, containing tight double plots and precise comic sequences, give way in the mid-1590s to the romantic atmosphere of his greatest comedies. *A Midsummer Night's Dream* is a witty mixture of romance, fairy magic, and comic lowlife scenes. Shakespeare's next comedy, the equally romantic *Merchant of Venice,* contains a portrayal of the vengeful Jewish moneylender Shylock, which reflects Elizabethan views but may appear derogatory to modern audiences. The wit and wordplay of *Much Ado About Nothing,* the charming rural setting of *As You Like It,* and the lively merrymaking of *Twelfth Night* complete Shakespeare's sequence of great comedies. After the lyrical *Richard II,* written almost entirely in verse, Shakespeare introduced prose comedy into the histories of the late 1590s, *Henry IV, parts 1* and 2, and *Henry V.* His characters become more complex and tender as he switches deftly between comic and serious scenes, prose and poetry, and achieves the narrative variety of his mature work. This period begins and ends with two tragedies: *Romeo and Juliet,* the famous romantic tragedy of sexually charged adolescence, love, and death; and *Julius Caesar*—based on Sir Thomas North's 1579 translation of Plutarch's *Parallel Lives*—which introduced a new kind of drama.

According to Shakespearean scholar James Shapiro, in *Julius Caesar* "the various strands of politics, character, inwardness, contemporary events, even Shakespeare's own reflections on the act of writing, began to infuse each other".

In the early 1600s, Shakespeare wrote the so-called "problem plays" *Measure for Measure, Troilus and Cressida,* and *All's Well That Ends Well* and a number of his best known tragedies. Many critics believe that Shakespeare's greatest tragedies represent the peak of his art. The titular hero of one of Shakespeare's most famous tragedies, *Hamlet,* has probably been discussed more than any other Shakespearean character, especially for his famous soliloquy "To be or not to be; that is the question." Unlike the introverted Hamlet, whose fatal flaw is hesitation, the heroes of the tragedies that followed, Othello and King Lear, are undone by hasty errors of judgement. The plots of Shakespeare's tragedies often hinge on such fatal errors or flaws, which overturn order and destroy the hero and those he loves. In *Othello,* the villain Iago stokes Othello's sexual jealousy to the point where he murders the innocent wife who loves him. In *King Lear,* the old king commits the tragic error of giving up his powers, initiating the events which lead to the murder of his daughter and the torture and blinding of the Earl of Gloucester. According to the critic Frank Kermode, "the play offers neither its good characters nor its audience any relief from its cruelty". In *Macbeth,* the shortest and most compressed of Shakespeare's tragedies, uncontrollable ambition incites Macbeth and his wife, Lady Macbeth, to murder the rightful king and usurp the throne, until their own guilt destroys them in turn. In this play, Shakespeare adds a supernatural element to the tragic structure. His last major tragedies, *Antony and Cleopatra* and *Coriolanus,* contain some of Shakespeare's finest poetry and were considered his most successful tragedies by the poet and critic T.S. Eliot. In his final period, Shakespeare turned to romance or tragicomedy and completed three more major plays: *Cymbeline, The Winter's Tale* and *The Tempest,* as well as the collaboration, *Pericles, Prince of Tyre.* Less bleak than the tragedies, these four plays are graver in tone than the comedies of the 1590s, but they end with reconciliation and the forgiveness of potentially tragic errors. Some commentators have seen this change in mood as evidence of a more serene view of life on Shakespeare's part, but it may merely reflect the theatrical fashion of the day. Shakespeare collaborated on two further surviving plays, *Henry VIII* and *The Two Noble Kinsmen,* probably with John Fletcher.

Performances

It is not clear for which companies Shakespeare wrote his early plays. The title page of the 1594 edition of *Titus Andronicus* reveals that the play had been acted by three different troupes. After the plagues of 1592–3, Shakespeare's plays were performed by his own company at The Theatre and the Curtain in Shoreditch, north of the Thames. Londoners flocked there to see the first part of *Henry IV,* Leonard Digges recording, "Let but Falstaff come, Hal, Poins, the rest...and you scarce shall have a room". When the company found themselves in dispute with their landlord, they pulled The Theatre down and used the timbers to construct the Globe Theatre, the first playhouse built by actors for actors, on the south bank of the Thames at Southwark. The Globe opened in autumn 1599, with *Julius Caesar* one of the first plays staged. Most of

Shakespeare's greatest post-1599 plays were written for the Globe, including *Hamlet, Othello* and *King Lear.* After the Lord Chamberlain's Men were renamed the King's Men in 1603, they entered a special relationship with the new King James. Although the performance records are patchy, the King's Men performed seven of Shakespeare's plays at court between 1 November 1604 and 31 October 1605, including two performances of *The Merchant of Venice.* After 1608, they performed at the indoor Blackfriars Theatre during the winter and the Globe during the summer. The indoor setting, combined with the Jacobean fashion for lavishly staged masques, allowed Shakespeare to introduce more elaborate stage devices. In *Cymbeline,* for example, Jupiter descends "in thunder and lightning, sitting upon an eagle: he throws a thunderbolt. The ghosts fall on their knees."

The actors in Shakespeare's company included the famous Richard Burbage, William Kempe, Henry Condell and John Heminges. Burbage played the leading role in the first performances of many of Shakespeare's plays, including *Richard III, Hamlet, Othello,* and *King Lear.* The popular comic actor Will Kempe played the servant Peter in *Romeo and Juliet* and Dogberry in *Much Ado About Nothing,* among other characters. He was replaced around the turn of the sixteenth century by Robert Armin, who played roles such as Touchstone in *As You Like It* and the fool in *King Lear.* In 1613, Sir Henry Wotton recorded that *Henry VIII* "was set forth with many extraordinary circumstances of pomp and ceremony". On 29 June, however, a cannon set fire to the thatch of the Globe and burned the theatre to the ground, an event which pinpoints the date of a Shakespeare play with rare precision.

Textual Sources

In 1623, John Heminges and Henry Condell, two of Shakespeare's friends from the King's Men, published the First Folio, a collected edition of Shakespeare's plays. It contained 36 texts, including 18 printed for the first time. Many of the plays had already appeared in quarto versions—flimsy books made from sheets of paper folded twice to make four leaves. No evidence suggests that Shakespeare approved these editions, which the First Folio describes as "stol'n and surreptitious copies". Alfred Pollard termed some of them "bad quartos" because of their adapted, paraphrased or garbled texts, which may in places have been reconstructed from memory. Where several versions of a play survive, each differs from the other. The differences may stem from copying or printing errors, from notes by actors or audience members, or from Shakespeare's own papers. In some cases, for example *Hamlet, Troilus and Cressida* and *Othello,* Shakespeare could have revised the texts between the quarto and folio editions. In the case of King Lear, however, while most modern additions do conflate them, the 1623 folio version is so different from the 1608 quarto, that the *Oxford Shakespeare* prints them both, arguing that they cannot be conflated without confusion.

Poems

In 1593 and 1594, when the theatres were closed because of plague, Shakespeare published two narrative poems on erotic themes, *Venus and Adonis* and *The Rape of Lucrece.* He dedicated them to Henry Wriothesley, Earl of Southampton. In *Venus and Adonis,* an innocent Adonis rejects the sexual advances of

Venus; while in *The Rape of Lucrece,* the virtuous wife Lucrece is raped by the lustful Tarquin. Influenced by Ovid's *Metamorphoses,* the poems show the guilt and moral confusion that result from uncontrolled lust. Both proved popular and were often reprinted during Shakespeare's lifetime. A third narrative poem, *A Lover's Complaint,* in which a young woman laments her seduction by a persuasive suitor, was printed in the first edition of the *Sonnets* in 1609. Most scholars now accept that Shakespeare wrote *A Lover's Complaint.* Critics consider that its fine qualities are marred by leaden effects. *The Phoenix and the Turtle,* printed in Robert Chester's 1601 *Love's Martyr,* mourns the deaths of the legendary phoenix and his lover, the faithful turtle dove. In 1599, two early drafts of sonnets 138 and 144 appeared in *The Passionate Pilgrim,* published under Shakespeare's name but without his permission.

Sonnets

Published in 1609, the *Sonnets* were the last of Shakespeare's non-dramatic works to be printed. Scholars are not certain when each of the 154 sonnets was composed, but evidence suggests that Shakespeare wrote sonnets throughout his career for a private readership. Even before the two unauthorised sonnets appeared in *The Passionate Pilgrim* in 1599, Francis Meres had referred in 1598 to Shakespeare's "sugred Sonnets among his private friends". Few analysts believe that the published collection follows Shakespeare's intended sequence. He seems to have planned two contrasting series: one about uncontrollable lust for a married woman of dark complexion (the "dark lady"), and one about conflicted love for a fair young man (the "fair youth"). It remains unclear if these figures represent real individuals, or if the authorial "I" who addresses them represents Shakespeare himself, though Wordsworth believed that with the sonnets "Shakespeare unlocked his heart". The 1609 edition was dedicated to a "Mr. W.H.", credited as "the only begetter" of the poems. It is not known whether this was written by Shakespeare himself or by the publisher, Thomas Thorpe, whose initials appear at the foot of the dedication page; nor is it known who Mr. W.H. was, despite numerous theories, or whether Shakespeare even authorised the publication. Critics praise the *Sonnets* as a profound meditation on the nature of love, sexual passion, procreation, death, and time. The production of Shakespeare's Sonnets was in some way influenced by the Italian sonnet:

> It was popularised by Dante and Petrarch and refined in Spain and France by DuBellay and Ronsard. Shakespeare probably had access to these last two authors, and read English poets as Richard Field and John Davies. The French and Italian poets gave preference to the Italian form of sonnet—two groups of four lines, or quatrains (always rhymed a-b-b-a a-b-b-a) followed by two groups of three lines, or tercets (variously rhymed c-c-d e-e-d or c-c-d e-d-e)—which created a sonorous music in the vowel rich Romance languages, but in Shakespeare it is artificial and monotonous for the English language. To overcome this problem derived from the difference of language, Shakespeare chose to follow the idiomatic rhyme scheme used by Philip Sidney in his *Astrophel and Stella* (published posthumously in 1591), where the rhymes are interlaced in two pairs of couplets to make the quatrain.

Style

Shakespeare's first plays were written in the

conventional style of the day. He wrote them in a stylised language that does not always spring naturally from the needs of the characters or the drama. The poetry depends on extended, sometimes elaborate metaphors and conceits, and the language is often rhetorical—written for actors to declaim rather than speak. The grand speeches in *Titus Andronicus*, in the view of some critics, often hold up the action, for example; and the verse in *Two Gentlemen of Verona* has been described as stilted.

Soon, however, Shakespeare began to adapt the traditional styles to his own purposes. The opening soliloquy of *Richard III* has its roots in the self-declaration of Vice in medieval drama. At the same time, Richard's vivid self-awareness looks forward to the soliloquies of Shakespeare's mature plays. No single play marks a change from the traditional to the freer style. Shakespeare combined the two throughout his career, with *Romeo and Juliet* perhaps the best example of the mixing of the styles. By the time of *Romeo and Juliet, Richard II*, and *A Midsummer Night's Dream* in the mid-1590s, Shakespeare had begun to write a more natural poetry. He increasingly tuned his metaphors and images to the needs of the drama itself.

Shakespeare's standard poetic form was blank verse, composed in iambic pentameter. In practice, this meant that his verse was usually unrhymed and consisted of ten syllables to a line, spoken with a stress on every second syllable. The blank verse of his early plays is quite different from that of his later ones. It is often beautiful, but its sentences tend to start, pause, and finish at the end of lines, with the risk of monotony. Once Shakespeare mastered traditional blank verse, he began to interrupt and vary its flow.

This technique releases the new power and flexibility of the poetry in plays such as *Julius Caesar* and *Hamlet*.

After *Hamlet*, Shakespeare varied his poetic style further, particularly in the more emotional passages of the late tragedies. The literary critic A.C. Bradley described this style as "more concentrated, rapid, varied, and, in construction, less regular, not seldom twisted or elliptical". In the last phase of his career, Shakespeare adopted many techniques to achieve these effects. These included run-on lines, irregular pauses and stops, and extreme variations in sentence structure and length. In *Macbeth*, for example, the language darts from one unrelated metaphor or simile to another: "was the hope drunk/ Wherein you dressed yourself?" (1.7.35–38); "...pity, like a naked new-born babe/ Striding the blast, or heaven's cherubim, hors'd/ Upon the sightless couriers of the air..." (1.7.21–25). The listener is challenged to complete the sense. The late romances, with their shifts in time and surprising turns of plot, inspired a last poetic style in which long and short sentences are set against one another, clauses are piled up, subject and object are reversed, and words are omitted, creating an effect of spontaneity.

Shakespeare's poetic genius was allied with a practical sense of the theatre. Like all playwrights of the time, Shakespeare dramatised stories from sources such as Petrarch and Holinshed. He reshaped each plot to create several centres of interest and show as many sides of a narrative to the audience as possible. This strength of design ensures that a Shakespeare play can survive translation, cutting and wide interpretation without loss to its core drama. As Shakespeare's mastery grew, he gave his characters clearer and more varied motivations and distinctive patterns of speech.

He preserved aspects of his earlier style in the later plays, however. In his late romances, he deliberately returned to a more artificial style, which emphasised the illusion of theatre.

Influence

Shakespeare's work has made a lasting impression on later theatre and literature. In particular, he expanded the dramatic potential of characterisation, plot, language, and genre. Until *Romeo and Juliet*, for example, romance had not been viewed as a worthy topic for tragedy. Soliloquies had been used mainly to convey information about characters or events; but Shakespeare used them to explore characters' minds. His work heavily influenced later poetry. The Romantic poets attempted to revive Shakespearean verse drama, though with little success. Critic George Steiner described all English verse dramas from Coleridge to Tennyson as "feeble variations on Shakespearean themes."

Shakespeare influenced novelists such as Thomas Hardy, William Faulkner, and Charles Dickens. The American novelist Herman Melville's soliloquies owe much to Shakespeare; his Captain Ahab in *Moby-Dick* is a classic tragic hero, inspired by *King Lear*. Scholars have identified 20,000 pieces of music linked to Shakespeare's works. These include two operas by Giuseppe Verdi, *Otello* and *Falstaff*, whose critical standing compares with that of the source plays. Shakespeare has also inspired many painters, including the Romantics and the Pre-Raphaelites. The Swiss Romantic artist Henry Fuseli, a friend of William Blake, even translated *Macbeth* into German. The psychoanalyst Sigmund Freud drew on Shakespearean psychology, in particular that of Hamlet, for his theories of human nature.

In Shakespeare's day, English grammar and spelling were less standardised than they are now, and his use of language helped shape modern English. Samuel Johnson quoted him more often than any other author in his *A Dictionary of the English Language*, the first serious work of its type. Expressions such as "with bated breath" (*Merchant of Venice*) and "a foregone conclusion" (*Othello*) have found their way into everyday English speech.

Reputation

Shakespeare was never revered in his lifetime, but he received his share of praise. In 1598, the cleric and author Francis Meres singled him out from a group of English writers as "the most excellent" in both comedy and tragedy. And the authors of the *Parnassus* plays at St John's College, Cambridge, numbered him with Chaucer, Gower and Spenser. In the First Folio, Ben Jonson called Shakespeare the "Soul of the age, the applause, delight, the wonder of our stage", though he had remarked elsewhere that "Shakespeare wanted art".

Between the Restoration of the monarchy in 1660 and the end of the seventeenth century, classical ideas were in vogue. As a result, critics of the time mostly rated Shakespeare below John Fletcher and Ben Jonson. Thomas Rymer, for example, condemned Shakespeare for mixing the comic with the tragic. Nevertheless, poet and critic John Dryden rated Shakespeare highly, saying of Jonson, "I admire him, but I love Shakespeare". For several decades, Rymer's view held sway; but during the eighteenth century, critics began to respond to Shakespeare on his own terms and acclaim what they termed his natural genius. A series of scholarly editions of his work, notably those of Samuel Johnson in 1765 and Edmond Malone in 1790, added to his growing reputation. By 1800, he was firmly enshrined as the national poet. In the eighteenth and nineteenth centuries, his reputation also spread abroad. Among those who championed him were the writers Voltaire, Goethe, Stendhal and Victor Hugo.

During the Romantic era, Shakespeare was praised by the poet and literary philosopher Samuel Taylor Coleridge; and the critic August Wilhelm Schlegel translated his plays in the spirit of German Romanticism. In the nineteenth century, critical admiration for Shakespeare's genius often bordered on adulation. "That King Shakespeare," the essayist Thomas Carlyle wrote in 1840, "does not he shine, in crowned sovereignty, over us all, as the noblest, gentlest, yet strongest of rallying signs; indestructible". The Victorians produced his plays as lavish spectacles on a grand scale. The playwright and critic George Bernard Shaw mocked the cult of Shakespeare worship as "bardolatry". He claimed that the new naturalism of Ibsen's plays had made Shakespeare obsolete.

The modernist revolution in the arts during the early twentieth century, far from discarding Shakespeare, eagerly enlisted his work in the service of the avant garde. The Expressionists in Germany and the Futurists in Moscow mounted productions of his plays. Marxist playwright and director Bertolt Brecht devised an epic theatre under the influence of Shakespeare. The poet and critic T.S. Eliot argued against Shaw that Shakespeare's "primitiveness" in fact made him truly modern. Eliot, along with G. Wilson Knight and the school of New Criticism, led a movement towards a closer reading of Shakespeare's imagery. In the 1950s, a wave of new critical approaches replaced modernism and paved the way for "post-modern" studies of Shakespeare.

Shakespeare's works include the 36 plays printed in the First Folio of 1623, listed below according to their folio classification as comedies, histories and tragedies. Two plays not included in the First Folio, *The Two Noble Kinsmen* and *Pericles, Prince of Tyre,* are now accepted as part of the canon, with scholars agreed that Shakespeare made a major contribution to their composition. No poems were included in the First Folio. In the late nineteenth century, Edward Dowden classified four of the late comedies as romances, and though many scholars prefer to call them *tragicomedies,* his term is often used. These plays and the associated *Two Noble Kinsmen* are marked with an asterisk below. In 1896, Frederick S. Boas coined the term "problem plays" to describe four plays:

> *All's Well That Ends Well, Measure for Measure, Troilus and Cressida* and *Hamlet.* "Dramas as singular in theme and temper cannot be strictly called comedies or tragedies", he wrote. "We may therefore borrow a convenient phrase from the theatre of today and class them together as Shakespeare's problem plays." The term, much debated and sometimes applied to other plays, remains in use, though *Hamlet* is definitively classed as a tragedy. The other problem plays are marked below with a double dagger.

Christopher Marlowe

Christopher Marlowe (c. 26 February 1564 – 30 May 1593) was an English dramatist, poet and translator of the Elizabethan era. The foremost Elizabethan tragedian next to William Shakespeare, he is known for his blank verse, his overreaching protagonists, and his mysterious death.

A warrant was issued for Marlowe's arrest on 18 May 1593. No reason for it was given, though it was thought to be connected to allegations of blasphemy—a manuscript believed to have been written by Marlowe was said to contain "vile heretical conceipts." He was brought before the Privy Council for questioning on 20 May, after which he had to report to them daily. Ten days later, he was stabbed to death by Ingram Frizer. Whether the stabbing was connected to his arrest has never been resolved

Marlowe was born to a shoemaker in Canterbury named John Marlowe and his wife Catherine. His date of birth is not known, but he was baptized on 26 February 1564, and thus born a few days before.

He attended The King's School, Canterbury (where a house is now named after him) and Corpus Christi College, Cambridge on a scholarship and received his Bachelor of Arts degree in 1584. In 1587 the university hesitated to award him his master's degree because of a rumour that he had converted to Roman Catholicism and intended to go to the English college at Rheims to prepare for the priesthood. However, his degree was awarded on schedule when the Privy Council intervened on his behalf, commending him for his "faithful dealing" and "good service" to the Queen. The nature of Marlowe's service was not specified by the Council, but its letter to the Cambridge authorities has provoked much speculation, notably the theory that Marlowe was operating as a secret agent working for Sir Francis Walsingham's intelligence service. No direct evidence supports this theory, although the Council's letter is evidence that Marlowe had served the government in some capacity.

Literary Career

Dido, Queen of Carthage was Marlowe's first drama. Marlowe's first play performed on stage in London stage was *Tamburlaine* (1587) about the conqueror Timur, who rises from shepherd to warrior. It is among the first English plays in blank verse, and, with Thomas Kyd's *The Spanish Tragedy*, generally is considered the beginning of the mature phase of the Elizabethan theatre. *Tamburlaine* was a success, and was followed with *Tamburlaine Part II*. The sequence of his plays is unknown; all deal with controversial themes.

The Jew of Malta, about a Maltese Jew's barbarous revenge against the city authorities, has a prologue delivered by a character representing Machiavelli.

Edward the Second is an English history play about the deposition of King Edward II by his barons and the Queen, who resent the undue influence the king's favourites have in court and state affairs.

The Massacre at Paris is a short and luridly written work, probably a reconstruction from memory of the original performance text, portraying the events of the Saint Bartholomew's Day Massacre in 1572, which English Protestants invoked as the blackest example of Catholic treachery. It features the silent "English Agent", whom subsequent tradition has identified with Marlowe himself and his connections to the secret service. Along with *The Tragical History of Doctor Faustus*, *The Massacre at Paris* is considered his most dangerous play, as agitators in London seized on its theme to advocate the murders of refugees from the low countries and, indeed, it warns Elizabeth I of this possibility in its last scene.

The Tragical History of Doctor Faustus, based on the German Faustbuch, was the first dramatised version of the Faust legend of a scholar's dealing with the devil. While versions of "The Devil's Pact" can be traced back to the 4th century, Marlowe deviates significantly by having his hero unable to "burn his books" or repenting to a merciful God in order to have his contract annulled at the end of the play. Marlowe's protagonist is instead torn apart by demons and dragged off screaming to hell. Dr Faustus is a textual problem for scholars as it was highly edited (and possibly censored) and rewritten after Marlowe's death. Two versions of the play exist: the 1604 quarto, also known as the A text, and the 1616 quarto or B text. Many scholars believe that the A text is more representative of Marlowe's original because it contains irregular character names and idiosyncratic spelling: the hallmarks of a text that used the author's handwritten manuscript, or "foul papers", as a major source.

Marlowe's plays were enormously successful, thanks in part, no doubt, to the imposing stage presence of Edward Alleyn. He was unusually tall for the time, and the haughty roles of Tamburlaine, Faustus, and Barabas were probably written especially for him. Marlowe's plays were the foundation of the repertoire of Alleyn's company, the Admiral's Men, throughout the 1590s.

Marlowe also wrote poetry, including a, possibly, unfinished minor epic, *Hero and Leander* (published with a continuation by George Chapman in 1598), the popular lyric *The Passionate Shepherd to His Love,* and translations of Ovid's *Amores* and the first book of Lucan's *Pharsalia.*

The two parts of *Tamburlaine* were published in 1590; all Marlowe's other works were published posthumously. In 1599, his translation of Ovid was banned and copies publicly burned as part of Archbishop Whitgift's crackdown on offensive material.

The Legend

As with other writers of the period, little is known about Marlowe. What little evidence there is can be found in legal records and other official documents. This has not stopped writers of both fiction and non-fiction from speculating about his activities and character. Marlowe has often been described as a spy, a brawler, a heretic and a homosexual, as well as a "magician," "duellist," "tobacco-user," "counterfeiter" and "rakehell." The evidence for most of these claims is slight. The bare facts of Marlowe's life have been embellished by many writers into colourful, and often fanciful, narratives of the Elizabethan underworld. However, J.B. Steane remarked, "it seems absurd to dismiss all of these Elizabethan rumours and accusations as 'the Marlowe myth'"

Spying

Marlowe is often alleged to have been a government spy. The author Charles Nicholl speculates this is so, and that Marlowe's recruitment took place when he was at Cambridge. Surviving college records from the period indicate Marlowe had a series of unusually lengthy absences from the university - much longer than permitted by university regulations - that began in the academic year 1584-1585. Surviving college buttery (dining room) accounts indicate he began spending lavishly on food and drink during the periods he was in attendance - more than he could have afforded on his known scholarship income.

As noted above, in 1587 the Privy Council ordered Cambridge University to award Marlowe his MA, denying rumours that he intended to go to the English Catholic college in Rheims, saying instead that he had been engaged in unspecified "affaires" on "matters touching the benefit of his country". This from a document dated 29 June 1587, from the Public Records Office - *Acts of Privy Council.*

It has sometimes been theorised that Marlowe was the "Morley" who was tutor to Arbella Stuart in 1589. This possibility was first raised in a *TLS* letter by E. St John Brooks in 1937; in a letter to *Notes and Queries,* John Baker has added that only Marlowe could be Arbella's tutor due to the absence of any other known "Morley" from the period with an MA and not otherwise occupied. If Marlowe was Arbella's tutor, (and some biographers think that the "Morley" in question may have been a brother of the musician Thomas Morley) it might indicate that he was a spy, since Arbella, niece of Mary Queen of Scots and cousin of James VI of Scotland, later James I of England, was at the time a strong candidate for the succession to Elizabeth's throne.

In 1592 Marlowe was arrested in the Dutch town of Flushing for attempting to counterfeit coins and use the proceeds to assist seditious Catholics. He was sent to be dealt with by the Lord Treasurer (Burghley) but no charge or imprisonment resulted. This arrest may have disrupted another of Marlowe's spying missions: by giving the resulting coinage to the Catholic cause he was to infiltrate the followers of the active Catholic plotter William Stanley and report back to Burghley.

Last Days

In early May 1593 several bills were posted about London threatening Protestant refugees from France and the Netherlands who had settled in the city. One of these, the "Dutch church libel," written in blank verse, contained allusions to several of Marlowe's plays and was signed, "Tamburlaine". On 11 May the Privy Council ordered the arrest of those responsible for the libels. The next day, Marlowe's colleague Thomas Kyd was arrested. Kyd's lodgings were searched and a fragment of a heretical tract was found. Kyd asserted, possibly under torture, that it had belonged to Marlowe. Two years earlier they had both been working for an aristocratic patron, probably Ferdinando Stanley, Lord Strange, and Kyd suggested that at this time, when they were sharing a workroom, the document had found its way among his papers. Marlowe's arrest was ordered on 18 May. Marlowe was not in London, but was staying with Thomas Walsingham, the cousin of the late Sir Francis Walsingham, Elizabeth's principal secretary in the 1580s and a man deeply involved in state espionage. However, he duly appeared before the Privy Council on 20 May and was instructed to "give his daily attendance on their Lordships, until he shall be licensed to the contrary". On 30 May, Marlowe was murdered.

Various versions of Marlowe's death were current at the time. Francis Meres says Marlowe was "stabbed to death by a bawdy serving-man, a rival of his in his lewd love" as punishment for his "epicurism and atheism." In 1917, in the *Dictionary of National Biography,* Sir Sidney Lee wrote that Marlowe was killed in a drunken fight, and this is still often stated as fact today.

The facts only came to light in 1925 when the scholar Leslie Hotson discovered the coroner's report on Marlowe's death in the Public Record Office. Marlowe had spent all day in a house in Deptford, owned by the widow Eleanor Bull. With him were three men: Ingram Frizer, Nicholas Skeres and Robert Poley. All three had been employed by the Walsinghams. Skeres and Poley had helped snare the conspirators in the Babington plot and Frizer was a servant of Thomas Walsingham. Witnesses testified that Frizer and Marlowe had earlier argued over the bill for their drink (now famously known as the 'Reckoning') exchanging "divers malicious words". Later, while Frizer was sitting at a table between the other two and Marlowe was lying behind him on a couch, Marlowe snatched Frizer's dagger and began attacking him. In the ensuing struggle, according to the coroner's report, Marlowe was accidentally stabbed above the right eye, killing him instantly. The jury concluded that Frizer acted in self-defence, and within a month he was pardoned. Marlowe was buried in an unmarked grave in the churchyard of St. Nicholas, Deptford, on 1 June 1593.

Marlowe's death is alleged by some to be an assassination for the following reasons:

1. The three men who were in the room with him when he died were all connected both to the state secret service and to the London underworld. Frizer and Skeres also had a long record as loan sharks and con-men, as shown by court records. Bull's house also had "links to the government's spy network".
2. Their story that they were on a day's pleasure outing to Deptford is alleged to be implausible. In

fact, they spent the whole day closeted together, deep in discussion. Also, Robert Poley was carrying confidential despatches to the Queen, who was at her palace of Nonsuch in Surrey, but instead of delivering them, he spent the day with Marlowe and the other two.

3. It seems too much of a coincidence that Marlowe's death occurred only a few days after his arrest for heresy.

4. The manner of Marlowe's arrest is alleged to suggest causes more tangled than a simple charge of heresy would generally indicate. He was released in spite of *prima facie* evidence, and even though the charges implicitly connected Sir Walter Raleigh and the Earl of Northumberland with the heresy. Thus, some contend it to be probable that the investigation was meant primarily as a warning to the politicians in the "School of Night", or that it was connected with a power struggle within the Privy Council itself.

5. The various incidents that hint at a relationship with the Privy Council, and by the fact that his patron was Thomas Walsingham, Sir Francis's second cousin, who was actively involved in intelligence work.

For these reasons and others, Charles Nicholl argues there was more to Marlowe's death than emerged at the inquest. There are different theories of some degree of probability. Since there are only written documents on which to base any conclusions, and since it is probable that the most crucial information about his death was never committed to writing at all, it is unlikely that the full circumstances of Marlowe's death will ever be known.

Atheism

Marlowe was reputed to be an atheist which, at that time, held the dangerous implication of being an enemy of God. Modern historians, however, consider that his professed atheism, as with his supposed Catholicism, may have been no more than an elaborate and sustained pretence adopted to further his work as a government spy. Contemporary evidence comes from Marlowe's accuser in Flushing, an informer called Richard Baines. The governor of Flushing had reported that both men had accused one "of malice one to another" of instigating the counterfeiting, and of intention to go over to Catholicism; such an action was considered atheistic by the Protestants, who constituted the dominant religious faction in England at that time. Following Marlowe's arrest on a charge of atheism in 1593, Baines submitted to the authorities a "note containing the opinion of one Christopher Marly concerning his damnable judgment of religion, and scorn of God's word." Baines attributes to Marlowe a total of eighteen items which "scoff at the pretensions of the Old and New Testament" such as, "Christ was a bastard and his mother dishonest [unchaste]," "the woman of Samaria and her sister were whores and that Christ knew them dishonestly," and, "St John the Evangelist was bedfellow to Christ and leaned always in his bosom", and, "that he used him as the sinners of Sodom". He also claims that Marlowe had Catholic sympathies. Other passages are merely sceptical in tone: "he persuades men to atheism, willing them not to be afraid of bugbears and hobgoblins". The final paragraph of Baines' document reads:

These thinges, with many other shall by good & honest witnes be aproved to be his opinions and Comon Speeches, and that this Marlow doth not only hould them himself, but almost into every Company he Cometh he perswades men to Atheism willing them not to be afeard of bugbeares and hobgoblins, and vtterly scorning both god and his ministers as I Richard Baines will Justify & approue both by mine oth and the testimony of many honest men, and almost al men with whome he hath Conversed any time will testify the same, and as I think all men in Cristianity ought to indevor that the mouth of so dangerous a member may be stopped, he saith likewise that he hath quoted a number of Contrarieties oute of the Scripture which he hath giuen to some great men who in Convenient time shalbe named. When these thinges shalbe Called in question the witnes shalbe produced.

Similar statements were made by Thomas Kyd after his imprisonment and possible torture; both Kyd and Baines connect Marlowe with the mathematician Thomas Harriot and Walter Raleigh's circle. Another document claims that Marlowe had read an "atheist lecture" before Raleigh; a man called Richard Chomley was charged with atheism and treason shortly after Marlowe's death, and noted in his testimony that "one Marlowe is able to show more sound reasons from atheism than any divine in England is able to give to prove divinity and that Marlowe told him that he hath read the atheist lecture to Sir Walter Raleigh and others".

Some critics believe that Marlowe sought to disseminate these views in his work and that he identified with his rebellious and iconoclastic protagonists. However, plays had to be approved by the Master of the Revels before they could be performed, and the censorship of publications was under the control of the Archbishop of Canterbury.

Presumably these authorities did not consider any of Marlowe's works to be unacceptable (apart from the *Amores*).

The public burning in 1589 of Francis Kett, a tutor at Corpus Christi College, was used by many informants to associate the playwright with the writing of seditious literature. Kett was charged with heresy based on his avowal of Unitarianism, a denial of the Holy Trinity, and this matches the content of the heretical material blamed on Marlowe by fellow playwright Thomas Kyd, but Kett's "fervent" religious beliefs seem at odds with Marlowe's supposed atheism. Kett had resigned his post only a few months after Marlowe joined the college.

Heresy and atheism were also used to describe those dealing in necromancy and alchemy. A common misconception about Marlowe, based solely upon *Doctor Faustus,* is that he himself was a proponent of the 'dark arts'. It is certainly true, when one considers the aforementioned play, that Marlowe had studied incantation rituals, but whether he practised them is another matter entirely.

Reputation

Whatever the particular focus of modern critics, biographers and novelists, for his contemporaries in the literary world, Marlowe was above all an admired and influential artist. Within weeks of his death, George Peele remembered him as "Marley, the Muses' darling"; Michael Drayton noted that he "Had in him those brave translunary things/That the first poets had", and Ben Jonson wrote of "Marlowe's mighty line". Thomas Nashe wrote warmly of his friend, "poor deceased Kit Marlowe". So too did the publisher

Edward Blount, in the dedication of *Hero and Leander* to Sir Thomas Walsingham.

Among the few contemporary dramatists to say anything negative about Marlowe was the anonymous author of the Cambridge University play *The Return From Parnassus* (1598) who wrote, "Pity it is that wit so ill should dwell,/Wit lent from heaven, but vices sent from hell."

The most famous tribute to Marlowe was paid by Shakespeare in *As You Like It,* where he not only quotes a line from *Hero and Leander* (Dead Shepherd, now I find thy saw of might, "Who ever loved that loved not at first sight?") but also gives to the clown Touchstone the words "When a man's verses cannot be understood, nor a man's good wit seconded with the forward child, understanding, it strikes a man more dead than a great reckoning in a little room." This appears to be a reference to Marlowe's murder which involved a fight over the "reckoning" – the bill.

Shakespeare was heavily influenced by Marlowe in his early work, as can be seen in the re-using of Marlowe themes in *Antony and Cleopatra, The Merchant of Venice, Richard II,* and *Macbeth* (*Dido, Jew of Malta, Edward II* and *Dr Faustus* respectively). In *Hamlet,* after meeting with the travelling actors, Hamlet requests the Player perform a speech about the Trojan War, which at 2.2.429-32 has an echo of Marlowe's *Dido, Queen of Carthage.* Indeed, in *Love's Labour's Lost,* echoing Marlowe's *The Massacre at Paris,* Shakespeare brings on a character called Marcade who arrives to interrupt the merriment with news of the King's death. This is a fitting tribute for one who delighted in destruction in his plays.

Given the murky inconsistencies concerning the account of Marlowe's death, a theory has arisen centred on the notion that Marlowe may have faked his death and then continued to write under the assumed name of William Shakespeare. Authors who have propounded this theory include:

- Wilbur Gleason Zeigler *It Was Marlowe* (1895)
- Calvin Hoffman, *The Man Who Was Shakespeare,* Mitre Press (1955)
- Calvin Hoffman, *The Murder of the Man Who Was Shakespeare,* Grosset & Dunlap (1960)
- Daryl Pinksen, *Marlowe's Ghost* (2008)
- Samuel Blumenfeld's *The Marlowe-Shakespeare Connection: A New Study of the Authorship Question*
- Louis Ule, *Christopher Marlowe (1564-1607): A Biography*
- A D Wraight, *The Story that the Sonnets Tell* (1994)
- Roderick L Eagle, *The Mystery of Marlowe's Death,* N&Q (1952)
- William Honey, *The Shakespeare Epitaph Deciphered,* Mitre Press (1969)

Ben Jonson

Benjamin Jonson was an English Renaissance dramatist, poet and actor. A contemporary of William Shakespeare, he is best known for his satirical plays, particularly *Volpone, The Alchemist,* and *Bartholomew Fair,* which are considered his best, and his lyric poems. A man of vast reading and a seemingly insatiable appetite for controversy, Jonson had an unparalleled breadth of influence on Jacobean and Caroline playwrights and poets.

Early Life

Although he was born in Westminster, London, Jonson claimed his family was of Scottish Border country descent, and this claim may have been supported by the fact that his coat of arms bears three spindles or rhombi, a device shared by a Borders family, the Johnstones of Annandale. His father died a month before Ben's birth, and his mother remarried two years later, to a master bricklayer. Jonson attended school in St. Martin's Lane, and was later sent to Westminster School, where one of his teachers was William Camden. Jonson remained friendly with Camden, whose broad scholarship evidently influenced his own style, until the latter's death in 1623. On leaving, Jonson was once thought to have gone on to the University of Cambridge; Jonson himself said that he did not go to university, but was put to a trade immediately: a legend recorded by Fuller indicates that he worked on a garden wall in Lincoln's Inn. He soon had enough of the trade, probably bricklaying, and spent some time in the Low Countries as a volunteer with the regiments of Francis Vere. In conversations with the poet William Drummond, subsequently published as the *Hawthornden Manuscripts*, Jonson reports that while in the Netherlands he killed an opponent in single combat and stripped him of his weapons.

Ben Jonson married, some time before 1594, a woman he described to Drummond as "a shrew, yet honest." His wife has not been definitively identified, but she is sometimes identified as the Ann Lewis who married a Benjamin Jonson at St Magnus-the-Martyr, near London Bridge. The registers of St. Martin's Church state that his eldest daughter Mary died in

November, 1593, when she was only six months old. His eldest son Benjamin died of the plague ten years later (Jonson's epitaph to him *On My First Sonne* was written shortly after), and a second Benjamin died in 1635. For five years somewhere in this period, Jonson lived separately from his wife, enjoying instead the hospitality of Lord Aubigny.

By the summer of 1597, Jonson had a fixed engagement in the Admiral's Men, then performing under Philip Henslowe's management at The Rose. John Aubrey reports, on uncertain authority, that Jonson was not successful as an actor; whatever his skills as an actor, he was evidently more valuable to the company as a writer.

By this time, Jonson had begun to write original plays for the Lord Admiral's Men; in 1598, he was mentioned by Francis Meres in his *Palladis Tamia* as one of "the best for tragedy." None of his early tragedies survive, however. An undated comedy, *The Case is Altered,* may be his earliest surviving play.

In 1597, a play co-written with Thomas Nashe entitled *The Isle of Dogs* was suppressed after causing great offence. Arrest warrants for Jonson and Nashe were subsequently issued by Elizabeth's so-called interrogator, Richard Topcliffe. Jonson was jailed in Marshalsea Prison and famously charged with "Leude and mutynous behavior", while Nashe managed to escape to Great Yarmouth. A year later, Jonson was again briefly imprisoned, this time in Newgate Prison, for killing another man, an actor Gabriel Spenser, in a duel on 22 September 1598 in Hogsden Fields, (today part of Hoxton). Tried on a charge of manslaughter, Jonson pleaded guilty but was subsequently released by benefit of clergy, a legal ploy through which he gained leniency by reciting a brief bible verse in Latin, forfeiting his 'goods and chattels' and being branded on his left thumb.

In 1598, Jonson produced his first great success, *Every Man in his Humour*, capitalising on the vogue for humour plays that had been begun by George Chapman with *An Humorous Day's Mirth*. William Shakespeare was among the first cast. This play was followed the next year by *Every Man Out of His Humour*, a pedantic attempt to imitate Aristophanes. It is not known whether this was a success on stage, but when published, it proved popular and went through several editions.

Jonson's other work for the theater in the last years of Elizabeth I's reign was unsurprisingly marked by fighting and controversy. *Cynthia's Revels* was produced by the Children of the Chapel Royal at Blackfriars Theatre in 1600. It satirized both John Marston, who Jonson believed had accused him of lustfulness, probably in *Histrio-Mastix*, and Thomas Dekker, against whom Jonson's animus is not known. Jonson attacked the same two poets again in 1601's *Poetaster*. Dekker responded with *Satiromastix*, subtitled "the untrussing of the humorous poet". The final scene of this play, whilst certainly not to be taken at face value as a portrait of Jonson, offers a caricature that is recognisable from Drummond's report - boasting about himself and condemning other poets, criticising performances of his plays, and calling attention to himself in any available way.

This "War of the Theatres" appears to have been concluded with reconciliation on all sides. Jonson collaborated with Dekker on a pageant welcoming James I to England in 1603 although Drummond reports that Jonson called Dekker a rogue. Marston dedicated *The Malcontent* to Jonson and the two collaborated with Chapman on *Eastward Ho,* a 1605 play whose anti-Scottish sentiment landed both authors in jail for a brief time.

At the beginning of the reign of James I of England in 1603 Jonson joined other poets and playwrights in welcoming the reign of the new king. Jonson quickly adapted himself to the additional demand for masques and entertainments introduced with the new reign and fostered by both the king and his consort Anne of Denmark.

Ascendance

Jonson flourished as a dramatist during the first decade or so of James's reign; by 1616, he had produced all the plays on which his reputation as a dramatist depends. These include the tragedy of *Catiline* (acted and printed 1611), which achieved only limited success, and the comedies *Volpone,* (acted 1605 and printed in 1607), *Epicoene, or the Silent Woman* (1609), *The Alchemist* (1610), *Bartholomew Fair* (1614) and *The Devil is an Ass* (1616). *The Alchemist* and *Volpone* appear to have been successful at once. Of *Epicoene,* Jonson told Drummond of a satirical verse which reported that the play's subtitle was appropriate, since its audience had refused to applaud the play (i.e., remained silent). Yet *Epicoene,* along with *Bartholomew Fair* and (to a lesser extent) *The Devil is an Ass* have in modern times achieved a certain degree of recognition. While his life during this period was apparently more settled than it had been in the 1590s, his financial security was still not assured. In 1603, Overbury reported that Jonson was living on Aurelian

Townsend and "scorning the world."His trouble with English authorities continued. In 1603, he was questioned by the Privy Council about *Sejanus,* a politically-themed play about corruption in the Roman Empire. He was again in trouble for topical allusions in a play, now lost, in which he took part. After the discovery of the Gunpowder Plot, he appears to have been asked by the Privy Council to attempt to prevail on a certain priest to cooperate with the government; the priest he found was Father Thomas Wright, who heard Fawkes's confession.

At the same time, Jonson pursued a more prestigious career as a writer of masques for James' court. *The Satyr* (1603) and *The Masque of Blackness* (1605) are but two of the some two dozen masques Jonson wrote for James or for Queen Anne; the latter was praised by Swinburne as the consummate example of this now-extinct genre, which mingled speech, dancing, and spectacle. On many of these projects he collaborated, not always peacefully, with designer Inigo Jones. Perhaps partly as a result of this new career, Jonson gave up writing plays for the public theaters for a decade. Jonson later told Drummond that he had made less than two hundred pounds on all his plays together.

1616 saw a pension of 100 marks (about £60) a year conferred upon him, leading some to identify him as England's first Poet Laureate. This sign of royal favour may have encouraged him to publish the first volume of the folio collected edition of his works that year. Other volumes followed in 1640–41 and 1692.

In 1618, Ben Jonson set out for his ancestral Scotland on foot. He spent over a year there, and the best-remembered hospitality which he enjoyed was that of the Scottish poet, Drummond of Hawthornden. Drummond undertook to record as much of Jonson's conversation as he could in his diary, and thus recorded aspects of Jonson's personality that would otherwise have been less clearly seen. Jonson delivers his opinions, in Drummond's terse reporting, in an expansive and even magisterial mood. In the postscript added by Drummond, he is described as "a great lover and praiser of himself, a contemner and scorner of others".

While in Scotland, he was made an honorary citizen of Edinburgh. On returning to England, he was awarded an honorary Master of Arts degree from Oxford University.

The period between 1605 and 1620 may be viewed as Jonson's heyday. In addition to his popularity on the public stage and in the royal hall, he enjoyed the patronage of aristocrats such as Elizabeth Sidney (daughter of Sir Philip Sidney) and Lady Mary Wroth. This connection with the Sidney family provided the impetus for one of Jonson's most famous lyrics, the country house poem *To Penshurst*.

Last Days

The 1620s began a lengthy and slow decline for Jonson. He was still well-known; from this time dates the prominence of the Sons of Ben or the "Tribe of Ben", those younger poets such as Robert Herrick, Richard Lovelace, and Sir John Suckling who took their bearing in verse from Jonson. However, a series of setbacks drained his strength and damaged his reputation.

Jonson returned to writing regular plays in the 1620s, but these are not considered among his best. They are of significant interest for the study of the culture of Charles I's England. *The Staple of News*, for example, offers a remarkable look at the earliest stage of English journalism. The lukewarm reception given that play was, however, nothing compared to the dismal failure of *The New Inn*; the cold reception given this play prompted Jonson to write a poem condemning his audience (the *Ode to Myself*), which in turn prompted Thomas Carew, one of the "Tribe of Ben," to respond in a poem that asks Jonson to recognize his own decline.

The principal factor in Jonson's partial eclipse was, however, the death of James and the accession of King Charles I in 1625. Justly or not, Jonson felt neglected by the new court. A decisive quarrel with Jones harmed his career as a writer of court masques, although he continued to entertain the court on an irregular basis. For his part, Charles displayed a certain degree of care for the great poet of his father's day: he increased Jonson's annual pension to £100 and included a tierce of wine.

Despite the strokes that he suffered in the 1620s, Jonson continued to write. At his death in 1637 he seems to have been working on another play, *The Sad Shepherd*. Though only two acts are extant, this represents a remarkable new direction for Jonson: a move into pastoral drama. During the early 1630s he also conducted a correspondence with James Howell, who warned him about disfavour at court in the wake of his dispute with Jones.

Jonson is buried in Westminster Abbey, with the inscription "O Rare Ben Johnson" *(sic)* set in the slab over his grave. It has been suggested that this could be read "Orare Ben Jonson" (pray for Ben Jonson), which would indicate a deathbed return to Catholicism, but the carving shows a distinct space between "O" and "rare". Researchers suggest that the tribute came from William D'Avenant, Jonson's successor as Poet Laureate, as the same phrase appears on his gravestone nearby. The fact that he was buried in an upright grave could be an indication of his reduced circumstances at the time of his death, although it has also been written that Jonson asked for a grave exactly 18 inches square from the monarch and received an upright grave to fit in the requested space. The same source claims that the epitaph came from the remark of a passerby to the grave.

Work

Drama

Apart from two tragedies, *Sejanus* and *Catiline,* that largely failed to impress Renaissance audiences, Jonson's work for the public theatres was in comedy. These plays vary in some respects. The minor early plays, particularly those written for the boy players, present somewhat looser plots and less-developed characters than those written later, for adult companies. Already in the plays which were his salvos in the Poet's War, he displays the keen eye for absurdity and hypocrisy that marks his best-known plays; in these early efforts, however, plot mostly takes second place to variety of incident and comic set-pieces. They are, also, notably ill-tempered. Thomas Davies called *Poetaster* "a contemptible mixture of the serio-comic, where the names of Augustus Caesar, Maecenas, Virgil, Horace, Ovid, and Tibullus, are all sacrificed upon the altar of private resentment." Another early comedy in a different vein, *The Case is Altered,* is markedly similar to Shakespeare's romantic comedies in its foreign setting, emphasis on genial wit, and love-plot. Henslowe's diary indicates that Jonson had a hand in numerous other plays, including many in genres such as English history with which he is not otherwise associated.

The comedies of his middle career, from *Eastward Ho* to *The Devil is an Ass* are for the most part city comedy, with a London setting, themes of trickery and money, and a distinct moral ambiguity, despite Jonson's professed aim in the Prologue to *Volpone* to "mix profit with your pleasure". His late plays or "dotages," particularly *The Magnetic Lady* and *The Sad Shepherd*, exhibit some signs of an accommodation with the romantic tendencies of Elizabethan comedy.

Within this general progression, however, Jonson's comic style remained constant and easily recognizable. He announces his programme in the prologue to the folio version of *Every Man in His Humour*; he promises to represent "deeds, and language, such as men do use." He planned to write comedies that revived the classical premises of Elizabethan dramatic theory—or rather, since all but the loosest English comedies could claim some descent from Plautus and Terence, he intended to apply those premises with rigour. This commitment entailed negations: after *The Case is Altered*, Jonson eschewed distant locations, noble characters, romantic plots, and other staples of Elizabethan comedy. Jonson focused instead on the satiric and realistic inheritance of new comedy. He sets his plays in contemporary settings, peoples them with recognizable types, and sets them to actions that, if not strictly realistic, involve everyday motives such as greed and jealousy. In accordance with the temper of his age, he was often so broad in his characterisation that many of his most famous scenes border on the farcical. He was, moreover, more diligent in adhering to the classical unities than many of his peers—although as Margaret Cavendish noted, the unity of action in the major comedies was rather compromised by Jonson's abundance of incident. To this classical model Jonson applies the two features of his style which save his classical imitations from mere pedantry: the vividness with which he depicts the lives of his characters, and the intricacy of his plots. Coleridge, for instance, claimed that *The Alchemist* had one of the three most perfect plots in literature.

Poetry

Jonson's poetry, like his drama, is informed by his classical learning. Some of his better-known poems are close translations of Greek or Roman models; all display the careful attention to form and style that often came naturally to those trained in classics in the humanist manner. Jonson, however, largely avoided the debates about rhyme and meter that had consumed Elizabethan classicists such as Campion and Harvey. Accepting both rhyme and stress, Jonson uses them to mimic the classical qualities of simplicity, restraint, and precision.

"Epigrams" is an entry in a genre that was popular among late-Elizabethan and Jacobean audiences, although Jonson was perhaps the only poet of his time to work in its full classical range. The epigrams explore various attitudes, most but not all of them from the satiric stock of the day: complaints against women, courtiers, and spies abound. The condemnatory poems are short and anonymous; Jonson's epigrams of praise, including a famous poem to Camden and lines to Lucy Harington, are somewhat longer and mostly addressed to specific individuals. Although it is an epigram in the classical sense of the genre, "On My First Son" is neither satirical nor very short; the poem, and others like it, resemble what a later age sometimes called "lyric poetry." The poems of "The Forest" also appeared in the first folio. Most of the fifteen poems are addressed to Jonson's aristocratic supporters, but the most famous are his country-house poem "To Penshurst" and the poem "To Celia" ("Come, my Celia, let us prove") that appears also in "Volpone."

"Underwood," published in the expanded folio of 1640, is a larger and more heterogeneous group of poems. It contains "A Celebration of Charis," Jonson's most extended effort at love poetry; various religious pieces; encomiastic poems including the poem to Shakespeare and a sonnet on Mary Wroth; the "Execration against Vulcan" and others. The 1640 volume also contains three elegies which have often been ascribed to Donne.

Relationship with Shakespeare

There are many legends about Jonson's rivalry with Shakespeare, some of which may be true. Drummond reports that during their conversation, Jonson scoffed at two apparent absurdities in Shakespeare's plays: a nonsensical line in *Julius Caesar*, and the setting of *The Winter's Tale* on the non-existent seacoast of Bohemia. Drummond also reports Jonson saying that Shakespeare "wanted art." Whether Drummond is viewed as accurate or not, the comments fit well with Jonson's well-known theories about literature.

In *Timber,* which was published posthumously and reflects his lifetime of practical experience, Jonson offers a fuller and more conciliatory comment. He recalls being told by certain actors that Shakespeare never blotted (i.e., crossed out) a line when he wrote. His own response, "Would he had blotted a thousand," was taken as malicious. However, Jonson explains, "He was, indeed, honest, and of an open and free nature, had an excellent phantasy, brave notions, and gentle expressions, wherein he flowed with that facility that sometimes it was necessary he should be stopped". Jonson concludes that "there was ever more in him to be praised than to be pardoned." Also when Shakespeare died he said "He was not of an age, but for all time."

Thomas Fuller relates stories of Jonson and Shakespeare engaging in debates in the Mermaid Tavern; Fuller imagines conversations in which Shakespeare would run rings around the more learned but more ponderous Jonson. That the two men knew each other personally is beyond doubt, not only because of the tone of Jonson's references to him but because Shakespeare's company produced a number of Jonson's plays, at least one of which (*Every Man in his Humour*) Shakespeare certainly acted in. However, it is now impossible to tell how much personal communication they had, and tales of their friendship cannot be substantiated in the present state of knowledge.

Jonson's most influential and revealing commentary on Shakespeare is the second of the two poems that he contributed to the prefatory verse that opens Shakespeare's First Folio. This poem, "To the memory of my beloved, The AUTHOR, Mr. William Shakespeare: And what he hath left us," did a good deal to create the traditional view of Shakespeare as a poet who, despite "small Latine, and lesse Greeke", had a natural genius. The poem has traditionally been thought to exemplify the contrast Jonson perceived between himself, the disciplined and erudite classicist, scornful of ignorance and skeptical of the masses, and Shakespeare, represented in the poem as a kind of natural wonder whose genius was not subject to any rules except those of the audiences for which he wrote. But the poem itself qualifies this view:

Yet must I not give Nature all: Thy Art,
My gentle Shakespeare, must enjoy a part.

Some view this elegy as a conventional exercise, but a rising number of critics see it as a heartfelt tribute to the "Sweet Swan Of Avon," the "Soul of the Age!" It has been compellingly argued that Jonson helped to edit the First Folio, and he may have been inspired to write this poem, surely one of his greatest, by reading his fellow playwright's works, a number of which had been previously either unpublished or available in less satisfactory versions, in a relatively complete form.

Influence

During most of the seventeenth century Jonson was a towering literary figure, and his influence was enormous. Before the civil war The Tribe of Ben touted his importance, and during the Restoration Jonson's satirical comedies and his theory and practice of "humour characters" was extremely influential, providing the blueprint for many Restoration comedies. In the eighteenth century Jonson's status began to decline. In the Romantic era, Jonson suffered the fate of being unfairly compared and contrasted to Shakespeare, as the taste for Jonson's type of satirical comedy decreased. Jonson was at times greatly appreciated by the Romantics, but overall he was denigrated for not writing in a Shakespearean vein. In the twentieth century, Jonson's status rose significantly.

As G. E. Bentley notes in *Shakespeare and Jonson: Their Reputations in the Seventeenth Century Compared,* Jonson's reputation was in some respects equal to Shakespeare's in the seventeenth century. After the English theatres were reopened on the Restoration of Charles II, Jonson's work, along with Shakespeare's and Fletcher's work, formed the initial core of the Restoration repertory. It was not until after 1710 that Shakespeare's plays (ordinarily in heavily revised forms) were more frequently performed than those of his Renaissance contemporaries. Many critics since the eighteenth century have ranked Jonson below only Shakespeare among English Renaissance dramatists. Critical judgment has tended to emphasize the very qualities that Jonson himself lauds in his prefaces, in Timber, and in his scattered prefaces and dedications: the realism and propriety of his language, the bite of his satire, and the care with which he plotted his comedies.

Though his stature declined during the eighteenth century, Jonson was still read and commented on throughout the century, generally in the kind of comparative and dismissive terms just described. Heinrich Wilhelm von Gerstenberg translated parts of Peter Whalley's edition into German in 1765. Shortly before the Romantic revolution, Edward Capell offered an almost unqualified rejection of Jonson as a dramatic poet, who (he writes) "has very poor pretensions to the high place he holds among the English Bards, as there is no original manner to distinguish him, and the tedious sameness visible in his plots indicates a defect of Genius." The disastrous failures of productions of *Volpone* and *Epicoene* in the early 1770s no doubt bolstered a widespread sense that Jonson had at last grown too antiquated for the contemporary public; if Jonson still attracted enthusiasts such as Earl Camden and William Gifford, he all but disappeared from the stage in the last quarter of the century.

The romantic revolution in criticism brought about an overall decline in the critical estimation of Jonson. Hazlitt refers dismissively to Jonson's "laborious caution." Coleridge, while more respectful, describes Jonson as psychologically superficial: "He was a very accurately observing man; but he cared only to observe what was open to, and likely to impress, the senses." Coleridge placed Jonson second only to Shakespeare; other romantic critics were less approving. The early nineteenth century was the great age for recovering Renaissance drama. Jonson, whose reputation had survived, appears to have been less interesting to some readers than writers such as Thomas Middleton or John Heywood, who were in some senses "discoveries" of the nineteenth century. Moreover, the emphasis the romantic writers placed on imagination, and their concomitant tendency to distrust studied art, lowered Jonson's status, if it also sharpened their awareness of the difference traditionally noted between Jonson and Shakespeare. This trend was by no means universal, however; William Gifford, Jonson's first editor of the nineteenth century, did a great deal to defend Jonson's reputation during this period of general decline. In the next era, Swinburne, who was more interested in Jonson than most Victorians, wrote, "The flowers of his growing have every quality but one which belongs to the rarest and finest among flowers: they have colour, form, variety, fertility, vigour: the one thing they want is fragrance"—by "fragrance," Swinburne means spontaneity.

In the twentieth century, Jonson's body of work has been subject to a more varied set of analyses, broadly consistent with the interests and programmes of modern literary criticism. In an essay printed in *The Sacred Wood* T.S. Eliot attempts to repudiate the charge that Jonson was an arid classicist by analysing the role of imagination in his dialogue. Eliot was appreciative of Jonson's overall conception and his "surface," a view consonant with the modernist reaction against Romantic criticism, which tended to denigrate playwrights who did not concentrate on representations of psychological depth. Around mid-century, a number of critics and scholars followed Eliot's lead, producing detailed studies of Jonson's verbal style. At the same time, study of Elizabethan themes and conventions, such as those by E. E. Stoll and M. C. Bradbrook, provided a more vivid sense of how Jonson's work was shaped by the expectations of his time.

The proliferation of new critical perspectives after mid-century touched on Jonson inconsistently. Jonas Barish was the leading figure in a group of critics that was appreciative of Jonson's artistry. On the other hand, Jonson received less attention from the new critics than did some other playwrights and his work was not of programmatic interest to psychoanalytic critics. But Jonson's career eventually made him a focal point for the revived sociopolitical criticism. Jonson's work, particularly his masques and pageants, offers significant information regarding the relations of literary production and political power, as do his contacts with and poems for aristocratic patrons;

moreover, his career at the centre of London's emerging literary world has been seen as exemplifying the development of a fully commodified literary culture. In this respect, Jonson has been seen as a transitional figure, an author whose skills and ambition led him to a leading role both in the declining culture of patronage and in the rising culture of mass consumption.

If Jonson's reputation as a playwright has traditionally been linked to Shakespeare, his reputation as a poet has, since the early twentieth century, been linked to that of John Donne. In this comparison, Jonson represents the cavalier strain of poetry, which emphasized grace and clarity of expression; Donne, by contrast, epitomized the metaphysical school of poetry, with its reliance on strained, baroque metaphors and often vague phrasing. Since the critics who made this comparison (Herbert Grierson for example), were to varying extents rediscovering Donne, this comparison often worked to the detriment of Jonson's reputation.

In his time, though, Jonson was at least as influential as Donne. In 1623, historian Edmund Bolton named him the best and most polished English poet. That this judgment was widely shared is indicated by the admitted influence he had on younger poets. The grounds for describing Jonson as the "father" of cavalier poets are clear: many of the cavalier poets described themselves as his "sons" or his "tribe." For some of this tribe, the connection was as much social as poetic; Herrick describes meetings at "the Sun, the Dog, the Triple Tunne." All of them, including those like Herrick whose accomplishments in verse are generally regarded as superior to Jonson's, took inspiration from Jonson's revival of classical forms and themes, his subtle melodies, and his disciplined use of wit. In all of these respects, Jonson may be regarded as among the most important figures in the prehistory of English neoclassicism.

The best of Jonson's lyrics have remained current since his time; periodically, they experience a brief vogue, as after the publication of Peter Whalley's edition of 1756. Jonson's poetry continues to interest scholars for the light it sheds on English literary history, particularly as regards politics, systems of patronage, and intellectual attitudes. For the general reader, Jonson's reputation rests on a few lyrics that, though brief, are surpassed for grace and precision by very few Renaissance poems: "On My First Sonne"; "To Celia"; "To Penshurst"; and the epitaph on boy player Solomon Pavy.

As with other English Renaissance dramatists, a portion of Ben Jonson's literary output has not survived. In addition to *The Isle of Dogs* (1597), the records suggest these lost plays as wholly or partially Jonson's work: *Richard Crookback* (1602); *Hot Anger Soon Cold* (1598), with Porter and Henry Chettle; *Page of Plymouth* (1599), with Dekker; and *Robert II, King of Scots* (1599), with Chettle and Dekker. Several of Jonson's masques and entertainments also are not extant:

> *The Entertainment at Merchant Taylors* (1607); *The Entertainment at Salisbury House for James I* (1608); *The Entertainment at Britain's Burse for James I* (1609); and *The May Lord* (1613–19).

Finally, there are questionable or borderline attributions. Jonson may have had a hand in *Rollo, Duke of Normandy, or The Bloody Brother,* a play in the canon of John Fletcher and his collaborators. The comedy *The Widow* was printed in 1652 as the work of Thomas Middleton, Fletcher and Jonson, though scholars have been intensely skeptical about Jonson's presence in the play. A few attributions of anonymous plays, like *The London Prodigal,* have been ventured by individual researchers, but have met with cool responses.

Edmund Spenser

Edmund Spenser (c. 1552 – 13 January 1599) was an English poet best known for *The Faerie Queene,* an epic poem celebrating, through fantastical allegory, the Tudor dynasty and Elizabeth I. He is recognized as one of the premier craftsmen of Modern English verse in its infancy.

Life

Edmund Spenser was born in London around 1552. As a young boy, he was educated in London at the Merchant Taylors' School and matriculated as a sizar at Pembroke College, Cambridge.

In July 1580 Spenser went to Ireland, in the service of the newly appointed lord deputy, Arthur Lord Grey de Wilton. Then he served with the English forces during the Second Desmond Rebellion. After the defeat of the rebels he was awarded lands in County Cork that had been confiscated in the Munster Plantation during the Elizabethan reconquest of Ireland. Among his acquaintances in the area was Walter Raleigh, a fellow colonist.

Through his poetry Spenser hoped to secure a place at court, which he visited in Raleigh's company to deliver his most famous work, the *Faerie Queene.* However, he boldly antagonized the queen's principal secretary, Lord Burghley, and all he received in recognition of his work was a pension in 1591. When it was proposed that he receive payment of 100 pounds for his epic poem, Burghley remarked, "What, all this for a song!"

In the early 1590s, Spenser wrote a prose pamphlet titled, *A View of the Present State of Ireland.* This piece remained in manuscript until its publication and print in the mid-seventeenth century. It is probable that it was kept out of print during the author's lifetime because of its inflammatory content. The pamphlet argued that Ireland would never be totally 'pacified' by the English until its indigenous language and customs had been destroyed, if necessary by violence. Spenser recommended scorched earth tactics, such as he had seen used in the Desmond Rebellions, to create famine. Although it has been highly regarded as a polemical piece of prose and valued as a historical source on 16th century Ireland, the *View* is seen today as genocidal in intent. Spenser did express some praise for the Gaelic poetic tradition, but also used much tendentious and bogus analysis to demonstrate that the Irish were descended from barbarian Scythian stock.

Two of Ireland's leading historians of the early modern period Ciaran Brady and Nicholas Canny exchange verbal blow on the topic of Spenser's View of the State of Ireland. Brady's essential proposition is that Spencer wished the English government to undertake the extermination of most of the Irish population, Brady writes that Spencer preferred to write in dialogue form so that the crudity of his proposals would be masked. Canny undermines Brady conclusion that Spencer opted for "a holocaust or a "blood-bath", because in spite of Brady claims he did not choose the sword as his preferred instrument of policy. Canny argues that Spencer indeed chose not the extermination of the Irish race but rather a policy of 'social reform pursued by drastic means'. Canny's ultimate contadiction was that Brady was over reacting and that Spencer did not propose a policy to exterminate the Irish race. Then within one page he moves on to argue that no 'English writer of the early modern period ever proposed such a drastic programme in social engineering for England, and it was even more dramatic than Brady allows for because all elements of the Irish population including the Old English of the towns, whom Brady seems to think were exempt were subject to some element of this scheme of dispersal, reintegration and re-education This was one of the weak points in Canny's argument, maintaining that this policy was more 'dramatic than Brady allows', when Brady's proposal was one of 'bloodshed', 'extermination' and 'holocaust' and Canny's one of dispersal, reintegration and re-education. It doesn't take any specifying that genocide is more dramatic than a policy of social reform pursued with drastic measures. Again he contradicts his previous comments by writing 'substantial loss of life, including loss of civilian life, was considered by Spencer'. For more details on this tantalizing Historical debate, read Brady's "Spencer's Irish Crisis: Humanism and Experience in the 1590s and Canny, Nicholas. "Spenser's Irish Crisis: Humanism and Experience in the 1590s, a response to the claims of Brady.

Later on, during the Nine Years War in 1598, Spenser was driven from his home by Irish rebels. His castle at Kilcolman, near Doneraile in North Cork was burned, and it is thought one of his infant children died in the blaze - though local legend has it that his wife also died. He possessed a second holding to the south, at Rennie, on a rock overlooking the river Blackwater in North Cork. The ruins of it are still visible today. A short distance away grew a tree, locally known as "Spenser's Oak" until it was destroyed in a lightning strike in the 1960s. Local legend has it that he penned some or all of *The Faerie Queene* under this tree. Queen Victoria is said to have visited the tree while staying in nearby Convamore House during her state visit to Ireland. In the following year Spenser traveled to London, where he died in distressed circumstances, aged forty-six. It was arranged for his coffin to be carried by other poets, upon which they threw many pens and pieces of poetry into his grave with many tears.

Spenser was admired by William Wordsworth, John Keats, Lord Byron and Alfred Lord Tennyson, among others. The language of his poetry is purposely archaic, reminiscent of earlier works such as *The Canterbury Tales* of Geoffrey Chaucer, whom Spenser greatly admired.

Spenser's *Epithalamion* is the most admired of its type in the English language. It was written for his wedding to his young bride, Elizabeth Boyle. The poem consists of 365 long lines, corresponding to the days of the year; 68 short lines, representing the sum of the 52 weeks, 12 months, and 4 seasons of the annual cycle; and 24 stanzas, corresponding to the diurnal and sidereal hours.

Spenserian Stanza and Sonnet

Spenser used a distinctive verse form, called the Spenserian stanza, in several works, including *The*

Faerie Queene. The stanza's main meter is iambic pentameter with a final line in iambic hexameter (having six feet or stresses, known as an Alexandrine), and the rhyme scheme is ababbcbcc.

The Spenserian Sonnet is based on a fusion of elements of both the Petrarchan sonnet and the Shakespearean sonnet. It is similar to the Shakespearan sonnet in the sense that its set up is based more on the 3 quatrains and a couplet,a system set up by Shakespeare; however it is more like the Petrarchan tradition in the fact that the conclusion follows from the argument or issue set up in the earlier quatrains. There is also a great use of the parody of the blason and the idealization or praise of the mistress, a literary device used by many poets. It is a way to look at a woman through the appraisal of her features in comparison to other things. In this description, the mistress's body is described part by part, i.e., much more of a scientific way of seeing one. As William Johnson states in his article "Gender Fashioning and Dynamics of Mutuality in Spenser's Amoretti," the poet-love in the scenes of Spenser's sonnets in Amoretti, is able to see his lover in an objectified manner by moving her to another, or more clearly, an item. The purpose of Spenser doing this is to bring the woman from the "transcendental ideal" to a woman in everyday life. "Through his use of metonymy and metaphor, by describing the lady not as a whole being but as bodily parts, by alluding to centuries of topoi which remove her in time as well as space, the poet transforms the woman into a text, the living 'other' into an inanimate object". The opposite of this also occurs in *The Faerie Queen*. The counter-blason, or the opposition of appraisal, is used to describe Duessa. She is not objectified, but instead all of her flaws are highlighted.

Without a Rhyme or Reason

Spenser is also the man believed to have crafted the phrase "without reason or a rhyme". He was promised payment from the Queen of one hundred pounds, a so called, "reason for the rhyme". The Lord High Treasurer William Cecil, however, considered the sum too much. After a long while without receiving his payment, he sent her this quatrain:

> I was promis'd on a time,
>
> To have a reason for my rhyme:
>
> But from that time unto this season,
>
> I had neither rhyme or reason.
>
> She immediately ordered Cecil to send Spenser his due sum.

John Fletcher

John Fletcher (1579 – 1625) was a Jacobean playwright. Following William Shakespeare as house playwright for the King's Men, he was among the most prolific and influential dramatists of his day; both during his lifetime and in the early Restoration, his fame rivaled Shakespeare's. Though his reputation has been eclipsed since, Fletcher remains an important transitional figure between the Elizabethan popular tradition and the popular drama of the Restoration.

Biography

Fletcher was born in December 1579 (baptised December 20) in Rye, Sussex, and died of the plague in August 1625 (buried August 29 in St. Saviour's, Southwark). His father Richard Fletcher was an ambitious and successful cleric who was in turn Dean of Peterborough, Bishop of Bristol, Bishop of Worcester, and Bishop of London (shortly before his death) as well as chaplain to Queen Elizabeth. As dean of Peterborough, Richard Fletcher, at the execution of Mary, Queen of Scots at Fotheringay "knelt down on the scaffold steps and started to pray out loud and at length, in a prolonged and rhetorical style as though determined to force his way into the pages of history" and who cried out at her death, "So perish all the Queen's enemies!" Richard Fletcher died shortly after falling out of favor with the queen, over a marriage the queen had advised against. He appears to have been partly rehabilitated before his death in 1596; however, Fletcher died substantially in debt. The upbringing of John Fletcher and his seven siblings was entrusted to his paternal uncle Giles Fletcher, a poet and minor official. His uncle's connections ceased to be a benefit, and may even have become a liability, after the rebellion of the Earl of Essex, who had patronized him.

Fletcher appears to have entered Corpus Christi College, Cambridge University in 1591, at the age of eleven. It is not certain that he took a degree, but evidence suggests that he was preparing for a career in the church. Little is known about his time at college, but he evidently followed the same path previously trod by the University wits before him, from Cambridge to the burgeoning commercial theater of London. In 1606, he began to appear as an author for the Children of the Queen's Revels, then performing at the Blackfriars Theatre. Commendatory verses by Richard Brome in the Beaumont and Fletcher 1647 folio place Fletcher in the company of Ben Jonson; a comment of Jonson's to Drummond corroborates this claim, although it is not known when this friendship began. At the beginning of his career, his most important association was with Francis Beaumont. The two wrote together for close to a decade, first for the children and then for the King's Men. According to a legend transmitted or invented by John Aubrey, they also lived together (in Bankside), sharing clothes and having "one wench in the house between them." This domestic arrangement, if it existed, was ended by Beaumont's marriage in 1613, and their dramatic partnership ended after Beaumont fell ill, probably of a stroke, the same year.

By this time, Fletcher had moved into a closer association with the King's Men. He is commonly assumed to have collaborated with Shakespeare on *Henry VIII, The Two Noble Kinsmen,* and the lost *Cardenio;* a play he wrote singly around this time. *The Woman's Prize or the Tamer Tamed,* is a sequel to *The Taming of the Shrew.* After Shakespeare's death, Fletcher appears to have entered into an exclusive arrangement with the King's Men similar to that with which Shakespeare had worked; Fletcher wrote only for that company between the death of Shakespeare and his own death nine years later. He never lost his habit of collaboration, working with Nathan Field and later with Philip Massinger, who succeeded him as house playwright for the King's Men. His popularity continued unabated throughout his life; during the winter of 1621, three of his plays were performed at court. He died in 1625, apparently of the plague. He seems to have been buried in what is now Southwark Cathedral, although the precise location is not known; there is a reference by Aston Cockayne to a single grave for Fletcher and Massinger (also buried in Southwark).

His mastery is most notable in two dramatic types, tragicomedy and comedy of manners, both of which exerted a pervasive influence on dramatists in the reign of Charles I and during the Restoration.

In the preface to the printed edition of his play, Fletcher explained the failure as due to his audience's faulty expectations. They expected a pastoral tragicomedy to feature dances, comedy, and murder, with the shepherds presented in conventional stereotypes — as Fletcher put it, wearing "gray cloaks, with curtailed dogs in strings." Fletcher's preface in defense of his play is best known for its pithy definition of tragicomedy: "A tragicomedy is not so called in respect of mirth and killing, but in respect it wants [i.e., lacks] deaths, which is enough to make it no tragedy; yet brings some near it, which is enough to make it no comedy." A comedy, he went on to say, must be "a representation of familiar people," and the preface is critical of drama which would feature characters whose action violates nature.

In that case, Fletcher appears to have been developing a new style faster than audiences could comprehend. By 1609, however, he had found his stride. With Beaumont, he wrote *Philaster*, which became a hit for the King's Men and began a profitable connection between Fletcher and that company. *Philaster* appears also to have initiated a vogue for tragicomedy; Fletcher's influence has been credited with inspiring some features of Shakespeare's late romances (Kirsch, 288-90), and his influence on the tragicomic work of other playwrights is even more marked. By the middle of the 1610s, Fletcher's plays had achieved a popularity that rivalled Shakespeare's and which cemented the preeminence of the King's Men in Jacobean London. After Beaumont's retirement and early death in 1616, Fletcher continued working, both singly and in collaboration, until his death in 1625. By that time, he had produced, or had been credited with, close to fifty plays. This body of work remained a major part of the King's Men's repertory until the closing of the theaters in 1642.

During the Commonwealth, many of the playwright's best-known scenes were kept alive as drolls, the brief performances devised to satisfy the taste for plays while the theaters were suppressed. At the re-opening of the theaters in 1660, the plays in the Fletcher canon, in original form or revised, were by far the most common fare on the English stage. The most frequently revived plays suggest the developing taste for comedies of manners. Among the tragedies, *The Maid's Tragedy* and, especially, *Rollo Duke of Normandy* held the stage. Four tragicomedies (*A King and No King, The Humorous Lieutenant, Philaster,* and *The Island Princess*) were popular, perhaps in part for their similarity to and foreshadowing of heroic drama. Four comedies (*Rule a Wife And Have a Wife, The Chances, Beggars' Bush,* and especially *The Scornful Lady*) were also popular.

Yet the popularity of these plays relative to those of Shakespeare and to new productions steadily eroded. By around 1710, Shakespeare's plays were more frequently performed, and the rest of the century saw a steady erosion in performance of Fletcher's plays. By 1784, Thomas Davies asserted that only *Rule a Wife* and *The Chances* were still current on stage; a generation later, Alexander Dyce mentioned only *The Chances*.

Since then Fletcher has increasingly become a subject only for occasional revivals and for specialists. Fletcher and his collaborators have been the subject of important bibliographic and critical studies, but the plays have been revived only infrequently.

Plays

Fletcher's canon presents unusual difficulties of attribution. He collaborated regularly and widely, most often with Beaumont and Massinger but also with Nathan Field, Shakespeare and others. Some of his early collaborations with Beaumont were later revised by Massinger, adding another layer of complexity to unravel. Fortunately for scholars and students of English literature, Fletcher also had highly distinctive mannerisms in his creative efforts; his texts reveal a range of peculiarities that effectively identify his presence. He frequently uses *ye* instead of *you,* at rates sometimes approaching 50%; he frequently employs *'em* for *them,* along with a set of other particular preferences in contractions; he adds a sixth stressed syllable to a standard pentameter verse line—most often *sir* but also *too* or *still* or *next;* he has various other specific habits and preferences. The detection of this pattern, this personal Fletcherian textual profile, has allowed researchers to penetrate the confusions of the Fletcher canon with good success—and has in turn encouraged the use of similar techniques more broadly in the study of literature.

Careful bibliography has established the authors of each play with some degree of certainty. Determination of the exact shares of each writer (for instance by Cyrus Hoy) in particular plays is ongoing, based on patterns of textual and linguistic preferences, stylistic grounds, and idiosyncrasies of spelling.

The Nice Valour may be a play by Fletcher revised by Thomas Middleton; *The Fair Maid of the Inn* is perhaps a play by Massinger, John Ford, and John Webster, either with or without Fletcher's involvement. *The Laws of Candy* has been variously attributed to

Fletcher and to John Ford. *The Night-Walker* was a Fletcher original, with additions by Shirley for a 1639 production. And some of the attributions given above are disputed by some scholars, as noted in connection with *Four Plays in One. Rollo Duke of Normandy,* an especially difficult case and a focus of much disagreement among scholars, may have been written around 1617, and later revised by Massinger.

The first Beaumont and Fletcher folio of 1647 collected 35 plays, most of which that had not been previously published. The second folio of 1679 added 18 more, for a total of 53. The first folio included *The Masque of the Inner Temple and Gray's Inn* (1613), and the second *The Knight of the Burning Pestle* (1607), widely considered to be Beaumont's solo works.

One play in the canon, *Sir John Van Olden Barnavelt,* existed in manuscript and was not published till 1883. In 1640 James Shirley's *The Coronation* was misattributed to Fletcher upon its initial publication, and was included in the second Beaumont and Fletcher folio of 1679.

Thomas Kyd

Thomas Kyd (baptised 6 November 1558 – buried 15 August 1594) was an English dramatist, the author of *The Spanish Tragedy,* and one of the most important figures in the development of Elizabethan drama.

Although well-known in his own time, Kyd fell into obscurity until 1773 when Thomas Hawkins (an early editor of the The Spanish Tragedie) discovered that Kyd was named as its author by Thomas Heywood in his *Apologie for Actors* (1612). A hundred years later, scholars in Germany and England began to shed light on his life and work, including the controversial finding that he may have been the author of a *Hamlet* play pre-dating Shakespeare's.

Early Life

Thomas Kyd was the son of Francis and Anna Kyd and was baptized in the church of St Mary Woolnoth in the Ward of Langborn, Lombard Street, London on 6 November 1558. The baptismal register at St Mary Woolnoth carries this entry: "Thomas, son of Francis Kydd, Citizen and Writer of the Courte Letter of London". Francis Kydd was a scrivener and in 1580 was warden of the Scriveners' Company.

In October 1565 the young Kyd was enrolled in the newly-founded Merchant Taylors' School, whose headmaster was Richard Mulcaster. Fellow students included Edmund Spenser and Thomas Lodge. Here, Kyd received a well-rounded education, thanks to Mulcaster's progressive ideas. Apart from Latin and Greek, the curriculum included music, drama, physical education, and "good manners". There is no evidence that Kyd went on to either of the English universities. He may have followed for a time his father's profession; two letters written by him are extant and his handwriting suggests the training of a scrivener.

Career

Title page of Kyd's *The Spanish Tragedy,* with a woodcut showing (left) the hung body of Horatio discovered by (center) Hieronymo and Bel-Imperia being taken from the scene by a blackface Lorenzo (right).

Evidence suggests that in the 1580s Kyd became an important playwright, but little is known about his activity. Francis Meres placed him among "our best for tragedy" and Heywood elsewhere called him "Famous Kyd". Ben Jonson mentions him in the same breath as Christopher Marlowe (with whom, in London, Kyd at one time shared a room) and John Lyly in the Shakespeare First Folio.

The Spanish Tragedie was probably written in the mid to late 1580s. The earliest surviving edition was printed in 1592; the full title being, *The Spanish Tragedie, Containing the lamentable end of Don Horatio, and Bel-imperia: with the pittifull death of olde Hieronimo.* However, the play was usually known simply as "Hieronimo", after the protagonist. It was arguably the most popular play of the "Age of Shakespeare" and set new standards in effective plot construction and character development. In 1602 a version of the play with "additions" was published. Philip Henslowe's diary records payment to Ben Jonson for additions that year, but it is disputed whether the published additions reflect Jonson's work or if they were actually composed for a 1597 revival of *The Spanish Tragedy* mentioned by Henslowe.

Other works by Kyd are his translations of Torquato Tasso's *Padre di Famiglia,* published as *The Householder's Philosophy* (1588); and Robert Garnier's *Cornelia* (1594). Plays attributed in whole or in part to Kyd include *Soliman and Perseda, King Leir, Arden of Feversham* and *Edward III.* A play related to *The Spanish Tragedy* called *The First Part of Hieronimo* (surviving in a quarto of 1605) may be a bad quarto or memorial reconstruction of a play by Kyd, or it may be an inferior writer's burlesque of *The Spanish Tragedy* inspired by that play's popularity. Kyd is more generally accepted to have been the author of a *Hamlet,* the precursor of the Shakespearean play. Some poems by Kyd exist, but it seems that most of his work is lost or unidentified.

The success of Kyd's plays extended to Europe. Versions of *The Spanish Tragedy* and his *Hamlet* were popular in Germany and the Netherlands for generations. The influence of these plays on European drama was largely the reason for the interest in Kyd among German scholars in the nineteenth century.

Later Years

From 1587 to 1593 Kyd was in the service of an unidentified noble, since, after his imprisonment in 1593, he wrote to have lost "the favors of my Lord, whom I haue servd almost theis vi yeres nowe". Proposed nobles include the Earl of Sussex, the Earl of Pembroke, and Lord Strange. He may have worked as a secretary, if he did not also write plays. Around 1591 Christopher Marlowe also joined this patron's service, and for a while Marlowe and Kyd shared lodgings, and perhaps even ideas.

On 11 May 1593 the Privy Council ordered the arrest of the authors of "divers lewd and mutinous libels" which had been posted around London. The next day, Kyd was among those arrested; he would later believe that he had been the victim of an informer. His lodgings were searched and instead of evidence of the "libels" there was found an Arianist tract, described by an investigator as "vile heretical conceits denying the eternal deity of Jesus Christ found amongst the papers of Thos. Kydd *(sic)*, prisoner ... which he affirmeth he had from C. Marley *(sic)*". It is believed that Kyd was tortured brutally to obtain this information. Marlowe was summoned by the Privy Council after the events of this, and, while waiting for a decision on his case, was killed in an incident involving known government agents.

Kyd was eventually released but was not accepted back into his lord's service. Believing he was under suspicion of atheism himself, he wrote to the Lord Keeper, Sir John Puckering, protesting his innocence, but his efforts to clear his name were apparently fruitless. The last we hear from the playwright is the publication of *Cornelia* early in 1594. In the dedication to the Countess of Sussex he alludes to the "bitter times and privy broken passions" he had endured. Kyd died later that year, and was buried on 15 August in London. He was only 35 years of age. In December of that same year, Kyd's mother legally renounced the administration of his estate, probably because it was debt-ridden.

Thomas Middleton

Thomas Middleton (18 April 1580-1627) was an English Jacobean playwright and poet. Middleton stands with John Fletcher and Ben Jonson as among the most successful and prolific of playwrights who wrote their best plays during the Jacobean period. He was one of the few Renaissance dramatists to achieve equal success in comedy and tragedy. Also a prolific writer of masques and pageants, he remains one of the most noteworthy and distinctive of Jacobean dramatists.

Life

Middleton was born in London and baptized on 18 April 1580. He was the son of a bricklayer who had raised himself to the status of a gentleman and who, interestingly, owned property adjoining the Curtain theatre in Shoreditch. Middleton was just five when his father died and his mother's subsequent remarriage dissolved into a fifteen year battle over the inheritance of Thomas and his younger sister: an experience which must surely have informed and perhaps even incited his repeated satirizing of the legal profession.

Middleton attended Queen's College, Oxford, matriculating in 1598, although he did not graduate. Before he left Oxford (sometime in 1600 or 1601), he wrote and published three long poems in popular Elizabethan styles; none appears to have been especially successful, and one, his book of satires, ran afoul of the Anglican Church's ban on verse satire and was burned. Nevertheless, his literary career was launched.

In the early 1600s, Middleton made a living writing topical pamphlets, including one—*Penniless Parliament of Threadbare Poets*—that enjoyed many reprintings as well as becoming the subject of a Parliamentary inquiry. At the same time, records in the diary of Philip Henslowe show that Middleton was writing for the Admiral's Men. Unlike Shakespeare, Middleton remained a free agent, able to write for whichever company hired him. His early dramatic career was marked by controversy. His friendship with Thomas Dekker brought him into conflict with Ben Jonson and George Chapman in the War of the Theatres. The grudge with Jonson continued as late as 1626, when Jonson's play *The Staple of News* indulges a slur on Middleton's great success, *A Game at Chess*. It has been argued that Middleton's *Inner Temple Masque* (1619) sneers at Jonson (then absent in Scotland) as a "silenced bricklayer."

In 1603, Middleton married. The same year, an outbreak of plague forced the closing of the theaters in

London, and James I assumed the English throne. These events marked the beginning of Middleton's greatest period as a playwright. Having passed the time during the plague composing prose pamphlets (including a continuation of Thomas Nashe's *Pierce Penniless*), he returned to drama with great energy, producing close to a score of plays for several companies and in several genres, most notably city comedy and revenge tragedy. He continued his collaborations with Dekker, and the two produced *The Roaring Girl,* a biography of contemporary thief Mary Frith.

In the 1610s, Middleton began his fruitful collaboration with the actor William Rowley, producing *Wit at Several Weapons* and *A Fair Quarrel;* working alone he produced his comic masterpiece, *A Chaste Maid in Cheapside,* in 1613. His own plays from this decade reveal a somewhat mellowed temper; certainly there is no comedy among them with the satiric depth of *Michaelmas Term* and no tragedy as bloodthirsty as *The Revenger's Tragedy*. Middleton was also branching out into other dramatic endeavors; he was apparently called on to help revise *Macbeth* and *Measure for Measure,* and at the same time he was increasingly involved with civic pageants. This last connection was made official when, in 1620, he was appointed City Chronologer of the City of London. He held this post until his death in 1627, at which time it was passed to Jonson.

Middleton's official duties did not interrupt his dramatic writings; the 1620s saw the production of his and Rowley's tragedy *The Changeling,* and several tragicomedies. In 1624, he reached a pinnacle of notoriety when his dramatic allegory *A Game at Chess* was staged by the King's Men. The play used the conceit of a chess game to present and satirize the recent intrigues surrounding the Spanish Match. Though Middleton's approach was strongly patriotic, the Privy Council shut down the play after nine performances on the complaint of the Spanish ambassador. Middleton faced an unknown, but likely frightening, degree of punishment. Since no play later than *A Game at Chess* is recorded, it has been hypothesized that his punishment included a ban on writing for the stage.

Works

Middleton wrote in many genres, including tragedy, history and city comedy. His best-known plays are the tragedies *The Changeling* (written with William Rowley) and *Women Beware Women*, and the cynically satirical city comedy *A Chaste Maid in Cheapside*. Although earlier editions of *The Revenger's Tragedy* attribute the play to Cyril Tourneur, or refused to arbitrate between Middleton and Tourneur, since the massive and widely acclaimed statistical studies by David Lake and MacDonald P. Jackson, Middleton's authorship has not been seriously contested, and no scholar has mounted a new defense of the discredited Tourneur attribution. The Oxford Middleton and its companion piece, *Thomas Middleton and Early Modern Textual Culture* offer the most extensive and decisive evidence to date not only for Middleton's authorship of *The Revenger's Tragedy*, but also for his collaboration with Shakespeare on *Timon of Athens* and his adaptation and revision of Shakespeare's *Macbeth* and *Measure for Measure*.

Middleton's work is diverse even by the standards of his age. He did not have the kind of official relationship with a particular company that

Shakespeare or Fletcher had; instead, he appears to have written on a freelance basis for any number of companies. Particularly in the early years of his career, this freedom led to a great diversity in his output, which ranges from the "snarling" satire of *Michaelmas Term* (performed by the Children of Paul's) to the bleak intrigues of *The Revenger's Tragedy* (performed by the King's Men), assuming he is the author of the latter. Also contributing to the variety of the works is the scope of Middleton's career. If his early work was informed by the flourishing of satire in the late-Elizabethan period,

His maturity was influenced by the ascendancy of Fletcherian tragicomedy. If many of these plays have been judged less compelling than his earlier work, his later work, in which satiric fury is tempered and broadened, also includes three of his acknowledged masterpieces. *A Chaste Maid in Cheapside,* produced by the Lady Elizabeth's Men, skillfully combines Middleton's typically cutting presentation of London life with an expansive view of the power of love to effect reconciliation. *The Changeling,* a late tragedy, returns Middleton to an Italianate setting like that in *The Revenger's Tragedy;* here, however, the central characters are more fully drawn and more compelling as individuals, again, assuming he wrote *The Revenger's Tragedy.*

Middleton's plays are characterized by their cynicism about the human race, a cynicism that is often very funny. True heroes are a rarity in Middleton; in his plays, almost every character is selfish, greedy, and self-absorbed. This quality is best observed in the *A Chaste Maid in Cheapside,* a panoramic view of a London populated entirely by sinners, in which no social rank goes unsatirized. It can also be seen in the tragedies *Women Beware Women* and *The Revenger's Tragedy,* in which enjoyably amoral Italian courtiers endlessly plot against each other, resulting in a climactic bloodbath. When Middleton does portray good people, the characters have very small roles, and are flawless to perfection. Thanks to a theological pamphlet attributed to him, Middleton is thought by some to have been a strong believer in Calvinism, among the dominant strains in the theology of the English church of his time, which rigidly divides humanity into the damned and the elect, which focuses on human sinfulness and inadequacy more than in the other denominations of Christianity.

Reputation

Middleton's work has long been praised by literary critics, among them Algernon Charles Swinburne and T. S. Eliot. The latter thought Middleton was second only to Shakespeare. In his own time, he was thought talented enough to revise Shakespeare's *Macbeth* and *Measure for Measure.*

Middleton's plays have been staged throughout the twentieth century and into the twenty-first, each decade offering more productions than the last. Even less familiar works have been staged: *A Fair Quarrel* was performed at the National Theatre, and *The Old Law* has been performed by the Royal Shakespeare Company. *The Changeling* has been adapted for film several times, and the tragedy *Women Beware Women* remains a stage favorite. *The Revenger's Tragedy* was adapted into Alex Cox's film *Revengers Tragedy,* the opening credits of which attribute the play's authorship to Middleton.

Thomas Nashe

Thomas Nashe (November 1567- 1601) was an English Elizabethan pamphleteer, poet and satirist. He was the son of the minister William Nashe and his wife Margaret.

Life and Career

Little is known with certainty of Nashe's life. He was baptized in Lowestoft, Suffolk, where his father was curate. The family moved to West Harling, near Thetford in 1573 after Nashe's father was awarded the living there at the church of All Saints. Around 1581 Thomas went up to St John's College, Cambridge as a sizar, gaining his bachelor's degree in 1586. From references in his own polemics and those of others, he does not seem to have proceeded Master of Arts there. Most of his biographers agree that he left his college about summer 1588, as his name appears on a list of students due to attend philosophy lectures in that year. His reasons for leaving are unclear; his father may have died the previous year, but Richard Lichfield maliciously reported that Nashe had fled possible expulsion for his role in *Terminus et non terminus,* one of the raucous student theatricals popular at the time. Some years later, William Covell wrote in *Polimanteia* that Cambridge "has been unkind to the one [ie, Nashe] to wean him before his time." Nashe himself claimed that he could have become a fellow had he wished (in *Have With You to Saffron-Walden*)

Then he moved to London and started his literary career in earnest. The remaining decade of his life was dominated by two concerns: finding an adequate patron and participating in controversies, most famously with Gabriel and Richard Harvey. He arrived in London with his one exercise in euphuism, *The Anatomy of Absurdity*. His first appearance in print was, however, his preface to Robert Greene's *Menaphon*, which offers a brief definition of art and overview of contemporary literature. After this (and the publication of *Anatomy*) he was drawn into the Martin Marprelate controversy on the side of the bishops. As with the other writers in the controversy, his share is difficult to determine. He was formerly credited with the three "pasquil" tracts of 1589-1590, which were included in R. B. McKerrow's standard edition of Nashe's works: however McKerrow himself later argued strongly against their being by Nashe. The anti-Martinist *An Almond for a Parrot* (1590), ostensibly credited to one "Cutbert Curry-knave," is now universally recognized as Nashe's work, although its author humorously claims, in its dedication to the comedian William Kempe, to have met Harlequin in Bergamo while returning from a trip to Venice in the summer of 1589. However, there is no evidence Nashe had either time or means to go abroad, and he never subsequently refers to having visited Venice elsewhere in his work.

In 1590, he contributed a preface to an unlicensed edition of Philip Sidney's *Astrophil and Stella*, but the edition was called in, and the authorized second edition removed Nashe's work.

At some time in the early 1590s Nashe produced an erotic poem, *The Choice of Valentines*, possibly for the private circle of Ferdinando Stanley, 5th Earl of Derby (then known as Lord Strange). This circulated only in manuscript. It describes the visit of a young man named 'Tomalin' to the brothel where his girlfriend Frances ('Frankie') is employed. Having paid ten gold pieces for her favours, Tomalin is embarrassed to find that merely lifting her skirts makes him lose his erection. She perseveres in arousing him however and they make love, but to her disappointment he has an orgasm before her. Frankie then decides to take matters into her own hands: hence the informal title by which the poem was known, *Nashe's Dildo*. It was sharply criticized for its obscenity by contemporary authors Joseph Hall and John Davies of Hereford, though Nashe had tried to pre-empt criticism by placing it in the tradition of classical erotica: "Yet Ovid's wanton muse did not offend".

His friendship with Greene drew Nashe into the Harvey controversy. In 1590, Richard's *The Lamb of God* complained of the anti-Martinist pamphleteers in general, including a side-swipe at the *Menaphon* preface. Two years later, Greene's *A Quip for an Upstart Courtier* contained a passage on "rope makers" that clearly refers to the Harveys (whose father made ropes). The passage, which was removed from subsequent editions, may have been Nashe's. After Harvey mocked Greene's death in *Four Letters*, Nashe wrote *Strange News* (1593). Nashe attempted to apologize in the preface to *Christ's Tears Over Jerusalem* (1593), but the appearance of *Pierce's Supererogation* shortly after offended Nashe anew. He replied with *Have With You to Saffron-Walden* (1596), with a possibly sardonic dedication to Richard Lichfield, a barber of Cambridge. Harvey did not publish a reply, but Lichfield answered in a tract called "The Trimming of Thomas Nash," (1597). This pamphlet also contained a crude woodcut portrait of Nashe, shown as a man disreputably dressed and in fetters.

Alongside this running dispute, Nashe produced his more famous works. While staying in the household of Archbishop John Whitgift at Croydon in October 1592 he wrote an entertainment called

Summer's Last Will and Testament, a "shew" with some resemblance to a masque. In brief, the plot describes the death of Summer, who, feeling himself to be dying, reviews the performance of his former servants and eventually passes the crown on to Autumn. The play was published in 1600.

In 1593 Nashe published *Christ's Tears Over Jerusalem*, a pamphlet dedicated to Lady Elizabeth Carey. Despite the work's apparently devotional nature it contained satirical material which gave offence to the London civic authorities and Nashe was briefly imprisoned in Newgate. The intervention of Lady Elizabeth's husband Sir George Carey gained his release.

He remained in London apart from periodic visits to the countryside to avoid the plague - a fear reflected in the play *Summers last will and Testament*, written in the autumn of 1592. William Sommers, whose comments frame the play, was Henry VIII's jester. It includes the famous lyric:

> Adieu, farewell earths blisse,
> This world uncertaine is,
> Fond are lifes lustful joyes,
> Death proves them all but toyes,
> None from his darts can flye;
> I am sick, I must dye:
> Lord, have mercy on us.

In 1597, following the suppression of *The Isle of Dogs* (co-written with Ben Jonson), Jonson was jailed, but Nashe was able to escape to the country. He remained for some time in Great Yarmouth before returning to London.

He was alive in 1599, when his last known work, *Nashes Lenten Stuffe,* was published, and dead by 1601, when he was memorialized in a Latin verse in *Affaniae* by Charles Fitzgeoffrey.

He was featured in Thomas Dekker's *News from Hell* and referred to in the anonymous Parnassus plays, of which the latter provides this epitaph:

Let all his faultes sleepe with his mournfull chest
And there for ever with his ashes rest.
His style was wittie, though it had some gall,
Some things he might have mended, so may all.
Yet this I say, that for a mother witt,
Few men have ever seene the like of it.

He is also credited with the erotic poem *The Choice of Valentines* and his name appears on the title page of Christopher Marlowe's *Dido, Queen of Carthage,* though there is uncertainty as to what Nashe's contribution was. Some editions of this play, still extant in the 18th century but now unfortunately lost, contained memorial verses on Marlowe by Nashe, who was his friend.

John Webster

John Webster (c.1580 – c.1634) was an English Jacobean dramatist best known for his tragedies *The White Devil* and *The Duchess of Malfi,* often regarded as masterpieces of the early 17th-century English stage. He was a contemporary of William Shakespeare.

Biography

Webster's life is obscure, and the dates of his birth and death are not known. His father, a coach maker also named John Webster, married a blacksmith's daughter named Elizabeth Coates on 4 November 1577, and it is likely that Webster was born not long after in or near London. On 1 August 1598, "John Webster, lately of the New Inn" was admitted to the Middle Temple, one of the Inns of Court; in view of the legal interests evident in his dramatic work; this is possibly the playwright. Webster married the 17-year-old Sara Peniall on 18 March 1606, and their first child, John, was baptized at the parish of St Dunstan-in-the-West on 8 May 1606. Bequests in the will of a neighbour who died in 1617 indicate that other children were born to him.

Most of what is otherwise known of him relates to his theatrical activities. Webster was still writing plays as late as the mid-1620s, but Thomas Heywood's *Hierarchie of the Blessed Angels* (licensed 7 November 1634) speaks of him in the past tense, implying he was then dead.

Early Collaborations

By 1602, Webster was working with teams of playwrights on history plays, most of which were never printed. These included a tragedy *Caesar's Fall* (written with Michael Drayton, Thomas Dekker, Thomas Middleton and Anthony Munday), and a collaboration with Thomas Dekker *Christmas Comes but Once a Year* (1602). With Dekker he also wrote *Sir Thomas Wyatt*, which was printed in 1607. He worked with Thomas Dekker again on two city comedies, *Westward Ho* in 1604 and *Northward Ho* in 1605. Also in 1604, he adapted John Marston's *The Malcontent* for staging by the King's Men.

Major Tragedies

Despite his ability to write comedy, Webster is best

known for his two brooding English tragedies based on Italian sources. *The White Devil,* a retelling of the intrigues involving Vittoria Accoramboni, an Italian woman assassinated at the age of 28, was a failure when staged at the Red Bull Theatre in 1612 (published the same year), being too unusual and intellectual for its audience. *The Duchess of Malfi,* first performed by the King's Men about 1614 and published nine years later, was more successful. He also wrote a play called *Guise,* based on French history, of which little else is known as no text has survived.

The White Devil was performed in the Red Bull Theatre, an open-air theatre that is believed to have specialised in providing simple, escapist drama for a largely working class audience, a factor that might explain why Webster's highly intellectual and complex play was unpopular with its audience. In contrast, *The Duchess of Malfi* was probably performed by the King's Men in the smaller, indoor Blackfriars Theatre, where it would have played to a more highly educated audience that might have appreciated it better. The two plays would thus have been very different in their original performances. *The White Devil* would have been performed, probably in one continuous action, by adult actors, with elaborate stage effects a possibility. *The Duchess of Malfi* was performed in a controlled environment, with artificial lighting, and musical interludes between acts, which allowed time, perhaps, for the audience to accept the otherwise strange rapidity with which the Duchess is able to have babies.

Late Plays

Webster wrote one more play on his own: *The Devil's Law Case* (c. 1617-1619), a tragicomedy. His later plays were collaborative city comedies: *Anything for a Quiet Life* (c. 1621), co-written with Thomas Middleton, and *A Cure for a Cuckold* (c. 1624), co-written with William Rowley. In 1624, he also co-wrote a topical play about a recent scandal, *Keep the Widow Waking* (with John Ford, Rowley and Dekker). The play itself is lost, although its plot is known from a court case. He is believed to have contributed to the tragicomedy *The Fair Maid of the Inn* with John Fletcher, Ford, and Phillip Massinger. His *Appius and Virginia,* probably written with Thomas Heywood, is of uncertain date.

Reputation

Webster's major plays, *The White Devil* and *The Duchess of Malfi,* are macabre, disturbing works that seem to prefigure the Gothic literature of the seventeenth century. Intricate, complex, subtle and learned, they are difficult but rewarding, and are still frequently staged today.

Webster has received a reputation for being the Elizabethan and Jacobean dramatist with the most unsparingly dark vision of human nature. Even more than John Ford, whose *'Tis Pity She's a Whore* is also very bleak, Webster's tragedies present a horrific vision of mankind. In his poem "Whispers of Immortality," T. S. Eliot memorably says that Webster always saw "the skull beneath the skin".

On the other hand, Webster's title character in *The Duchess of Malfi* is presented as a figure of virtue by comparison to her malevolent brothers, and in facing death she exemplifies classical Stoic courage. Her martyr-like death scene has been compared to that of the titular king in Christopher Marlowe's play *Edward II.* Webster's use of a strong, virtuous woman as his central character was rare for his time and represents a deliberate reworking of some of the original historical event on which his play was based. The character of the duchess recalls the Victorian poet and essayist Algernon Charles Swinburne's comment in *A Study of Shakespeare* that in tragedies such as *King Lear* Shakespeare had shown such a bleak world as a foil or backdrop for virtuous heroines such as Ophelia and Imogen, so that their characterization would not seem too incredible. Swinburne describes such heroines as shining in the darkness.

While Webster's drama was generally dismissed in the eighteenth and nineteenth centuries, many twentieth century critics and theatregoers find *The White Devil* and *The Duchess of Malfi* to be brilliant plays of great poetic quality and dark themes. One explanation for this change is that only after the horrors of war in the early twentieth century could their desperate protagonists be portrayed on stage again, and understood. W. A. Edwards wrote of Webster's plays in *Scrutiny* II (1933–4): "Events are not within control, nor are our human desires; let's snatch what comes and clutch it, fight our way out of tight corners, and meet the end without squealing." The violence and pessimism of Webster's tragedies have seemed to some analysts close to modern sensibilities.

John Donne

John Donne, (21 January 1572-31 March 1631) was an English Jacobean poet, preacher and a major representative of the metaphysical poets of the period. His works are notable for their realistic and sensual style and include sonnets, love poetry, religious poems, Latin translations, epigrams, elegies, songs, satires and sermons. His poetry is noted for its vibrancy of language and inventiveness of metaphor, especially as compared to those of his contemporaries.

Despite his great education and poetic talents, he lived in poverty for several years, relying heavily on wealthy friends. In 1615 he became an Anglican priest and, in 1621, was appointed the Dean of St Paul's Cathedral in London.

Early Life

John Donne was born on Bread Street in London, England, into a Catholic family at a time when Catholicism was illegal in England. Donne was the third of six children. His father, also named John Donne, was of Welsh descent, and a warden of the Ironmongers Company in the City of London. Donne's father was a respected Catholic who avoided unwelcome government attention out of fear of being persecuted for his religious faith.

Donne's father died in 1576, leaving his wife, Elizabeth Heywood, the responsibility of raising their children. Elizabeth Heywood, also from a noted Catholic family, was the daughter of John Heywood, the playwright, and sister of Jasper Heywood, the translator and Jesuit. She was a great-niece of the Catholic martyr Thomas More. This tradition of martyrdom would continue among Donne's closer relatives, many of whom were executed or exiled for religious reasons. Despite the obvious dangers, Donne's family arranged for his education by the Jesuits, which gave him a deep knowledge of his religion that equipped him for the ideological religious conflicts of his time. Donne's mother married Dr. John Syminges, a wealthy widower with three children, a few months after Donne's father died. In 1577, his mother died, followed by two more of his sisters, Mary and Katherine, in 1581.

Donne was a student at Hart Hall, now Hertford College, Oxford, from the age of 11. After three years at Oxford he was admitted to the University of Cambridge, where he studied for another three years. He was unable to obtain a degree from either institution because of his Catholicism, since he could not take the Oath of Supremacy required of graduates.

In 1591 he was accepted as a student at the Thavies Inn legal school, one of the Inns of Chancery in London. In 1592 he was admitted to Lincoln's Inn, one of the Inns of Court, where he held the office of Master of the Revels. His brother Henry was also a university student prior to his arrest in 1593 for harbouring a Catholic priest, William Harrington, whom Henry betrayed under torture. Harrington was tortured on the rack, hanged until not quite dead, and then was subjected to live disembowelment. Henry Donne died in Newgate prison of bubonic plague, leading John Donne to begin questioning his Catholic faith.

During and after his education, Donne spent much of his considerable inheritance on women, literature, pastimes and travel. Although there is no record detailing precisely where he traveled, it is known that he traveled across Europe and later fought with the Earl of Essex and Sir Walter Raleigh against the Spanish at Cádiz (1596) and the Azores (1597) and witnessed the loss of the Spanish flagship, the *San Felipe*. According to Izaak Walton, who wrote a biography of Donne in 1640:

During the next four years he fell in love with Egerton's niece Anne More, and they were married just before Christmas in 1601 against the wishes of both Egerton and her father, George More, Lieutenant of the Tower. This ruined his career and earned him a short stay in Fleet Prison, along with the priest who married them and the man who acted as a witness to the wedding. Donne was released when the marriage was proven valid, and soon secured the release of the other two. Walton tells us that when he wrote to his wife to tell her about losing his post, he wrote after his name: *John Donne, Anne Donne, Un-done.* It was not until 1609 that Donne was reconciled with his father-in-law and received his wife's dowry.

Following his release, Donne had to accept a retired country life in Pyrford, Surrey. Over the next few years he scraped a meagre living as a lawyer, depending on his wife's cousin Sir Francis Wolly to house him, his wife, and their children. Since Anne Donne had a baby almost every year, this was a very generous gesture. Though he practised law and worked as an assistant pamphleteer to Thomas Morton, he was in a state of constant financial insecurity, with a growing family to provide for.

Anne bore him 12 children in 16 years of marriage (including two stillbirths - their eighth and then in 1617 their last child); indeed, she spent most of her married life either pregnant or nursing. The 10 surviving children were named Constance, John, George, Francis, Lucy (after Donne's patroness Lucy, Countess of Bedford, her godmother), Bridget, Mary, Nicholas, Margaret and Elizabeth. Francis, Nicholas and Mary died before they were ten. In a state of despair, Donne noted that the death of a child would mean one less mouth to feed, but he could not afford the burial expenses. During this time Donne wrote, but did not publish, *Biathanatos,* his defense of suicide. His wife died on 15 August 1617, five days after giving birth to their twelfth child, a still-born baby. Donne mourned her deeply, including writing the 17th Holy Sonnet. He never remarried; this was quite unusual for the time, especially as he had a large family to bring up.

Early Poetry

Donne's earliest poems showed a developed knowledge of English society coupled with sharp criticism of its problems. His satires dealt with common Elizabethan topics, such as corruption in the legal system, mediocre poets, and pompous courtiers. His images of sickness, vomit, manure, and plague assisted in the creation of a strongly satiric world populated by all the fools and knaves of England. His third satire, however, deals with the problem of true religion, a matter of great importance to Donne. He argued that it was better to examine carefully one's religious convictions than blindly to follow any established tradition, for none would be saved at the Final Judgment, by claiming "A Harry, or a Martin taught [them] this."

Donne's early career was also notable for his erotic poetry, especially his elegies, in which he employed unconventional metaphors, such as a flea biting two lovers being compared to sex. In *Elegy XIX: To His Mistress Going to Bed,* he poetically undressed his mistress and compared the act of fondling to the exploration of America. In *Elegy XVIII,* he compared the gap between his lover's breasts to the Hellespont. Donne did not publish these poems, although did allow them to circulate widely in manuscript form.

Career and Later Life

Donne was elected as Member of Parliament for the constituency of Brackley in 1602, but this was not a paid position and Donne struggled to provide for his family, relying heavily upon rich friends. The fashion for coterie poetry of the period gave him a means to seek patronage and many of his poems were written for wealthy friends or patrons, especially Sir Robert Drury, who came to be Donne's chief patron in 1610. Donne wrote the two *Anniversaries, An Anatomy of the World* (1611) and *Of the Progress of the Soul,* (1612), for Drury. While historians are not certain as to the precise reasons for which Donne left the Catholic Church, he was certainly in communication with the King, James I of England, and in 1610 and 1611 he wrote two anti-Catholic polemics: *Pseudo-Martyr* and *Ignatius his Conclave.* Although James was pleased with Donne's work, he refused to reinstate him at court and instead urged him to take holy orders. At length, Donne acceded to the King's wishes and in 1615 was ordained into the Church of England.

A few months before his death, Donne commissioned this portrait of himself as he expected to appear when he rose from the grave at the Apocalypse. He hung the portrait on his wall as a reminder of the transience of life.

Donne became a Royal Chaplain in late 1615, Reader of Divinity at Lincoln's Inn in 1616, and received a Doctor of Divinity degree from Cambridge University in 1618. Later in 1618 he became chaplain to Viscount Doncaster, who was on an embassy to the princes of Germany. Donne did not return to England until 1620. In 1621 Donne was made Dean of St Paul's, a leading (and well-paid) position in the Church of

England and one he held until his death in 1631. During his period as Dean his daughter Lucy died, aged eighteen. It was in late November and early December of 1623 that he suffered a nearly fatal illness, thought to be either typhus or a combination of a cold followed by the seven-day relapsing fever. During his convalescence he wrote a series of meditations and prayers on health, pain, and sickness that were published as a book in 1624 under the title of *Devotions upon Emergent Occasions*. Meditation XVII later became well known for its phrase "for whom the bell tolls" and the statement that "no man is an island". In 1624 he became vicar of St Dunstan-in-the-West, and 1625 a Royal Chaplain to Charles I. He earned a reputation as an eloquent preacher and 160 of his sermons have survived, including the famous Death's Duel sermon delivered at the Palace of Whitehall before King Charles I in February 1631.

Later Poetry

Some have speculated that Donne's numerous illnesses, financial strain, and the deaths of his friends all contributed to the development of a more somber and pious tone in his later poems. The change can be clearly seen in "An Anatomy of the World" (1611), a poem that Donne wrote in memory of Elizabeth Drury, daughter of his patron, Sir Robert Drury. This poem treats Elizabeth's demise with extreme gloominess, using it as a symbol for the Fall of Man and the destruction of the universe.

The poem "A Nocturnal upon S. Lucy's Day," being the shortest day of the year, concerns the poet's despair at the death of a loved one. In it Donne expresses a feeling of utter negation and hopelessness, saying that "I am every dead thing...re-begot / Of absence, darkness, death." This famous work was probably written in 1627 when both Donne's friend Lucy, Countess of Bedford, and his daughter Lucy Donne died. Three years later, in 1630, Donne wrote his will on Saint Lucy's day (December 13), the date the poem describes as "Both the year's, and the day's deep midnight."

The increasing gloominess of Donne's tone may also be observed in the religious works that he began writing during the same period. His early belief in the value of skepticism now gave way to a firm faith in the traditional teachings of the Bible. Having converted to the Anglican Church, Donne focused his literary career on religious literature. He quickly became noted for his sermons and religious poems. The lines of these sermons would come to influence future works of English literature, such as Ernest Hemingway's *For Whom the Bell Tolls,* which took its title from a passage in Meditation XVII, and Thomas Merton's *No Man is an Island,* which took its title from the same source.

Towards the end of his life Donne wrote works that challenged death, and the fear that it inspired in many men, on the grounds of his belief that those who die are sent to Heaven to live eternally. One example of this challenge is his Holy Sonnet X, from which come the famous lines "Death, be not proud, though some have called thee / Mighty and dreadful, for thou art not so." Even as he lay dying during Lent in 1631, he rose from his sickbed and delivered the Death's Duel sermon, which was later described as his own funeral sermon. Death's Duel portrays life as a steady descent to suffering and death, yet sees hope in salvation and immortality through an embrace of God, Christ and the Resurrection.

Death

It is thought that his final illness was stomach cancer. He died on 31 March 1631 having written many poems in his lifetime (though only in manuscript - his poems would not be printed and published until two years after his death); but having left a body of work fiercely engaged with the emotional and intellectual conflicts of his age. John Donne is buried in St Paul's, where a memorial statue of him was erected (carved from a drawing of him in his shroud), with a Latin epigraph probably composed by himself.

Style

John Donne was famous for his metaphysical poetry in the 17th century. His work suggests a healthy appetite for life and its pleasures, while also expressing deep emotion. He did this through the use of conceits, wit and intellect — as seen in the poems "The Sun Rising" and "Batter My Heart".

Donne is considered a master of the metaphysical conceit, an extended metaphor that combines two vastly different ideas into a single idea, often using imagery. An example of this is his equation of lovers with saints in "The Canonization." Unlike the conceits found in other Elizabethan poetry, most notably Petrarchan conceits, which formed clichéd comparisons between more closely related objects (such as a rose and love), metaphysical conceits go to a greater depth in comparing two completely unlike objects, although sometimes in the mode of Shakespeare's radical paradoxes and imploded contraries. One of the most famous of Donne's conceits is found in "A Valediction: Forbidding Mourning" where he compares two lovers who are separated to the two legs of a compass.

Donne's works are also witty, employing paradoxes, puns, and subtle yet remarkable analogies. His pieces are often ironic and cynical, especially regarding love and human motives. Common subjects of Donne's poems are love (especially in his early life), death (especially after his wife's death), and religion.

John Donne's poetry represented a shift from classical forms to more personal poetry. Donne is noted for his poetic metre, which was structured with changing and jagged rhythms that closely resemble casual speech (it was for this that the more classically-minded Ben Jonson commented that "Donne, for not keeping of accent, deserved hanging").

Some scholars believe that Donne's literary works reflect the changing trends of his life, with love poetry and satires from his youth and religious sermons during his later years. Other scholars, such as Helen Gardner, question the validity of this dating - most of his poems were published posthumously (1633). The exception to these is his *Anniversaries* which were published in 1612 and *Devotions upon Emergent Occasions* published in 1624. His sermons are also dated, sometimes specifically by date and year.

Philip Sidney

Sir Philip Sidney (30 November 1554 – 17 October 1586) became one of the Elizabethan Age's most prominent figures. Famous in his day in England as a poet, courtier and soldier, he remains known as the author of *Astrophel and Stella* (1581, pub. 1591), *The Defence of Poetry* (or *An Apology for Poetry*, 1581, pub. 1595), and *The Countess of Pembroke's Arcadia* (1580, pub. 1590).

Biography

Born at Penshurst Place, Kent, he was the eldest son of Sir Henry Sidney and Lady Mary Dudley. His mother was the daughter of John Dudley, 1st Duke of Northumberland, and the sister of Robert Dudley, 1st Earl of Leicester. His younger sister, Mary Sidney, married Henry Herbert, 2nd Earl of Pembroke. Mary Sidney, who upon her marriage became the Countess of Pembroke, was a writer, translator and literary patron. Sidney dedicated his longest work, the *Arcadia,* to her. After her brother's death, Mary Sidney Herbert reworked the Arcadia, now known as The Countess of Pembroke's Arcadia.

Philip was educated at Shrewsbury School and Christ Church, Oxford. He was much travelled and highly learned. In 1572, he travelled to France as part of the embassy to negotiate a marriage between Elizabeth I and the Duc D'Alençon. He spent the next several years in mainland Europe, moving through Germany, Italy, Poland, and Austria. On these travels, he met a number of prominent European intellectuals and politicians.

Returning to England in 1575, Sidney met Penelope Devereux, the future Lady Rich; though much younger, she would inspire his famous sonnet sequence of the 1580s, *Astrophel and Stella.* Her father, the Earl of Essex, is said to have planned to marry his daughter to Sidney, but he died in 1576. In England, Sidney occupied himself with politics and art. He defended his father's administration of Ireland in a lengthy document. More seriously, he quarrelled with Edward de Vere, 17th Earl of Oxford, probably because of Sidney's opposition to the French marriage, which de Vere championed. In the aftermath of this episode, Sidney challenged de Vere to a duel, which Elizabeth forbade. He then wrote a lengthy letter to the Queen detailing the foolishness of the French marriage. Characteristically, Elizabeth bristled at his presumption, and Sidney prudently retired from court.

His artistic contacts were more peaceful and more significant for his lasting fame. During his absence from court, he wrote the first draft of *The Arcadia* and *A Defense of Poetry*. Somewhat earlier, he had met Edmund Spenser, who dedicated the Shepheardes Calendar to him. Other literary contacts included membership, along with his friends and fellow poets Fulke Greville, Edward Dyer, Edmund Spenser and Gabriel Harvey, of the (possibly fictitious) 'Areopagus', a humanist endeavour to classicize English verse.

Sidney had returned to court by the middle of 1581. That same year Penelope Devereux was married, apparently against her will, to Lord Rich. Sidney was knighted in 1583. An early arrangement to marry Anne Cecil, daughter of Sir William Cecil and eventual wife of de Vere, had fallen through in 1571. In 1583, he married Frances, teenage daughter of Sir Francis Walsingham. The next year, he met Giordano Bruno who subsequently dedicated two books to Sidney.

Both through his family heritage and his personal experience (he was in Walsingham's house in Paris during the St. Bartholomew's Day Massacre), Sidney was a keenly militant Protestant. In the 1570s, he had persuaded John Casimir to consider proposals for a united Protestant effort against the Roman Catholic Church and Spain. In the early 1580s, he argued unsuccessfully for an assault on Spain itself. In 1585, his enthusiasm for the Protestant struggle was given a free rein when he was appointed governor of Flushing in the Netherlands. In the Netherlands, he consistently urged boldness on his superior, his uncle the Earl of Leicester. He conducted a successful raid on Spanish forces near Axel in July, 1586.

Later that year, he joined Sir John Norris in the Battle of Zutphen. During the siege, he was shot in the thigh and died twenty-six days later. According to the story, while lying wounded he gave his water-bottle to another wounded soldier, saying, "Thy necessity is yet greater than mine". This became possibly the most famous story about Sir Phillip, intended to illustrate his noble character.

Sidney's body was returned to London and interred in St. Paul's Cathedral on 16 February 1587. Already during his own lifetime, but even more after his death, he had become for many English people the very epitome of a courtier: learned and politic, but at the same time generous, brave, and impulsive. Never more than a marginal figure in the politics of his time, he was memorialized as the flower of English manhood in Edmund Spenser's *Astrophel,* one of the greatest English Renaissance elegies.

In Zutphen, the Netherlands, a street has been named after Sir Philip. A statue for him can be found in the park at the Coehoornsingel, where the English soldiers who fell in the Battle of Zutphen were also temporarily buried. A memorial at the location where he was mortally wounded by the Spanish can be found at the entrance of a footpath at the Warnsveldseweg, southeast of the Catholic cemetery.

Works

The Lady of May — This is one of Sidney's lesser-known works, a masque written and performed for Queen Elizabeth in 1578 or 1579.

Astrophel and Stella — The first of the famous English sonnet sequences, *Astrophel and Stella* was probably composed in the early 1580s. The sonnets were well-circulated in manuscript before the first (apparently pirated) edition was printed in 1591; only in 1598 did an authorised edition reach the press. The sequence was a watershed in English Renaissance poetry. In it, Sidney partially nativised the key features of his Italian model, Petrarch: variation of emotion from poem to poem, with the attendant sense of an ongoing, but partly obscure, narrative; the philosophical trappings; the musings on the act of poetic creation itself. His experiments with rhyme scheme were no less notable; they served to free the English sonnet from the strict rhyming requirements of the Italian form.

The Countess of Pembroke's Arcadia — The *Arcadia*, by far Sidney's most ambitious work, was as significant in its own way as his sonnets. The work is a romance that combines pastoral elements with a mood derived from the Hellenistic model of Heliodorus. In the work, that is, a highly idealized version of the shepherd's life adjoins (not always naturally) with stories of jousts, political treachery, kidnappings, battles, and rapes. As published in the sixteenth century, the narrative follows the Greek model: stories are nested within each other, and different story-lines are intertwined. The work enjoyed great popularity for more than a century after its publication. William Shakespeare borrowed from it for the Gloucester subplot of *King Lear*; parts of it were also dramatized by John Day and James Shirley. According to a widely-told story, King Charles I quoted lines from the book as he mounted the scaffold to be executed; Samuel Richardson named the heroine of his first novel after Sidney's Pamela. *Arcadia* exists in two significantly different versions. Sidney wrote an early version (The Old Arcadia) during a stay at Mary Herbert's house; this version is narrated in a straightforward, sequential manner. Later, Sidney began to revise the work on a more ambitious plan, with much more backstory about the princes, and a much more complicated story line, with many more characters. He completed most of the first three books, but the project was unfinished at the time of his death—the third book breaks off in the middle of a swordfight. There were several early editions of the book. Fulke Greville published the revised version alone, in 1590. The Countess of Pembroke, Sidney's sister, published a version in 1593, which pasted the last two books of the first version onto the first three books of the revision. In the 1621 version, Sir William Alexander provided a bridge to bring the two stories back into agreement. It was known in this cobbled-together fashion until the discovery, in the early twentieth century, of the earlier version.

An Apology for Poetry — Sidney wrote the *Defence* before 1583. It is generally believed that he was at least partly motivated by Stephen Gosson, a former playwright who dedicated his attack on the English stage, *The School of Abuse*, to Sidney in 1579, but Sidney primarily addresses more general objections to poetry, such as those of Plato. In his essay, Sidney integrates a number of classical and Italian precepts on fiction. The essence of his defense is that poetry, by combining the liveliness of history with the ethical focus of philosophy, is more effective than either history or philosophy in rousing its readers to virtue. The work also offers important comments on Edmund Spenser and the Elizabethan stage.

7

Renaissance Poetry

The Renaissance was slow in coming to England, with the generally accepted start date being around 1509. It is also generally accepted that the English Renaissance extended until the Restoration in 1660. However, a number of factors had prepared the way for the introduction of the new learning long before this start date. A number of medieval poets had, as already noted, shown an interest in the ideas of Aristotle and the writings of European Renaissance precursors such as Dante.

The introduction of movable-block printing by Caxton in 1474 provided the means for the more rapid dissemination of new or recently rediscovered writers and thinkers. Caxton also printed the works of Chaucer and Gower and these books helped establish the idea of a native poetic tradition that was linked to its European counterparts. In addition, the writings of English humanists like Thomas More and Thomas Elyot helped bring the ideas and attitudes associated with the new learning to an English audience.

Three other factors in the establishment of the English Renaissance were the Reformation, Counter Reformation, and the opening of the era of English naval power and overseas exploration and expansion. The establishment of the Church of England in 1535 accelerated the process of questioning the Catholic world-view that had previously dominated intellectual and artistic life. At the same time, long-distance sea voyages helped provide the stimulus and information that underpinned a new understanding of the nature of the universe which resulted in the theories of Nicolaus Copernicus and Johannes Kepler.

Early Renaissance Poetry

With a small number of exceptions, the early years of the 16th century are not particularly notable. The Douglas *Aeneid* was completed in 1513 and John Skelton wrote poems that were transitional between the late Medieval and Renaissance styles. The new king, Henry VIII, was something of a poet himself. The most significant English poet of this period was Thomas Wyatt, who was among the first poets to write sonnets in English. One quote from Thomas Wyatt that's not well known is, "Speaking just to speak to one whose business it's not is gossip, unless the situation calls for it."

The Elizabethans

The Elizabethan period (1558 to 1603) in poetry is characterized by a number of frequently overlapping developments. The introduction and adaptation of themes, models and verse forms from other European traditions and classical literature, the Elizabethan song tradition, the emergence of a courtly poetry often centred around the figure of the monarch and the growth of a verse-based drama are among the most important of these developments.

Elizabethan Song

A wide range of Elizabethan poets wrote songs, including Nicholas Grimald, Thomas Nashe and Robert Southwell. There are also a large number of extant anonymous songs from the period. Perhaps the greatest of all the songwriters was Thomas Campion. Campion is also notable because of his experiments with metres based on counting syllables rather than stresses. These quantitative metres were based on classical models and should be viewed as part of the wider Renaissance revival of Greek and Roman artistic methods.

The songs were generally printed either in miscellanies or anthologies such as Richard Tottel's 1557 *Songs and Sonnets* or in songbooks that included printed music to enable performance. These performances formed an integral part of both public and private entertainment. By the end of the 16th century, a new generation of composers, including John Dowland, William Byrd, Orlando Gibbons, Thomas Weelkes and Thomas Morley were helping to bring the art of Elizabethan song to an extremely high musical level.

Courtly Poetry

With the consolidation of Elizabeth's power, a genuine court sympathetic to poetry and the arts in general emerged. This encouraged the emergence of a poetry aimed at, and often set in, an idealised version of the courtly world.

Among the best known examples of this are Edmund Spenser's *The Faerie Queene,* which is effectively an extended hymn of praise to the queen, and Philip Sidney's *Arcadia.* This courtly trend can also be seen in Spenser's *Shepheardes Calender*. This poem marks the introduction into an English context of the classical pastoral, a mode of poetry that assumes an aristocratic audience with a certain kind of attitude to the land and peasants. The explorations of love found in the sonnets of William Shakespeare and the poetry of Walter Raleigh and others also implies a courtly audience.

Elizabethan Verse Drama

Elizabethan verse drama is widely considered to be one of the major achievements of literature in English, and its most famous exponent, William Shakespeare, is revered as the greatest poet in the language. This drama, which served both as courtly masque and popular entertainment, deals with all the major themes of contemporary literature and life.

There are plays on European, classical, and religious themes reflecting the importance of humanism and the Reformation. There are also a number of plays dealing with English history that may be read as part of an effort to strengthen the British national myth and as artistic underpinnings for Elizabeth's resistance to the Spanish and other foreign threats. A number of the comic works for the stage also use bucolic themes connected with the pastoral genre.In addition to Shakespeare, other notable dramatists of the period include Christopher Marlowe, Thomas Middleton, Thomas Dekker and Ben Jonson.

Classicism

Gavin Douglas' *Aeneid*, Thomas Campion's metrical experiments, and Spenser's *Shepheardes Calender* and plays like Shakespeare's *Antony and Cleopatra* are all examples of the influence of classicism on Elizabethan poetry. It remained common for poets of the period to write on themes from classical mythology; Shakespeare's *Venus and Adonis* and the Christopher Marlowe/George Chapman *Hero and Leander* are examples of this kind of work.

Translations of classical poetry also became more widespread, with the versions of Ovid's *Metamorphoses* by Arthur Golding (1565–67) and George Sandys (1626), and Chapman's translations of Homer's *Iliad* (1611) and *Odyssey* (c.1615), among the outstanding examples.

Canons of Renaissance English Poetry

Canons of Renaissance English poetry (i.e. in the 16th and early 17th century). While the canon has always been in some form of flux, it is only towards the late 20th century that concerted efforts were made to challenge the canon and the very concept of a canon. Questions that once did not even have to be made, such as where to put the limitations of periods, what geographical areas to include, what genres to include, what writers and what kinds of writers to include, are now central to writers of histories, anthology editors, curriculum designers, and individual teachers and learners. For example the customary exclusion of women writers has been successfully challenged over the last twenty years.

Canonical Canon

Who some of the central figures of the Elizabethan canon are, has long been established. They are Edmund Spenser, Sir Philip Sidney, Christopher Marlowe, William Shakespeare, Ben Jonson, and John

Donne. This list is so established that there seem to be few attempts to change it, simply because the cultural importance of these six is so great that even re-evaluations on grounds of literary merit has not dared to dislodge them from the curriculum. For this reason the challenges to the canon that have been made during the last century have mainly been concerned with the so-called "minor" poets.

This distinction between "major" and "minor" poets, and between "major" and "minor" works by individual poets, is one of the mainstays of the canonical tradition. Its aim can be summed up in the words of F. T. Palgrave who in his The Golden Treasury aimed to pass over *"extreme or temporary phases in style"* in favour of *"something neither modern, nor ancient, but true in all ages"*. This anachronistic ideal has curiously enough been prevalent throughout two hundred years of literary history whose ostensible goal has been to describe the period.

Canons before 20th Century

Donne, Ben Jonson, and Spenser were major influences on 17th century poetry. Spenser was the primary English influence on John Milton; while Donne was imitated by the Metaphysical poets and Jonson by the Cavalier poets. Both Donne and Jonson influenced the leading poet of the late 17th century, John Dryden. However, Dryden condemned the Metaphysical tendency in his criticism. Metaphysical poetry fell further into disrepute in the 18th century, while the interest in Renaissance verse was rekindled through the scholarship of Thomas Warton and others. The Lake Poets and subsequent Romantics were well-read in Renaissance poetry; Coleridge admired Donne, which is slightly unusual for this period. However, the canon of Renaissance poetry was formed only in the Victorian period, with anthologies like Palgrave's Golden Treasury. A fairly representative idea of the "Victorian canon" is given by Sir Arthur Quiller-Couch's Oxford Book of English Verse (1919). The poems from this period are largely songs; apart from the major names, one sees the two pioneers Sir Thomas Wyatt and the Earl of Surrey, and a scattering of poems by other writers of the period. The dominant figure is Anonymous. Some poems, such as Thomas Sackville's Induction to the *Mirror for Magistrates,* were highly regarded (and therefore "in the canon") but omitted as non-lyric.

The canon was also redistributed after Jacob Burckhardt's *The Civilization of the Renaissance in Italy* from 1860 formulated a view of the Renaissance as an aristocratic court culture. Consequently, later anthologies such as Arthur Symons's *A Sixteenth-Century Anthology* from 1905 focused on lyric poetry at the expense of other genres, a preference which remained throughout the first half of the 20th century.

Eliot's Changes to Canon

T. S. Eliot's many essays on Elizabethan subjects were mainly concerned with the drama, but there are attempts to bring back long-forgotten poets to general attention, for example Sir John Davies, whose cause he championed in an article in The Times Literary Supplement in 1926. Eliot's writing did much to bring the metaphysical poets, Donne in particular, back into favour.

Winters's Alternative Canon

The American critic Yvor Winters suggested in 1939,

an alternative canon of Elizabethan poetry . In this canon he excludes the famous representatives of the Petrarchan school of poetry, represented by Sir Philip Sidney and Edmund Spenser, and instead turns his eye to a Native or Plain Style *anti-Petrarchan* movement, which he claims has been overlooked and undervalued. The most underrated member of this movement he deems to have been George Gascoigne (1525-1577), who "deserves to be ranked...among the six or seven greatest lyric poets of the century, and perhaps higher" . Other members were Sir Walter Raleigh (1552-1618), Thomas Nashe (1567-1601), Barnabe Googe (1540-1594), and George Turberville (1540-1610).

Characteristic of this movement is that a poem has "a theme usually broad, simple, and obvious, even tending toward the proverbial, but usually a theme of some importance, humanly speaking; a feeling restrained to the minimum required by the subject; a rhetoric restrained to a similar minimum, the poet being interested in his rhetoric as a means of stating his matter as economically as possible, and not, as are the Petrarchans, in the pleasures of rhetoric for its own sake There is also in the school a strong tendency towards aphoristic statement" .

This attempt at rewriting a canon should not be seen as a challenge to the concept of the canon as such, but rather as an attempt to emulate T. S. Eliot's modernist revisions of the tradition. As with Eliot's canon, it may for today's reader say more about Winters and his time than about Elizabethan literature, but the list of poems he names among the best should still be of interest to the student who has already read the established, "Petrarchan," canon.

Winters compares the situation in Renaissance studies with that of the canon of eighteenth century poets, where he claims, *"the two greatest poetic talents of the period, those of Samuel Johnson and of Charles Churchill"* were obscured by the rising Romantic school and such poets as Thomas Gray and William Collins. The poems he mentions by Johnson and Churchill have been added to the list below.

An alternative Canon

These are some of the poems Winters recommends (in general the ones Winters considers to be the best are put first).From the anti-Petrarchan school:

- Sir Thomas Wyatt: "Tagus Farewell", "Is it possible", "I abide and abide", "They flee from me", "It may be good", "Your looks so often cast", "Disdain me not", "Perdie I said it not", "If thou wilt mightly be", "I have sought long", "And wilt thou leave me thus", "It was my choice", "Forget not yet", "What should I say", "Hate whom ye list", "Sighs are my food", "Madam withouten many words", "Within my breast I never thought it gain", "It burneth yet, alas!", "Speak thou and speed", "Under this stone".
- Thomas, Lord Vaux: "I loath that I did love", "When I look back", "When all is done and said".
- Nicholas Grimald: "Mirror of matrons".
- George Gascoigne: "Gascoigne's Woodmanship", "Gascoigne's De Profundis", "Gascoigne's Memories" II and III, "The Constancy of a Lover", "Dan Bartholomew's Dolorous Discourses" (from *Dan Bartholomew of Bath*), "In Praise of a Gentlewoman Who though She Was not very Fair Yet Was She as Hard-Favored as Might Be" (1).

- Barnabe Googe: "Of Nicholas Grimald", "To Dr. Balle", "To Mistress A.", "To the Translation of Palingenius", "Of Mistress D. S.", "Of Money", "Coming Homeward Out of Spain".
- George Turberville: "To the Roving Pirate", "To One that Had Little Wit", "To an Old Gentlewoman Who Painted Her Face", "Of the Clock and the Cock", "That All Things Are as They Are Used".
- Sir Walter Raleigh: "The Lie", "What is our life", "Even such is time".
- Jasper Heywood: "My friend if thou wilt credit me in ought".
- Thomas Nashe: "In Time of Pestilence", "Autumn hath all the fruitful summer's treasure".

From the Petrarchan school:

- Sir Thomas Wyatt: "My lute, awake", "All heavy minds", "Comfort thyself", "Lo what it is to love", "Leave then to slander love", "Ah, my heart, what aileth thee", and "Whoso list to hunt" (as the only interesting sonnet). In many ways, however, Wyatt's poems might be - and were by Winters - classified as Native Style.
- Sir Fulke Greville: "Down in the depths of my iniquity", Sonnets i, vii, xii, xxii, xliv, lii, xliv, lii, lvi from *Caelica, Epitaph to Sidney. Greville's poems migrated chronologically from the Petrarchan to the Plain Style to religious meditation.*
- Sir Philip Sidney: "Who hath his fancy pleased", "Doubt you to whom my Muse these notes entendeth", "Only joy, now here you are", "O you that hear this voice", "Who is it that this dark night", "The nightingale as soon as April

bringeth", "Ring out your bells", "What tongue can her perfection tell", sonnets xxxi, xxxix, xli, lxxiv, lxxxiv, xcviii, xcix, cv, cix, cx from *Astrophel and Stella.*

- Thomas Morley: "Ladies, you see time flieth", "No, no, Nigella!".
- Samuel Daniel: "Beauty, sweet love".
- William Shakespeare: Sonnets 66, 116, 129, 146.
- Thomas Campion: "Now winter nights enlarge", "When thou must home to shades of underground", "Shall I come, sweet love, to thee", "Sleep, angry beauty", "There is a garden in her face", "Thou art not fair for all thy red and white", What then is love but morning", "Whether men do laugh or weep".
- Ben Jonson: "To Heaven", "Though beauty be the mark of praise", "Where dost thou careless lie", "High-spirited friend", "From death and dark oblivion, near the same", "False world, good night", "Good and Great God, can I not think of Thee", "To draw no envy, Shakespeare, on thy name", "This morning, timely rapt with holy fire", To Charis I & II, "The Hour Glass", "My Picture Left in Scotland", "Joy, joy to mortals the rejoicing fires" from *Love's Triumph Through Callipolis,* "Drink to me only with thine eyes", "Come, my Celia", "Queen and huntress, chaste and fair". But Winters classified much of Jonson's best work as of the Plain Style ("My Picture Left in Scotland," "On His First Son").
- John Donne: "Valediction of His Name in a Window", "A Valediction: Forbidding Mourning", Holy Sonnet No. 1.

- Anonymous: "Come away, come, sweet love".

Winters also mentions these poems from the Eighteenth century as the best of that century:

- Samuel Johnson: "Prologue to Comus" and "Prologue to A Word to the Wise"
- Charles Churchill: "Dedication to Warburton"

Harold Bloom's Western Canon

Harold Bloom's version of the Western canon includes the poems of Sir Thomas Wyatt and Henry Howard, Earl of Surrey, Sir Philip Sidney's The Countess of Pembroke's Arcadia and Astrophel and Stella, Fulke Grèville's poems, Edmund Spenser's The Faerie Queene and "minor" poems, the poems of Sir Walter Ralegh, Christopher Marlowe, Michael Drayton, Samuel Daniel, William Shakespeare, Thomas Campion, John Donne and Ben Jonson. It will be noted that this list is very much author-centred, rather than work-centred, including, as it does, every poem by a relatively little-known poet like Drayton, but not a single one by George Gascoigne.

8

Restoration Literature

Restoration literature is the English literature written during the historical period commonly referred to as the English Restoration (1660–1689), which corresponds to the last years of the direct Stuart reign in England, Scotland, Wales, and Ireland. In general, the term is used to denote roughly homogeneous styles of literature that centre on a celebration of or reaction to the restored court of Charles II. It is a literature that includes extremes, for it encompasses both *Paradise Lost* and the Earl of Rochester's *Sodom,* the high-spirited sexual comedy of *The Country Wife* and the moral wisdom of *The Pilgrim's Progress.* It saw Locke's *Treatises of Government,* the founding of the Royal Society, the experiments and holy meditations of Robert Boyle, the hysterical attacks on theatres from Jeremy Collier, and the pioneering of literary criticism from John Dryden and John Dennis. The period witnessed news become a commodity, the essay develop into a periodical art form, and the beginnings of textual criticism.

The dates for Restoration literature are a matter of convention, and they differ markedly from genre to genre. Thus, the "Restoration" in drama may last until

1700, while in poetry it may last only until 1666 and the *annus mirabilis;* and in prose it might end in 1688, with the increasing tensions over succession and the corresponding rise in journalism and periodicals, or not until 1700, when those periodicals grew more stabilised. In general, scholars use the term "Restoration" to denote the literature that began and flourished under Charles II, whether that literature was the laudatory ode that gained a new life with restored aristocracy, the eschatological literature that showed an increasing despair among Puritans, or the literature of rapid communication and trade that followed in the wake of England's mercantile empire.

Historical Context

During the Interregnum, England had been dominated by Puritan literature and the intermittent presence of official censorship (for example, Milton's *Areopagitica* and his later retraction of that statement). While some of the Puritan ministers of Oliver Cromwell wrote poetry that was elaborate and carnal (such as Andrew Marvell's "Mower" poem, "To His Coy Mistress"), such poetry was not published. Similarly, some of the poets who published with the Restoration produced their poetry during the Interregnum. The official break in literary culture caused by censorship and radically moralist standards effectively created a gap in literary tradition. At the time of the Civil War, poetry had been dominated by metaphysical poetry of the John Donne, George Herbert, and Richard Lovelace sort. Drama had developed the late Elizabethan theatre traditions and had begun to mount increasingly topical and political plays (for example, the drama of Thomas Middleton). The Interregnum put a stop, or at least a caesura, to these lines of influence and allowed a seemingly fresh start for all forms of literature after the Restoration.

The last years of the Interregnum were turbulent, as were the last years of the Restoration period, and those who did not go into exile were called upon to change their religious beliefs more than once. With each religious preference came a different sort of literature, both in prose and poetry (the theatres were closed during the Interregnum). When Cromwell died and his son, Richard Cromwell, threatened to become Lord Protector, politicians and public figures scrambled to show themselves as allies or enemies of the new regime. Printed literature was dominated by odes in poetry, and religious writing in prose. The industry of religious tract writing, despite official efforts, did not reduce its output. Figures such as the founder of the Society of Friends, George Fox, were jailed by the Cromwellian authorities and published at their own peril.

During the Interregnum, the royalist forces attached to the court of Charles I went into exile with the twenty-year-old Charles II and conducted a brisk business in intelligence and fund-raising for an eventual return to England. Some of the royalist ladies installed themselves in convents in Holland and France that offered safe haven for indigent and travelling nobles and allies. The men similarly stationed themselves in Holland and France, with the court-in-exile being established in The Hague before setting up more permanently in Paris. The nobility who travelled with (and later travelled to) Charles II were therefore lodged for more than a decade in the midst of the continent's literary scene. As Holland and France in the 17th century were little alike, so the influences picked up by courtiers in exile and the travellers who sent intelligence and money to them were not monolithic. Charles spent his time attending plays in France, and he developed a taste for Spanish plays. Those nobles living in Holland began to learn about mercantile exchange as well as the tolerant, rationalist prose debates that circulated in that officially tolerant nation. John Bramhall, for example, had been a strongly high church theologian, and yet, in exile, he debated willingly with Thomas Hobbes and came into the Restored church as tolerant in practice as he was severe in argument. Courtiers also received an exposure to the Roman Catholic Church and its liturgy and pageants, as well as, to a lesser extent, Italian poetry.

Initial Reaction

When Charles II became king in 1660, the sense of novelty in literature was tempered by a sense of suddenly participating in European literature in a way that England had not before. One of Charles's first moves was to reopen the theatres and to grant letters patent giving mandates for the theatre owners and managers. Thomas Killigrew received one of the patents, establishing the King's Company and opening the first patent theatre at the Theatre Royal, Drury Lane; Sir William Davenant received the other, establishing the Duke of York's theatre company and opening his patent theatre in Lincoln's Inn Fields. Drama was public and a matter of royal concern, and therefore both theatres were charged with producing a certain number of old plays, and Davenant was charged with presenting material that would be morally uplifting. Additionally, the position of Poet Laureate was recreated, complete with payment by a barrel of "sack" (Spanish white wine), and the requirement for birthday odes.

Charles II was a man who prided himself on his wit and his worldliness. He was well known as a philanderer as well. Highly witty, playful, and sexually wise poetry thus had court sanction. Charles and his brother James, the Duke of York and future King of England, also sponsored mathematics and natural philosophy, and so spirited scepticism and investigation into nature were favoured by the court. Charles II sponsored the Royal Society, which courtiers were eager to join, just as Royal Society members moved in court. Charles and his court had also learned the lessons of exile. Charles was High Church (and secretly vowed to convert to Roman Catholicism on his death) and James was crypto-Catholic, but royal policy was generally tolerant of religious and political dissenters. While Charles II did have his own version of the Test Act, he was slow to jail or persecute Puritans, preferring merely to keep them from public office (and therefore to try to rob them of their Parliamentary positions). As a consequence, the prose literature of dissent, political theory, and economics increased in Charles II's reign.

Authors moved in two directions in reaction to Charles's return. On the one hand, there was an attempt at recovering the English literature of the Jacobean period, as if there had been no disruption; but, on the other, there was a powerful sense of novelty, and authors approached Gallic models of literature and elevated the literature of wit (particularly satire and parody). The novelty would show in the literature of sceptical inquiry, and the Gallicism would show in the introduction of Neoclassicism into English writing and criticism.

Top-down History

The Restoration is an unusual historical period, as its literature is bounded by a specific political event: the restoration of the Stuart monarchy. It is unusual in another way, as well, for it is a time when the influence of that king's presence and personality permeated literary society to such an extent that, almost uniquely, literature reflects the court. The adversaries of the restoration, the Puritans and democrats and republicans, similarly respond to the peculiarities of the king and the king's personality. Therefore, a top-down view of the literary history of the Restoration has more validity than that of most literary epochs. "The Restoration" as a critical concept covers the duration of the effect of Charles and Charles's manner. This effect extended beyond his death, in some instances, and not as long as his life, in others.

Poetry

The Restoration was an age of poetry. Not only was poetry the most popular form of literature, but it was also the most *significant* form of literature, as poems affected political events and immediately reflected the times. It was, to its own people, an age dominated only by the king, and not by any single genius. Throughout the period, the lyric, ariel, historical, and epic poem was being developed.

The English Epic

Even without the introduction of Neo-classical criticism, English poets were aware that they had no national epic. Edmund Spenser's *Faerie Queene* was well known, but England, unlike France with *The Song of Roland* or Spain with the *Cantar de Mio Cid* or, most of all, Italy with the *Aeneid,* had no epic poem of national origins. Several poets attempted to supply this void.

Sir William Davenant was the first Restoration poet to attempt an epic. His unfinished *Gondibert* was of epic length, and it was admired by Hobbes. However, it also used the ballad form, and other poets, as well as critics, were very quick to condemn this rhyme scheme as unflattering and unheroic (Dryden *Epic*). The prefaces to *Gondibert* show the struggle for a formal epic structure, as well as how the early Restoration saw themselves in relation to Classical literature.

Although today he is studied separately from the Restoration period, John Milton's *Paradise Lost* was published during that time. Milton no less than Davenant wished to write the English epic, and chose blank verse as his form. Milton rejected the cause of English exceptionalism: his *Paradise Lost* seeks to tell the story of all mankind, and his pride is in Christianity rather than Englishness.

Significantly, Milton began with an attempt at writing an epic on King Arthur, for that was the matter of English national founding. While Milton rejected that subject, in the end, others made the attempt. Richard Blackmore wrote both a *Prince Arthur* and *King Arthur*. Both attempts were long, soporific, and failed both critically and popularly. Indeed, the poetry was so slow that the author became known as "Never-ending Blackmore."

The Restoration period ended without an English epic. *Beowulf* may now be called the English epic, but the work was unknown to Restoration authors, and Old English was incomprehensible to them.

Poetry, Verse, and Odes

Lyric poetry, in which the poet speaks of his or her own feelings in the first person and expresses a mood, was not especially common in the Restoration period. Poets expressed their points of view in other forms, usually public or formally disguised poetic forms such as odes, pastoral poetry, and ariel verse. One of the characteristics of the period is its devaluation of individual sentiment and psychology in favour of public utterance and philosophy. The sorts of lyric poetry found later in the Churchyard Poets would, in the Restoration, only exist as pastorals.

Formally, the Restoration period had a preferred rhyme scheme. Rhyming couplets in iambic pentameter was by far the most popular structure for poetry of all types. Neo-Classicism meant that poets attempted adaptations of Classical meters, but the rhyming couplet in iambic pentameter held a near monopoly. According to Dryden, the rhyming couplet in iambic pentameter has the right restraint and dignity for a lofty subject, and its rhyme allowed for a complete, coherent statement to be made. Dryden was struggling with the issue of what later critics in the Augustan period would call "decorum": the fitness of form to subject. It is the same struggle that Davenant faced in his *Gondibert*.

Dryden's solution was a closed couplet in iambic pentameter that would have a minimum of enjambment. This form was called the "heroic couplet," because it was suitable for heroic subjects. Additionally, the age also developed the mock-heroic couplet. After 1672 and Samuel Butler's *Hudibras*, iambic tetrameter couplets with unusual or unexpected rhymes became known as Hudibrastic verse. It was a formal parody of heroic verse, and it was primarily used for satire. Jonathan Swift would use the Hudibrastic form almost exclusively for his poetry.

Although Dryden's reputation is greater today, contemporaries saw the 1670s and 1680s as the age of courtier poets in general, and Edmund Waller was as praised as any. Dryden, Rochester, Buckingham, and Dorset dominated verse, and all were attached to the court of Charles. Aphra Behn, Matthew Prior, and Robert Gould, by contrast, were outsiders who were profoundly royalist. The court poets follow no one particular style, except that they all show sexual awareness, a willingness to satirise, and a dependence upon wit to dominate their opponents. Each of these poets wrote for the stage as well as the page. Of these, Behn, Dryden, Rochester, and Gould deserve some separate mention.

Dryden was prolific; and he was often accused of plagiarism. Both before and after his Laureateship, he wrote public odes. He attempted the Jacobean pastoral along the lines of Walter Raleigh and Philip Sidney, but his greatest successes and fame came from his attempts at apologetics for the restored court and the Established Church. His *Absalom and Achitophel* and *Religio Laici* both served the King directly by making controversial royal actions seem reasonable. He also pioneered the mock-heroic. Although Samuel Butler had invented the mock-heroic in English with *Hudibras* (written during the Interregnum but published in the Restoration), Dryden's *MacFlecknoe* set up the satirical parody. Dryden was himself not of noble blood, and he was never awarded the honours that he had been promised by the King (nor was he repaid the loans he had made to the King), but he did as much as any peer to serve Charles II. Even when James II came to the throne and Roman Catholicism was on the rise, Dryden attempted to serve the court, and his *The Hind and the Panther* praised the Roman church above all others. After that point, Dryden suffered for his conversions, and he was the victim of many satires.

Buckingham wrote some court poetry, but he, like Dorset, was a patron of poetry more than a poet. Rochester, meanwhile, was a prolix and outrageous poet. Rochester's poetry is almost always sexually frank and is frequently political. Inasmuch as the Restoration came after the Interregnum, the very sexual explicitness of Rochester's verse was a political statement and a thumb in the eye of Puritans. His poetry often assumes a lyric pose, as he pretends to write in sadness over his own impotence or sexual conquests, but most of Rochester's poetry is a parody of an existing, Classically-authorised form. He has a mock topographical poem, several mock odes, and mock pastorals. Rochester's interest was in inversion, disruption, and the superiority of wit as much as it was in hedonism. Rochester's venality led to an early death, and he was later frequently invoked as the exemplar of a Restoration rake.

Aphra Behn modelled the rake Willmore in her play *The Rover* on Rochester; and while she was best known publicly for her drama (in the 1670s, only Dryden's plays were staged more often than hers), Behn wrote a great deal of poetry that would be the basis of her later reputation. Edward Bysshe would include numerous quotations from her verse in his *Art of English Poetry* (1702). While her poetry was occasionally sexually frank, it was never as graphic or intentionally lurid and titillating as Rochester's. Rather, her poetry was, like the court's ethos, playful and honest about sexual desire. One of the most remarkable aspects of Behn's success in court poetry, however, is that Behn was herself a commoner. She had no more relation to peers than Dryden, and possibly quite a bit less. As a woman, a commoner, and Kentish, she is remarkable for her success in moving in the same circles as the King himself. As Janet Todd and others have shown, she was likely a spy for the Royalist side during the Interregnum. She was certainly a spy for Charles II in the Second Anglo-Dutch War, but found her services unrewarded (in fact, she may have spent time in debtor's prison) and turned to writing to support herself. Her ability to write poetry that stands among the best of the age gives some lie to the notion that the Restoration was an age of female illiteracy and verse composed and read only by peers.

If Behn is a curious exception to the rule of noble verse, Robert Gould breaks that rule altogether. Gould was born of a common family and orphaned at the age of thirteen. He had no schooling at all and worked as a domestic servant, first as a footman and then, probably, in the pantry. However, he was attached to the Earl of Dorset's household, and Gould somehow learned to read and write, as well as possibly to read and write Latin. In the 1680s and 1690s, Gould's poetry was very popular. He attempted to write odes for money, but his great success came with *Love Given O'er, or A Satyr Upon ... Woman* in 1692. It was a partial adaptation of a satire by Juvenal, but with an immense amount of explicit invective against women. The misogyny in this poem is some of the harshest and most visceral in English poetry: the poem sold out all editions. Gould also wrote a *Satyr on the Play House* (reprinted in Montagu Sommers's *The London Stage*) with detailed descriptions of the actions and actors involved in the Restoration stage. He followed the success of *Love Given O'er* with a series of misogynistic poems, all of which have specific, graphic, and witty denunciations of female behaviour. His poetry has "virgin" brides who, upon their wedding nights, have "the straight gate so wide/ It's been leapt by all mankind," noblewomen who have money but prefer to pay the coachman with oral sex, and noblewomen having sex in their coaches and having the cobblestones heighten their pleasures. Gould's career was brief, but his success was not a novelty of subliterary misogyny. After Dryden's conversion to Roman Catholicism, Gould even engaged in a poison pen battle with the Laureate. His "Jack Squab" (the Laureate getting paid with squab as well as sack and implying that Dryden would sell his soul for a dinner) attacked Dryden's faithlessness viciously, and Dryden and his friends replied. That a footman even *could* conduct a verse war is remarkable. That he did so without, apparently, any prompting from his patron is astonishing.

Translations

Roger L'Estrange was a significant translator, and he also produced verse translations. Others, such as Richard Blackmore, were admired for their "sentence" but have not been remembered. Also, Elkannah Settle was, in the Restoration, a lively and promising political satirist, though his reputation has not fared well since his day. After booksellers began hiring authors and sponsoring specific translations, the shops filled quickly with poetry from hirelings. Similarly, as periodical literature began to assert itself as a political force, a number of now anonymous poets produced topical, specifically occasional verse.The largest and most important form of *incunabula* of the era was satire. There were great dangers in being associated with satire and its publication was generally done anonymously. To begin with, defamation law cast a wide net, and it was difficult for a satirist to avoid prosecution if he were proven to have written a piece that seemed to criticise a noble. More dangerously, wealthy individuals would often respond to satire by having the suspected poet physically attacked by ruffians. John Dryden was set upon for being merely *suspected* of having written the *Satire on Mankind.* A consequence of this anonymity is that a great many poems, some of them of merit, are unpublished and largely unknown. Political satires against The Cabal, against Sunderland's government, and, most especially, against James II's rumoured conversion to Roman Catholicism, are uncollected. However, such poetry was a vital part of the vigorous Restoration scene, and it was an age of energetic and voluminous satire.

Prose Genres

Prose in the Restoration period is dominated by Christian religious writing, but the Restoration also saw the beginnings of two genres that would dominate later periods: fiction and journalism. Religious writing often strayed into political and economic writing, just as political and economic writing implied or directly addressed religion.

Philosophical Writing

The Restoration saw the publication of a number of significant pieces of political and philosophical writing that had been spurred by the actions of the Interregnum. Additionally, the court's adoption of Neo-classicism and empirical science led to a receptiveness toward significant philosophical works.

Thomas Sprat wrote his *History of the Royal Society* in 1667 and set forth, in a single document, the goals of empirical science ever after. He expressed grave suspicions of adjectives, nebulous terminology, and all language that might be subjective. He praised a spare, clean, and precise vocabulary for science and explanations that are as comprehensible as possible. In Sprat's account, the Royal Society explicitly rejected anything that seemed like scholasticism. For Sprat, as for a number of the founders of the Royal Society, science was Protestant: its reasons and explanations had to be comprehensible to all. There would be no priests in science, and anyone could reproduce the experiments and hear their lessons. Similarly, he emphasised the need for conciseness in description, as well as reproducibility of experiments.

William Temple, after he retired from being what today would be called Secretary of State, wrote several bucolic prose works in praise of retirement, contemplation, and direct observation of nature. He also brought the Ancients and Moderns quarrel into English with his *Reflections on Ancient and Modern Learning*. The debates that followed in the wake of this quarrel would inspire many of the major authors of the first half of the 18th century.

The Restoration was also the time when John Locke wrote many of his philosophical works. Locke's empiricism was an attempt at understanding the basis of human understanding itself and thereby devising a proper manner for making sound decisions. These same scientific methods led Locke to his *Two Treatises of Government*, which later inspired the thinkers in the American Revolution. As with his work on understanding, Locke moves from the most basic units of society toward the more elaborate, and, like Thomas Hobbes, he emphasises the plastic nature of the social contract. For an age that had seen absolute monarchy overthrown, democracy attempted, democracy corrupted, and limited monarchy restored; only a flexible basis for government could be satisfying.

Religious Writing

The Restoration moderated most of the more strident sectarian writing, but radicalism persisted after the Restoration. Puritan authors such as John Milton were forced to retire from public life or adapt, and those Diggers, Fifth Monarchist, Leveller, Quaker, and Anabaptist authors who had preached against monarchy and who had participated directly in the regicide of Charles I were partially suppressed. Consequently, violent writings were forced underground, and many of those who had served in the Interregnum attenuated their positions in the Restoration.

Fox, and William Penn, made public vows of pacifism and preached a new theology of peace and love. Other Puritans contented themselves with being able to meet freely and act on local parishes. They distanced themselves from the harshest sides of their religion that had led to the abuses of Cromwell's reign. Two religious authors stand out beyond the others in this time: John Bunyan and Izaak Walton.

Bunyan's *The Pilgrim's Progress* is an allegory of personal salvation and a guide to the Christian life.

Instead of any focus on eschatology or divine retribution, Bunyan instead writes about how the individual saint can prevail against the temptations of mind and body that threaten damnation. The book is written in a straightforward narrative and shows influence from both drama and biography, and yet it also shows an awareness of the allegorical tradition found in Edmund Spenser.

Izaak Walton's *The Compleat Angler* is similarly introspective. Ostensibly, his book is a guide to fishing, but readers treasured its contents for their descriptions of nature and serenity. There are few analogues to this prose work. On the surface, it appears to be in the tradition of other guide books, but, like *Pilgrim's Progress,* its main business is guiding the individual.

More court-oriented religious prose included sermon collections and a great literature of debate over the convocation and issues before the House of Lords. The Act of First Fruits and Fifths, the Test Act, the Act of Uniformity 1662, and others engaged the leading divines of the day. Robert Boyle, notable as a scientist, also wrote his *Meditations* on God, and this work was immensely popular as devotional literature well beyond the Restoration. Devotional literature in general sold well and attests a wide literacy rate among the English middle classes.

Restoration Journalism

During the Restoration period, the most common manner of getting news would have been a broadsheet publication. A single, large sheet of paper might have a written, usually partisan, account of an event. However, the period saw the beginnings of the first professional and periodical (meaning that the publication was regular) journalism in England. Journalism develops late, generally around the time of William of Orange's claiming the throne in 1689. Coincidentally or by design, England began to have newspapers just when William came to court from Amsterdam, where there were already newspapers being published.

The early efforts at news sheets and periodicals were spotty. Roger L'Estrange produced both *The News* and *City Mercury*, but neither of them was a sustained effort. Henry Muddiman was the first to succeed in a regular news paper with the *London Gazette*. In 1665, Muddiman produced the *Oxford Gazette* as a digest of news of the royal court, which was in Oxford to avoid the plague in London. When the court moved back to Whitehall later in the year, the title *London Gazette* was adopted (and is still in use today). Muddiman had begun as a journalist in the Interregnum and had been the official journalist of the Long Parliament (in the form of *The Parliamentary Intelligencer*). Although Muddiman's productions are the first regular news accounts, they are still not the first modern newspaper, as the work was sent in manuscript by post to subscribers and was not a printed sheet for general sale to the public. That had to wait for *The Athenian Mercury*.

Sporadic essays combined with news had been published throughout the Restoration period, but *The Athenian Mercury* was the first regularly published periodical in England. John Dunton and the "Athenian Society" (actually a mathematician, minister, and philosopher paid by Dunton for their work) began publishing in 1691, just after the reign of William and Mary began. In addition to news reports, *The Athenian*

Mercury allowed readers to send in questions anonymously and receive a printed answer. The questions mainly dealt with love and health, but there were some bizarre and intentionally amusing questions as well (e.g. a question on why a person shivers after urination, written in rhyming couplets). The questions section allowed the journal to sell well and to be profitable. Therefore, it ran for six years, produced four books that spun off from the columns, and then received a bound publication as *The Athenian Oracle.*

The Athenian Mercury set the stage for the later *Spectator, Gray's Inn Journal, Temple Bar Journal,* and scores of politically oriented journals, such as the original *The Guardian, The Observer, The Freeholder, Mist's Journal,* and many others. Also, *The Athenian Mercury* published poetry from contributors, and it was the first to publish the poetry of Jonathan Swift and Elizabeth Singer Rowe. The trend of newspapers would similarly explode in subsequent years; a number of these later papers had runs of a single day and were composed entirely as a method of planting political attacks.

Fiction

Although it is impossible to satisfactorily date the beginning of the novel in English, long fiction and fictional biographies began to distinguish themselves from other forms in England during the Restoration period. An existing tradition of *Romance* fiction in France and Spain was popular in England. Ludovico Ariosto's *Orlando Furioso* engendered prose narratives of love, peril, and revenge, and Gauthier de Costes, seigneur de la Calprenède's novels were quite popular during the Interregnum and beyond.

The "Romance" was considered a feminine form, and women were taxed with reading "novels" as a vice. Inasmuch as these novels were largely read in French or in translation from French, they were associated with effeminacy. However, novels slowly divested themselves of the Arthurian and chivalric trappings and came to centre on more ordinary or picaresque figures. One of the most significant figures in the rise of the novel in the Restoration period is Aphra Behn. She was not only the first professional female novelist, but she may be among the first professional novelists of either sex in England.

Behn's first novel was *Love-Letters Between a Nobleman and His Sister* in 1684. This was an epistolary novel documenting the amours of a scandalous nobleman who was unfaithful to his wife with her sister (thus making his lover his sister-in-law rather than biological sister). The novel is highly romantic, sexually explicit, and political.

Behn wrote the novel in two parts, with the second part showing a distinctly different style from the first. Behn also wrote several "Histories" of fictional figures, such as her *The History of a Nun*. As the genre of "novel" did not exist, these histories were prose fictions based on biography. However, her most famous novel was *Oroonoko* in 1688. This was a fictional biography, published as a "true history", of an African king who had been enslaved in Suriname, a colony Behn herself had visited.

Behn's novels show the influence of tragedy and her experiences as a dramatist. Later novels by Daniel Defoe would adopt the same narrative framework, although his choice of biography would be tempered by his experience as a journalist writing "true histories" of criminals.

Other forms of fiction were also popular. Available to readers were versions of the stories of *Reynard the Fox,* as well as various indigenous folk tales, such as the various Dick Whittington and Tom Thumb fables. Most of these were in verse, but some circulated in prose. These largely anonymous or folk compositions circulated as chapbooks.

Subliterary Genres and Writers

Along with the figures mentioned above, the Restoration period saw the beginnings of explicitly political writing and hack writing. Roger L'Estrange was a pamphleteer who became the surveyor of presses and licenser of the press after the Restoration. In 1663–6, L'Estrange published *The News.* When he was implicated in the Popish Plot and fled England, he published *The Observator* (1681–1687) to attack Titus Oates and the Puritans. L'Estrange's most important contributions to literature, however, came with his translations. He translated Erasmus in 1680, Quevedo in 1668, and, most famously and importantly, Aesop's *Fables* in 1692 and 1699. This last set off a small craze for writing new fables, and particularly political fables.

Also during the later part of the period, Charles Gildon and Edmund Curll began their work on hireling "Lives." Curll was a bookseller (what today would be called a publisher), and he paid authors to produce biographies, translations, and the like. Similarly, Gildon, who was an occasional friend of Restoration authors, produced biographies with wholesale inventions in them. This writing for pay was despised by the literary authors, who called it "hack" writing.

Theatre

Duke's Theatre at Dorset Gardens

The return of the stage-struck Charles II to power in 1660 was a major event in English theatre history. As soon as the previous Puritan regime's ban on public stage representations was lifted, the drama recreated itself quickly and abundantly. Two theatre companies, the King's and the Duke's Company, were established in London, with two luxurious playhouses built to designs by Christopher Wren and fitted with moveable scenery and thunder and lightning machines.

Traditionally, Restoration plays have been studied by genre rather than chronology, more or less as if they were all contemporary, but scholars today insist on the rapid evolvement of drama in the period and on the importance of social and political factors affecting it. The influence of theatre company competition and playhouse economics is also acknowledged, as is the significance of the appearance of the first professional actresses.

In the 1660s and 1670s, the London scene was vitalised by the competition between the two patent companies. The need to rise to the challenges of the other house made playwrights and managers extremely responsive to public taste, and theatrical fashions fluctuated almost week by week. The mid-1670s were a high point of both quantity and quality, with John Dryden's *Aureng-zebe* (1675), William Wycherley's *The Country Wife* (1675) and *The Plain Dealer* (1676), George Etherege's *The Man of Mode* (1676), and Aphra Behn's *The Rover* (1677), all within a few seasons.

From 1682 the production of new plays dropped sharply, affected both by a merger between the two companies and by the political turmoil of the Popish Plot (1678) and the Exclusion crisis (1682). The 1680s were especially lean years for comedy, the only exception being the remarkable career of Aphra Behn, whose achievement as the first professional British woman dramatist has been the subject of much recent study. There was a swing away from comedy to serious political drama, reflecting preoccupations and divisions following on the political crisis. The few comedies produced also tended to be political in focus, the whig dramatist Thomas Shadwell sparring with the tories John Dryden and Aphra Behn.

In the calmer times after 1688, Londoners were again ready to be amused by stage performance, but the single "United Company" was not well prepared to offer it. No longer powered by competition, the company had lost momentum and been taken over by predatory investors, while management in the form of the autocratic Christopher Rich attempted to finance a tangle of "farmed" shares and sleeping partners by slashing actors' salaries. The upshot of this mismanagement was that the disgruntled actors set up their own co-operative company in 1695. A few years of re-invigorated two-company competition followed which allowed a brief second flowering of the drama, especially comedy. Comedies like William Congreve's *Love For Love* (1695) and *The Way of the World* (1700), and John Vanbrugh's *The Relapse* (1696) and *The Provoked Wife* (1697) were "softer" and more middle class in ethos, very different from the aristocratic extravaganza twenty years earlier, and aimed at a wider audience. If "Restoration literature" is the literature that reflects and reflects upon the court of

Charles II, Restoration drama arguably ends before Charles II's death, as the playhouse moved rapidly from the domain of courtiers to the domain of the city middle classes. On the other hand, Restoration drama shows altogether more fluidity and rapidity than other types of literature, and so, even more than in other types of literature, its movements should never be viewed as absolute. Each decade has brilliant exceptions to every rule and entirely forgettable confirmations of it.

Drama

Genre in Restoration drama is peculiar. Authors labelled their works according to the old tags, "comedy" and "drama" and, especially, "history", but these plays defied the old categories. From 1660 onwards, new dramatic genres arose, mutated, and intermixed very rapidly. In tragedy, the leading style in the early Restoration period was the male-dominated heroic drama, exemplified by John Dryden's *The Conquest of Granada* (1670) and *Aureng-Zebe* (1675) which celebrated powerful, aggressively masculine heroes and their pursuit of glory both as rulers and conquerors, and as lovers. These plays were sometimes called by their authors' histories or tragedies, and contemporary critics will call them after Dryden's term of "Heroic drama". Heroic dramas centred on the actions of men of decisive natures, men whose physical and (sometimes) intellectual qualities made them natural leaders. In one sense, this was a reflection of an idealised king such as Charles or Charles's courtiers might have imagined. However, such dashing heroes were also seen by the audiences as occasionally standing in for noble rebels who would redress injustice with the sword. The plays were, however, tragic in the strictest definition, even though they were not necessarily sad.

In the 1670s and 1680s, a gradual shift occurred from heroic to pathetic tragedy, where the focus was on love and domestic concerns, even though the main characters might often be public figures. After the phenomenal success of Elizabeth Barry in moving the audience to tears in the role of Monimia in Thomas Otway's *The Orphan* (1680), "she-tragedies" (a term coined by Nicholas Rowe), which focused on the sufferings of an innocent and virtuous woman, became the dominant form of pathetic tragedy. Elizabeth Howe has argued that the most important explanation for the shift in taste was the emergence of tragic actresses whose popularity made it unavoidable for dramatists to create major roles for them. With the conjunction of the playwright "master of pathos" Thomas Otway and the great tragedienne Elizabeth Barry in *The Orphan,* the focus shifted from hero to heroine. Prominent she-tragedies include John Banks's *Virtue Betrayed, or, Anna Bullen* (1682) (about the execution of Anne Boleyn), Thomas Southerne's *The Fatal Marriage* (1694), and Nicholas Rowe's *The Fair Penitent* (1703) and *Lady Jane Grey,* 1715.

While she-tragedies were more comfortably tragic, in that they showed women who suffered for no fault of their own and featured tragic flaws that were emotional rather than moral or intellectual, their success did not mean that more overtly political tragedy was not staged. The Exclusion crisis brought with it a number of tragic implications in real politics, and therefore any treatment of, for example, the Earl of Essex (several versions of which were circulated and briefly acted at non-patent theatres) could be read as seditious. Thomas Otway's *Venice Preserv'd* of 1682 was a royalist political play that, like Dryden's *Absalom and Achitophel,* seemed to praise the king for his actions in the *meal tub plot.*

Otway's play had the floating city of Venice stand in for the river town of London, and it had the dark senatorial plotters of the play stand in for the Earl of Shaftesbury. It even managed to figure in the Duke of Monmouth, Charles's illegitimate, war-hero son who was favoured by many as Charles's successor over the Roman Catholic James.

Venice Preserv'd is, in a sense, the perfect synthesis of the older politically royalist tragedies and histories of Dryden and the newer she-tragedies of feminine suffering, for, although the plot seems to be a political allegory, the action centres on a woman who cares for a man in conflict, and most of the scenes and dialogue concern her pitiable sufferings at his hands.

Comedy

Restoration comedy is notorious for its sexual explicitness, a quality encouraged by Charles II personally and by the rakish aristocratic ethos of his court. The best-known plays of the early Restoration period are the unsentimental or "hard" comedies of John Dryden, William Wycherley, and George Etherege, which reflect the atmosphere at Court, and celebrate an aristocratic macho lifestyle of unremitting sexual intrigue and conquest.

The Earl of Rochester, real-life Restoration rake, courtier and poet, is flatteringly portrayed in Etherege's *Man of Mode* (1676) as a riotous, witty, intellectual, and sexually irresistible aristocrat, a template for posterity's idea of the glamorous Restoration rake (actually never a very common character in Restoration comedy).

Wycherley's *The Plain Dealer* (1676), a variation on the theme of Molière's *Le misanthrope,* was highly regarded for its uncompromising satire and earned Wycherley the appellation "Plain Dealer" Wycherley or "Manly" Wycherley, after the play's main character Manly. The single writer who most supports the charge of obscenity levelled then and now at Restoration comedy is probably Wycherley.

During the second wave of Restoration comedy in the 1690s, the "softer" comedies of William Congreve and John Vanbrugh reflected mutating cultural perceptions and great social change. The playwrights of the 1690s set out to appeal to more socially mixed audiences with a strong middle-class element, and to female spectators, for instance by moving the war between the sexes from the arena of intrigue into that of marriage.

The focus in comedy is less on young lovers outwitting the older generation, more on marital relations after the wedding bells. In Congreve's plays, the give-and-take set pieces of couples still testing their attraction for each other have mutated into witty prenuptial debates on the eve of marriage, as in the famous "Proviso" scene in *The Way of the World* (1700).

Restoration drama had a bad reputation for three centuries. The "incongruous" mixing of comedy and tragedy beloved by Restoration audiences was execrated on all hands. The Victorians denounced the comedy as too indecent for the stage, and the standard reference work of the early 20th century, *The Cambridge*

History of English and American Literature, dismissed the tragedy as being of "a level of dulness and lubricity never surpassed before or since". Today, the Restoration total theatre experience is again valued, both by postmodern literary critics and on the stage. The comedies of Aphra Behn in particular, long condemned as especially offensive in coming from a woman's pen, have become academic and repertory favourites.

9

Augustan Literature

Augustan literature is a style of English literature produced during the reigns of Queen Anne, King George I, and George II in the first half of the 18th century, ending in the 1740s with the deaths of Pope and Swift. It is a literary epoch that featured the rapid development of the novel, an explosion in satire, the mutation of drama from political satire into melodrama, and an evolution toward poetry of personal exploration. In philosophy, it was an age increasingly dominated by empiricism, while in the writings of political-economy it marked the evolution of mercantilism as a formal philosophy, the development of capitalism, and the triumph of trade.

The chronological boundary points of the era are generally vague, largely since the label's origin in contemporary 18th century criticism has made it a shorthand designation for a somewhat nebulous age of satire. This new Augustan period exhibited exceptionally bold political writings in all genres, with the satires of the age marked by an arch, ironic pose, full of nuance, and a superficial air of dignified calm that hid sharp criticisms beneath. As literacy grew, literature began to appear from all over the kingdom.

Authors gradually began to accept literature that went in unique directions rather than the formerly monolithic conventions and, through this, slowly began to honor and recreate various folk compositions. Beneath the appearance of a placid and highly regulated series of writing modes, many developments of the later Romantic era were beginning to take place—while politically, philosophically, and literarily, modern consciousness was being hewn out of hitherto feudal and courtly notions of ages past.

Enlightenment

"Augustan" derives from George I wishing to be seen as Augustus Caesar. Alexander Pope, who had been imitating Horace, wrote an *Epistle to Augustus* that was to George II and seemingly endorsed the notion of his age being like that of Augustus, when poetry became more mannered, political and satirical than in the era of Julius Caesar. Later, Voltaire and Oliver Goldsmith (in his *History of Literature* in 1764) used the term "Augustan" to refer to the literature of the 1720s and '30s. Outside of poetry, however, the Augustan era is generally known by other names. Partially because of the rise of empiricism and partially due to the self-conscious naming of the age in terms of Ancient Rome, two imprecise labels have been affixed to the age. One is that it is the age of neoclassicism. The other is that it is the Age of Reason. Both terms have some usefulness, but both also obscure much. While neoclassical criticism from France was imported to English letters, the English had abandoned their strictures in all but name by the 1720s. As for whether the era was "the Enlightenment" or not, the critic Donald Greene wrote vigorously against it, arguing persuasively that the age should be known as "The

Age of Exuberance," while T.H. White made a case for "The Age of Scandal". Most recently, Roy Porter attempted again to argue for the developments of science dominating all other areas of endeavor in the age unmistakably making it the Enlightenment.

An auctioneer sells books from the estate of a condemned doctor, *c.* 1700, in Moorfields. The books contain pornography, medicine, and Classics. The print satirizes "new men" wanting to collect libraries without collecting learning.

One of the most critical elements of the 18th century was the increasing availability of printed material, both for readers and authors. Books fell in price dramatically, and used books were sold at Bartholomew Fair and other fairs. Additionally, a brisk trade in chapbooks and broadsheets carried London trends and information out to the farthest reaches of the kingdom. This was only furthered with the establishment of periodicals, including *The Gentleman's Magazine* and the *London Magazine*. Not only, therefore, were people in York aware of the happenings of Parliament and the court, but people in London were more aware than before of the happenings of York. Furthermore, in this age before copyright, pirate editions were commonplace, especially in areas without frequent contact with London. Pirate editions thereby encouraged booksellers to increase their shipments to outlying centers like Dublin, which increased, again, awareness across the whole realm. This was compounded by the end of the Press Restriction Act in 1693, which allowed for provincial printing presses to be established, creating a printing structure that was no longer under government control.

All types of literature were spread quickly in all directions. Newspapers not only began, but they multiplied. Furthermore, the newspapers were immediately compromised, as the political factions created their own newspapers, planted stories, and bribed journalists.

Leading clerics had their sermon collections printed, and these were top selling books. Since dissenting, Establishment, and Independent divines were in print, the constant movement of these works helped defuse any one region's religious homogeneity and fostered emergent latitudinarianism. Periodicals were exceedingly popular, and the art of essay writing was at nearly its apex.

Furthermore, the happenings of the Royal Society were published regularly, and these events were digested and explained or celebrated in more popular presses. The latest books of scholarship had "keys" and "indexes" and "digests" made of them that could popularize, summarize, and explain them to a wide audience.

The cross-index, now commonplace, was a novelty in the 18th century, and several persons created indexes for older books of learning, allowing anyone to find what an author had to say about a given topic at a moment's notice. Books of etiquette, of correspondence, and of moral instruction and hygiene multiplied.

Economics began as a serious discipline, but it did so in the form of numerous "projects" for solving England's (and Ireland's, and Scotland's) ills. Sermon collections, dissertations on religious controversy, and prophecies, both new and old and explained, cropped up in endless variety. In short, readers in the 18th century were overwhelmed by competing voices. True and false sat side by side on the shelves, and anyone could be a published author, just as anyone could quickly pretend to be a scholar by using indexes and digests.

The positive side of the explosion in information was that the 18th century was markedly more generally educated than the centuries before. Education was less confined to the upper classes than it had been in prior centuries, and consequently contributions to science, philosophy, economics, and literature came from all parts of the newly United Kingdom.

It was the first time when literacy and a library were all that stood between a person and education. It was an age of "enlightenment" in the sense that the insistence and drive for reasonable explanations of nature and mankind was a rage. It was an "age of reason" in that it was an age that accepted clear, rational methods as superior to tradition. However, there was a dark side to such literacy as well, a dark side which authors of the 18th century felt at every turn, and that was that nonsense and insanity were also getting more adherents than ever before.

Charlatans and mountebanks were fooling more, just as sages were educating more, and alluring and lurid apocalypses vied with sober philosophy on the shelves. As with the world-wide web in the 21st century, the democratization of publishing meant that older systems for determining value and uniformity of view were both in shambles. Thus, it was increasingly difficult to trust books in the 18th century, because books were increasingly easy to make and buy.

Political and Religious Context

The Restoration period ended with the exclusion crisis and the Glorious Revolution, where Parliament set up a new rule for succession to the British throne that would always favor Protestantism over sanguinity. This had brought William and Mary to the throne instead of James II, and was codified in the Act of Settlement 1701. James had fled to France from where his son James Francis Edward Stuart launched an attempt to retake the throne in 1715. Another attempt was launched by the latter's son Charles Edward Stuart in 1745. The attempted invasions are often referred to as "the 15" and "the 45". When William died, Anne Stuart came to the throne. Anne was reportedly immoderately stupid: Thomas Babington Macaulay would say of Anne that "when in good humour, [she] was meekly stupid and, when in bad humour, was sulkily stupid." Anne's reign saw two wars and great triumphs by John Churchill, the Duke of Marlborough.

Marlborough's wife, Sarah Churchill, was Anne's best friend, and many supposed that she secretly controlled the Queen in every respect. With a weak ruler and the belief that true power rested in the hands of the leading ministers, the two factions of politics stepped up their opposition to each other, and Whig and Tory were at each others' throats. This weakness at the throne would lead quickly to the expansion of the powers of the party leader in Parliament and the establishment in all but name of the Prime Minister office in the form of Robert Walpole. When Anne died without issue, George I, Elector of Hanover, came to the throne. George I never bothered to learn the English language, and his isolation from the English people was instrumental in keeping his power relatively irrelevant. His son, George II, on the other hand, spoke some English and some more French, and his was the first full Hanoverian rule in England. By that time, the powers of Parliament had silently expanded, and George II's power was perhaps equal only to that of Parliament.

London's population exploded spectacularly. During the Restoration, it grew from around 350,000 to 600,000 in 1700 (*Old Bailey*) (*Millwall history*). By 1800, it had reached 950,000. Not all of these residents were prosperous. The enclosure act had destroyed lower-class farming in the countryside, and rural areas experienced painful poverty. When the Black Act was expanded to cover all protestors to enclosure, the communities of the country poor were forced to migrate or suffer. Therefore, young people from the country often moved to London with hopes of achieving success, and this swelled the ranks of the urban poor and cheap labor for city employers. It also meant an increase in numbers of criminals, prostitutes and beggars. The fears of property crime, rape, and starvation found in Augustan literature should be kept in the context of London's growth, as well as the depopulation of the countryside.

William Hogarth's *Gin Lane* is not entirely caricature, for in 1750, over a fourth of all houses in St Giles were gin shops, all unlicensed. Partially because of these population pressures, property crime became a business both for the criminals and for those who fed off of the criminals. Major crime lords like Jonathan Wild invented new schemes for stealing, and the newspapers were eager to report crime. Biographies of the daring criminals became popular, and these spawned fictional biographies of fictional criminals.

Cautionary tales of country women abused by sophisticated rakes (such as Anne Bond) and libertines in the city were popular fare, and these prompted fictional accounts of exemplary women abused (or narrowly escaping abuse).

The population pressure also meant that urban discontent was never particularly difficult to find for political opportunists, and London suffered a number of riots, most of them against supposed Roman Catholic agent provocateurs. When highly potent, inexpensive distilled spirits were introduced, matters worsened, and authors and artists protested the innovation of gin.

From 1710, the government encouraged distilling as a source of revenue and trade goods, and there were no licenses required for the manufacturing or selling of gin. There were documented instances of women drowning their infants to sell the child's clothes for gin, and so these facilities created both the fodder for riots and the conditions against which riots would occur.

Dissenters (those radical Protestants who would not join with the Church of England) recruited and preached to the poor of the city, and various offshoots of the Puritan and "Independent" (Baptist) movements increased their numbers substantially. One theme of these ministers was the danger of the Roman Catholic Church, which they frequently saw as the Whore of Babylon. While Anne was high church, George I came from a far more Protestant nation than England, and George II was almost low church, as the events of the Bangorian Controversy would show. The convocation was effectively disbanded by George I (who was struggling with the House of Lords), and George II was pleased to keep it in abeyance. Additionally, both of the first two Hanoverians were concerned with James Francis Edward Stuart and Charles Edward Stuart who had considerable support in Scotland and Ireland, and anyone too high church was suspected of being a closet Jacobite, thanks in no small part to Walpole's inflating fears of Stuart sympathizers among any group that did not support him.

History and Literature

The literature of the 18th century—particularly the early 18th century, which is what "Augustan" most commonly indicates—is explicitly political in ways that few others are. Because the professional author was still not distinguishable from the hack-writer, those who wrote poetry, novels, and plays were frequently either politically active or politically funded. At the same time, an aesthetic of artistic detachment from the everyday world had yet to develop, and the aristocratic ideal of an author so noble as to be above political concerns was largely archaic and irrelevant. The period may be an "Age of Scandal," for it is an age when authors dealt specifically with the crimes and vices of their world.

Satire, both in prose, drama, and poetry, was the genre that attracted the most energetic and voluminous writing. The satires produced during the Augustan period were occasionally gentle and non-specific—commentaries on the comically flawed human condition—but they were at least as frequently specific critiques of specific policies, actions, and persons. Even those works studiously non-topical were, in fact, transparently political statements in the 18th century. Consequently, readers of 18th-century literature today need to understand the history of the period more than most readers of other literature do. The authors were writing for an informed audience and only secondarily for posterity. Even the authors who criticized writing that lived for only a day (e.g. Jonathan Swift and Alexander Pope, in *The Dedication to Prince Posterity* of *A Tale of a Tub* and *Dunciad,* among other pieces) were criticizing specific authors who are unknown without historical knowledge of the period. 18th-century poetry of all forms was in constant dialog: each author was responding and commenting upon the others. 18th-century novels were written against other 18th-century novels (e.g. the battles between Henry Fielding and Samuel Richardson and between Laurence Sterne and Tobias Smollett). Plays were written to make fun of plays, or to counter the success of plays (e.g. the reaction against and for *Cato* and, later, Fielding's *The Authors Farce*). Therefore, history and literature are linked in a way rarely seen at other times. On the one hand, this metropolitan and political writing can seem like coterie or salon work, but, on the other, it was the literature of people deeply committed to sorting out a new type of government, new technologies, and newly vexatious challenges to philosophical and religious certainty.

Prose

The essay, satire, and dialogue (in philosophy and religion) thrived in the age, and the English novel was truly begun as a serious art form. Literacy in the early 18th century passed into the working classes, as well as the middle and upper classes (Thompson, *Class*). Furthermore, literacy was not confined to men, though rates of female literacy are very difficult to establish. For those who were literate, circulating libraries in

England began in the Augustan period. Libraries were open to all,

Essays and Journalism

English essayists were aware of Continental models, but they developed their form independently from that tradition, and periodical literature grew between 1692 and 1712. Periodicals were inexpensive to produce, quick to read, and a viable way of influencing public opinion, and consequently there were many broadsheet periodicals headed by a single author and staffed by hirelings (so-called "Grub Street" authors). One periodical outsold and dominated all others, however, and that was *The Spectator*, written by Joseph Addison and Richard Steele (with occasional contributions from their friends). *The Spectator* developed a number of pseudonymous characters, including "Mr. Spectator," Roger de Coverley, and "Isaac Bickerstaff", and both Addison and Steele created fictions to surround their narrators. The dispassionate view of the world (the pose of a spectator, rather than participant) was essential for the development of the English essay, as it set out a ground wherein Addison and Steele could comment and meditate upon manners and events.

Rather than being philosophers like Montesquieu, the English essayist could be an honest observer and his reader's peer. After the success of *The Spectator*, more political periodicals of comment appeared. However, the political factions and coalitions of politicians very quickly realized the power of this type of press, and they began funding newspapers to spread rumors. The Tory ministry of Robert Harley (1710–1714) reportedly spent over 50,000 pounds sterling on creating and bribing the press (Butt); we know this figure because their successors publicized it, but they (the Walpole government) were suspected of spending even more. Politicians wrote papers, wrote into papers, and supported papers, and it was well known that some of the periodicals, like *Mist's Journal*, were party mouthpieces.

Philosophy and Religious Writing

The Augustan period showed less literature of controversy than the Restoration. There were Puritan authors, however, and one of the names usually associated with the novel is perhaps the most prominent in Puritan writing: Daniel Defoe. After the coronation of Anne, dissenter hopes of reversing the Restoration were at an ebb, and dissenter literature moved from the offensive to the defensive, from revolutionary to conservative. Defoe's infamous volley in the struggle between high and low church came in the form of *The Shortest Way with the Dissenters; Or, Proposals for the Establishment of the Church*. The work is satirical, attacking all of the worries of Establishment figures over the challenges of dissenters. It is, in other words, defensive. Later still, the most majestic work of the era, and the one most quoted and read, was William Law's *A Serious Call to a Devout and Holy Life* (1728). The *Meditations* of Robert Boyle remained popular as well. Both Law and Boyle called for revivalism, and they set the stage for the later development of Methodism and George Whitefield's sermon style. However, their works aimed at the individual, rather than the community. The age of revolutionary divines and militant evangelists in literature was over for a considerable time.

Also in contrast to the Restoration, when philosophy in England was fully dominated by John Locke, the 18th century had a vigorous competition among followers of Locke. Bishop Berkeley extended Locke's emphasis on perception to argue that perception entirely solves the Cartesian problem of subjective and objective knowledge by saying "to be is to be perceived." Only, Berkeley argued, those things that are perceived by a consciousness are real. For Berkeley, the persistence of matter rests in the fact that God perceives those things that humans are not, that a living and continually aware, attentive, and involved God is the only rational explanation for the existence of objective matter. In essence, then, Berkeley's skepticism leads to faith. David Hume, on the other hand, took empiricist skepticism to its extremes, and he was the most radically empiricist philosopher of the period. He attacked surmise and unexamined premises wherever he found them, and his skepticism pointed out metaphysics in areas that other empiricists had assumed were material. Hume doggedly refused to enter into questions of his personal faith in the divine, but his assault on the logic and assumptions of theodicy and cosmogeny was devastating, and he concentrated on the provable and empirical in a way that would lead to utilitarianism and naturalism later.

In social and political philosophy, economics underlies much of the debate. Bernard de Mandeville's *The Fable of the Bees* (1714) became a center point of controversy regarding trade, morality, and social ethics. Mandeville argued that wastefulness, lust, pride, and all the other "private" vices were good for the society at large, for each led the individual to employ others, to spend freely, and to free capital to flow through the economy. Mandeville's work is full of paradox and is meant, at least partially, to problematize what he saw as the naive philosophy of human progress and inherent virtue. However, Mandeville's arguments, initially an attack on graft of the War of the Spanish Succession, would be quoted often by economists who wished to strip morality away from questions of trade.

Adam Smith is remembered by lay persons as the father of capitalism, but his *Theory of Moral Sentiments* of 1759 also attempted to strike out a new ground for moral action. His emphasis on "sentiment" was in keeping with the era, as he emphasized the need for "sympathy" between individuals as the basis of fit action. These ideas, and the psychology of David Hartley, were influential on the sentimental novel and even the nascent Methodist movement. If sympathetic sentiment communicated morality, would it not be possible to induce morality by providing sympathetic circumstances? Smith's greatest work was *An Inquiry into the Nature and Causes of the Wealth of Nations* in 1776. What it held in common with de Mandeville, Hume, and Locke was that it began by analytically examining the history of material exchange, without reflection on morality. Instead of deducing from the ideal or moral to the real, it examined the real and tried to formulate inductive rules.

Satire

A single name overshadows all others in 18th-century prose satire: Jonathan Swift. Swift wrote poetry as well as prose, and his satires range over all topics. Critically, Swift's satire marked the development of prose parody away from simple satire or burlesque. A burlesque or lampoon in prose would imitate a despised author and quickly move to *reductio ad absurdum* by having the victim say things coarse or idiotic. On the other hand, other satires would argue against a habit, practice, or policy by making fun of its reach or composition or methods. What Swift did was to combine parody, with its imitation of form and style of another, and satire in prose. Swift's works would pretend to speak in the voice of an opponent and imitate the style of the opponent and have the parodic work itself be the satire. Swift's first major satire was *A Tale of a Tub* (1703–1705), which introduced an ancients/moderns division that would serve as a distinction between the old and new conception of value. The "moderns" sought trade, empirical science, the individual's reason above the society's, while the "ancients" believed in inherent and immanent value of birth, and the society over the individual's determinations of the good.

In Swift's satire, the moderns come out looking insane and proud of their insanity, and dismissive of the value of history. In Swift's most significant satire, *Gulliver's Travels* (1726), autobiography, allegory, and philosophy mix together in the travels. Thematically, *Gulliver's Travels* is a critique of human vanity, of pride. Book one, the journey to Liliput, begins with the world as it is. Book two shows that the idealized nation of Brobdingnag with a philosopher king is no home for a contemporary Englishman. Book four depicts the land of the Houyhnhnms, a society of horses ruled by pure reason, where humanity itself is portrayed as a group of "yahoos" covered in filth and dominated by base desires. It shows that, indeed, the very desire for reason may be undesirable, and humans must struggle to be neither Yahoos nor Houyhnhnms, for book three shows what happens when reason is unleashed without any consideration of morality or utility (i.e. madness, ruin, and starvation).

There were other satirists who worked in a less virulent way, who took a bemused pose and only made lighthearted fun. Tom Brown, Ned Ward, and Tom D'Urfey were all satirists in prose and poetry whose works appeared in the early part of the Augustan age. Tom Brown's most famous work in this vein was *Amusements Serious and Comical, Calculated for the Meridian of London* (1700). Ned Ward's most memorable work was *The London Spy* (1704–1706). *The London Spy,* before *The Spectator,* took up the position of an observer and uncomprehendingly reporting back. Tom D'Urfey's *Wit and Mirth: or Pills to Purge Melancholy* (1719) was another satire that attempted to offer entertainment, rather than a specific bit of political action, in the form of coarse and catchy songs.

Particularly after Swift's success, parodic satire had an attraction for authors throughout the 18th century. A variety of factors created a rise in political writing and political satire, and Robert Walpole's success and domination of House of Commons was a very effective proximal cause for polarized literature and thereby the rise of parodic satire. The parodic satire takes apart the cases and plans of policy without necessarily contrasting a normative or positive set of values. Therefore, it was an ideal method of attack for ironists and conservatives—those who would not be able to enunciate a set of values to change toward but could condemn present changes as ill-considered. Satire was present in all genres during the Augustan period. Perhaps primarily, satire was a part of political and religious debate. Every significant politician and political act had satires to attack it. Few of these were parodic satires, but parodic satires, too, emerged in political and religious debate. So omnipresent and powerful was satire in the Augustan age that more than one literary history has referred to it as the "Age of satire" in literature.

Poetry

In the Augustan era, poets wrote in direct counterpoint and direct expansion of one another, with each poet writing satire when in opposition. There was a great struggle over the nature and role of the pastoral in the early part of the century, reflecting two simultaneous movements: the invention of the subjective self as a worthy topic, with the emergence of a priority on *individual* psychology, against the insistence on all acts of art being *performance* and public gesture designed for the benefit of society at large. The development seemingly agreed upon by both sides was a gradual adaptation of all forms of poetry from their older uses. Odes would cease to be encomium, ballads cease to be narratives, elegies cease to be sincere memorials, satires no longer be specific entertainments, parodies no longer be performance pieces without sting, song no longer be pointed, and the lyric would become a celebration of the individual rather than a lover's complaint. These developments can be seen as extensions of Protestantism, as Max Weber argued, for they represent a gradual increase in the implications of Martin Luther's doctrine of the priesthood of all believers, or they can be seen as a growth of the power and assertiveness of the bourgeoisie and an echo of the displacement of the worker from the home in growing industrialization, as Marxists such as E.P. Thompson have argued. It can be argued that the development of the subjective individual against the social individual was a natural reaction to trade over other methods of economic production. Whatever the prime cause, a largely conservative set of voices argued for a social person and largely emergent voices argued for the individual person.

The entire Augustan age's poetry was dominated by Alexander Pope. His lines were repeated often enough to lend quite a few clichés and proverbs to modern English usage. Pope had few poetic rivals, but he had many personal enemies and political, philosophical, or religious opponents, and Pope himself was quarrelsome in print. Pope and his enemies (often called "the Dunces" because of Pope's successful satirizing of them in *The Dunciad*) fought over central matters of the proper subject matter for poetry and the proper pose of the poetic voice.

There was a great struggle over the nature and role of the pastoral in the early part of the century. After Pope published his *Pastorals* of the four seasons in 1709, an evaluation in the *Guardian* praised Ambrose Philips's pastorals above Pope's, and Pope replied with a mock praise of Philips's *Pastorals* that heaped scorn on them. Pope quoted Philips's worst lines, mocked his execution, and delighted in pointing out his empty lines. Pope later explained that any depictions of shepherds and their mistresses in the pastoral must not be updated shepherds, that they must be icons of the Golden Age: "we are not to describe our shepherds as shepherds at this day really are, but as they may be conceived then to have been, when the best of men followed the employment" (Gordon). Philips's *Pastorals* were not particularly awful poems, but they did reflect his desire to "update" the pastoral. In 1724, Philips would update poetry again by writing a series of odes dedicated to "all ages and characters, from Walpole, the steerer of the realm, to Miss Pulteney in the nursery." Henry Carey was one of the best at satirizing these poems, and his *Namby Pamby* became a hugely successful obliteration of Philips and Philips's endeavor. What is notable about Philips against Pope, however, is the fact that *both* poets were adapting the pastoral and the ode, both altering it. Pope's insistence upon a Golden Age pastoral no less than Philips's desire to update it meant making a political statement. While it is easy to see in Ambrose Philips an effort at modernist triumph, it is no less the case that Pope's artificially restricted pastoral was a statement of what the ideal should be.

Pope's friend John Gay also adapted the pastoral. Gay, working at Pope's suggestion, wrote a parody of the updated pastoral in *The Shepherd's Week.* He also imitated the Satires of Juvenal with his *Trivia.* In 1728, his *The Beggar's Opera* was an enormous success, running for an unheard-of eighty performances. All of these works have in common a gesture of compassion. In *Trivia,* Gay writes as if commiserating with those who live in London and are menaced by falling masonry and bedpan slops, and *The Shepherd's Week* features great detail of the follies of everyday life and eccentric character. Even *The Beggar's Opera,* which is a satire of Robert Walpole, portrays its characters with compassion: the villains have pathetic songs in their own right and are acting out of exigency rather than boundless evil.

Throughout the Augustan era the "updating" of Classical poets was a commonplace. These were not translations, but rather they were imitations of Classical models, and the imitation allowed poets to veil their responsibility for the comments they made. Alexander Pope would manage to refer to the King himself in unflattering tones by "imitating" Horace in his *Epistle to Augustus*. Similarly, Samuel Johnson wrote a poem that falls into the Augustan period in his "imitation of Juvenal" entitled *London*. The imitation was inherently conservative, since it argued that all that was good was to be found in the old classical education, but these imitations were used for progressive purposes, as the poets who used them were often doing so to complain of the political situation.

In satire, Pope achieved two of the greatest poetic satires of all time in the Augustan period. *The Rape of the Lock* (1712 and 1714) was a gentle mock-heroic. Pope applies Virgil's heroic and epic structure to the story of a young woman (Arabella Fermor) having a lock of hair snipped by an amorous baron (Lord Petre). The *structure* of the comparison forces Pope to invent mythological forces to overlook the struggle, and so he creates an epic battle, complete with a mythology of sylphs and metempsychosis, over a game of Ombre, leading to a fiendish appropriation of the lock of hair. Finally, a deux ex machina appears and the lock of hair experiences an apotheosis. To some degree, Pope was adapting Jonathan Swift's habit, in *A Tale of a Tub*, of pretending that metaphors were literal truths, and he was inventing a mythos to go with the everyday. The poem was an enormous public success.

A decade after the gentle, laughing satire of *The Rape of the Lock*, Pope wrote his masterpiece of invective and specific opprobrium in *The Dunciad*. The story is that of the goddess Dulness choosing a new avatar. She settles upon one of Pope's personal enemies, Lewis Theobald, and the poem describes the coronation and heroic games undertaken by all of the dunces of Great Britain in celebration of Theobald's ascension. When Pope's enemies responded to *The Dunciad* with attacks, Pope produced the *Dunciad Variorum,* with a "learned" commentary upon the original *Dunciad.* In 1743, he added a fourth book and changed the hero from Lewis Theobald to Colley Cibber. In the fourth book of the new *Dunciad,* Pope expressed the view that, in the battle between light and dark (enlightenment and the Dark Ages), Night and Dulness were fated to win, that all things of value were soon going to be subsumed under the curtain of unknowing.

John Gay and Alexander Pope belong on one side of a line separating the celebrants of the individual and the celebrants of the social. Pope wrote *The Rape of the Lock,* he said, to settle a disagreement between two great families, to laugh them into peace. Even *The Dunciad,* which seems to be a serial killing of everyone on Pope's enemies list, sets up these figures as expressions of dangerous and *antisocial* forces in letters. Theobald and Cibber are marked by vanity and pride, by having no care for morality. The hireling pens Pope attacks mercilessly in the heroic games section of the *Dunciad* are all embodiments of avarice and lies. Similarly, Gay writes of political society, of social dangers, and of follies that must be addressed to protect the greater whole. Gay's individuals are microcosms of the society at large. On the other side of this line were people who agreed with the *politics* of Gay and Pope (and Swift), but not in approach. They include, early in the Augustan Age, James Thomson and Edward Young. Thomson's *The Seasons* (1730) is poetry of natural description, but they are unlike

Pope's notion of the Golden Age pastoral. Thomson's poet speaks in the first person from direct observation, and his own mood and sentiment color the descriptions of landscape. Unlike Pope's *Windsor Forest,* Thomson's seasons have no mythology, no celebration of Britain or the crown. *Winter,* in particular, is melancholy and meditative. Edward Yonge's *Night Thoughts* (1742–1744) was immediately popular. It was, even more than *Winter,* a poem of deep solitude, melancholy, and despair. In these two poets, there are the stirrings of the lyric as the Romantics would see it: the celebration of the private individual's idiosyncratic, yet paradigmatic, responses to the visions of the world.

These hints at the solitary poet were carried into a new realm with Thomas Gray, whose *Elegy Written in a Country Church-Yard* (1750) set off a new craze for poetry of melancholy reflection. It was written in the "country," and not in or as opposed to London, and the poem sets up the solitary observer in a privileged position. It is only by being solitary that the poet can speak of a truth that is wholly individually realized. After Gray, a group often referred to as the Churchyard Poets began imitating his pose, if not his style. Oliver Goldsmith (*The Deserted Village*), Thomas Warton, and even Thomas Percy (*The Hermit of Warkworth*), each conservative by and large and Classicist (Gray himself was a professor of Greek), took up the new poetry of solitude and loss.

When the Romantics emerged at the end of the 18th century, they were not assuming a radically new invention of the subjective self themselves, but merely formalizing what had gone before. Similarly, the later 18th century saw a ballad revival, with Thomas Percy's

Reliques of Ancient English Poetry. The relics were not always very ancient, as many of the ballads dated from only the 17th century (e.g. the Bagford Ballads or The Dragon of Wantley in the Percy Folio), and so what began as an antiquarian movement soon became a folk movement. When this folk-inspired impulse combined with the solitary and individualistic impulse of the Churchyard Poets, Romanticism was nearly inevitable.

Drama

The "Augustan era" is difficult to define chronologically in prose and poetry, but it is very easy to date its end in drama. The Augustan era's drama ended definitively in 1737, with the Licensing Act. Prior to 1737, however, the English stage was changing rapidly from the Restoration comedy and Restoration drama and their noble subjects to the quickly developing melodrama.

George Lillo and Richard Steele wrote the trend-setting plays of the early Augustan period. Lillo's plays consciously turned from heroes and kings and toward shopkeepers and apprentices. They emphasized drama on a household scale, rather than a national scale, and the hamartia and agon in his tragedies are the common flaws of yielding to temptation and the commission of Christian sin. The plots are resolved with Christian forgiveness and repentance. Steele's *The Conscious Lovers* (1722) hinges upon his young hero avoiding fighting a duel. These plays set up a new set of values for the stage. Instead of amusing the audience or inspiring the audience, they sought to instruct the audience and ennoble it. Further, the plays were popular precisely because they seemed to reflect the audience's own lives and concerns.

Joseph Addison also wrote a play, entitled *Cato,* in 1713. *Cato* concerned the Roman statesman. The year of its première was important, for Queen Anne was in serious illness at the time, and both the Tory ministry of the day and the Whig opposition were concerned about the succession. Both groups were contacting the Old Pretender about bringing the Young Pretender over. Londoners sensed this anxiety, for Anne had no heirs, and all of the natural successors in the Stuart family were Roman Catholic or unavailable. Therefore, the figure of Cato was a transparent symbol of Roman integrity, and the Whigs saw in him a champion of Whig values, while the Tories saw in him an embodiment of Tory sentiments or, like the Tory *Examiner,* tried to claim that Cato was above political "faction". Both sides cheered the play, even though Addison was himself clearly Whig (Bloom and Bloom 266, 269). John Home's play *Douglas* (1756) would have a similar fate to *Cato* in the next generation, after the Licensing Act.

A print by William Hogarth entitled *A Just View of the British Stage* from 1724 depicting the managers of Drury Lane (Robert Wilks, Colley Cibber, and Barton Booth) rehearsing a play consisting of nothing but special effects, while they used the scripts for *Macbeth, Hamlet, Julius Caesar* and *The Way of the World* for toilet paper. This battle of effects was a common subject of satire for the literary wits, including Pope in *The Dunciad.*

As during the Restoration, economics drove the stage in the Augustan period. Under Charles II court patronage meant economic success, and therefore the Restoration stage featured plays that would suit the monarch and/or court. The drama that celebrated kings and told the history of Britain's monarchs was fit fare for the crown and courtiers. Charles II was a philanderer, and so Restoration comedy featured a highly sexualized set of plays. However, after the reign of William and Mary, the court and crown stopped taking a great interest in the playhouse. Theaters had to get their money from the audience of city dwellers, therefore, and consequently plays that reflected city anxieties and celebrated the lives of citizens drew and were staged.

Thus, there were quite a few plays that were, in fact, not literary that were staged more often than the literary plays. John Rich and Colley Cibber duelled over special theatrical effects. They put on plays that were actually just spectacles, where the text of the play was almost an afterthought. Dragons, whirlwinds, thunder, ocean waves, and even actual elephants were on stage. Battles, explosions, and horses were put on the boards. Rich specialized in pantomime and was famous as the character "Lun" in harlequin presentations. The plays put on in this manner are not generally preserved or studied, but their monopoly on the theaters infuriated established literary authors.

Additionally, opera made its way to England during this period. Inasmuch as opera combined singing with acting, it was a mixed genre, and this violated all the strictures of neo-classicism. Further, high melodies would cover the singers' expressions of grief or joy, thus breaking "decorum."

John Gay parodied the opera with his satirical *Beggar's Opera* (1728) and offered up a parody of Robert Walpole's actions during the South Sea Bubble. Superficially, the play is about a man named Macheath who keeps being imprisoned by a thief named

Peachum and who escapes prison over and over again because the daughter of the jailor, Lucy Lockitt, is in love with him. This is an obvious parallel with the case of Jonathan Wild (Peachum) and Jack Sheppard (Macheath). However, it was also the tale of Robert Walpole (Peachum) and the South Sea directors (Macheath). The play was a hit, and its songs were printed up and sold. However, when Gay wrote a follow up called *Polly,* Walpole had the play suppressed before performance (Winn 112-114).

Playwrights were therefore in straits. On the one hand, the playhouses were doing without plays by turning out hack-written pantomimes. On the other hand, when a satirical play appeared, the Whig ministry would suppress it. This antagonism was picked up by Henry Fielding, who was not afraid to fight Walpole.

His *Tom Thumb* (1730) was a satire on all of the tragedies written before him, with quotations from all the worst plays patched together for absurdity, and the plot concerned the eponymous tiny man attempting to run things. It was, in other words, an attack on Robert Walpole and the way that he was referred to as "the Great Man." Here, the Great Man is made obviously deficient by being a midget. Walpole responded, and Fielding's revision of the play was in print only. It was written by "Scribblerus Secundus," its title page announced, and it was the *Tragedy of Tragedies,* which functioned as a clearly Swiftian parodic satire. Anti-Walpolean sentiment also showed in increasingly political plays, and the theaters began to stage them. A particular play of unknown authorship entitled *A Vision of the Golden Rump* was cited when Parliament passed the Licensing Act of 1737.

The Licensing Act required all plays to go to a censor before staging, and only those plays passed by the censor were allowed to be performed. The first play to be banned by the new Act was *Gustavus Vasa,* by Henry Brooke. Samuel Johnson wrote a Swiftian parodic satire of the licensers, entitled *A Complete Vindication of the Licensers of the English Stage.* The satire was, of course, not a vindication at all, but rather a *reductio ad absurdum* of the position for censorship. Had the licensers not exercised their authority in a partisan manner, the Act might not have chilled the stage so dramatically, but the public was well aware of the bannings and censorship, and consequently any play that *did* pass the licensers was regarded with suspicion by the public. Therefore, the playhouses had little choice but to present old plays and pantomime and plays that had no conceivable political content. In other words, William Shakespeare's reputation grew enormously as his plays saw a quadrupling of performances, and sentimental comedy and melodrama were the only choices.

Very late in the Augustan period, Oliver Goldsmith attempted to resist the tide of sentimental comedy with *She Stoops to Conquer* (1773), and Richard Brinsley Sheridan would mount several satirical plays after Walpole's death, but to a large degree the damage had been done and would last for a century.

10

Victorian Literature

Victorian literature is the literature produced during the reign of Queen Victoria (1837-1901) and corresponds to the Victorian era. It forms a link and transition between the writers of the romantic period and the very different literature of the 20th century.

The 19th century saw the novel become the leading form of literature in English. The works by pre-Victorian writers such as Jane Austen and Walter Scott had perfected both closely-observed social satire and adventure stories. Popular works opened a market for the novel amongst a reading public. The 19th century is often regarded as a high point in British literature as well as in other countries such as France, the United States and Russia. Books, and novels in particular, became ubiquitous, and the "Victorian novelist" created legacy works with continuing appeal.

Significant Victorian novelists and poets include: Matthew Arnold, the Brontë sisters, (Emily, Anne and Charlotte Brontë), Christina Rossetti, Robert Browning, Elizabeth Barrett Browning, Joseph Conrad, Edward Bulwer-Lytton, Wilkie Collins, Charles Dickens, Benjamin Disraeli, George Eliot, George Meredith, Elizabeth Gaskell, George Gissing, Thomas Hardy, A.

E. Housman, Rudyard Kipling, Robert Louis Stevenson, Bram Stoker, Algernon Charles Swinburne, Philip Meadows Taylor, Alfred Lord Tennyson, William Thackeray, Anthony Trollope, George MacDonald, G.M. Hopkins, Oscar Wilde, Lewis Carrol and H. G. Wells (although many people consider his writing to be more of the Edwardian age).

Victorian Novels

Charles Dickens is a prime exemplar of Victorian novelists. Extraordinarily popular in his day with his characters taking on a life of their own beyond the page, Dickens is still the most popular and read author of that time. His first real novel, *The Pickwick Papers,* written at only twenty-five, was an overnight success, and all his subsequent works sold extremely well. He worked diligently and prolifically to produce entertaining writing the public wanted, but also to offer commentary on social challenges of the era. The comedy of his first novel has a satirical edge which pervades his writings. These deal with the plight of the poor and oppressed and end with a ghost story cut short by his death. The slow trend in his fiction towards darker themes is mirrored in much of the writing of the century, and literature after his death in 1870 is notably different from that at the start of the era.

William Thackeray was Dickens's great rival at the time. With a similar style but a slightly more detached, acerbic and barbed satirical view of his characters, he also tended to depict situations of a more middle class flavour than Dickens. He is best known for his novel *Vanity Fair,* subtitled *A Novel without a Hero,* which is also an example of a form popular in Victorian literature: the historical novel, in which very recent history is depicted. Anthony Trollope tended to write about a slightly different part of the structure, namely the landowning and professional classes.

Away from the big cities and the literary society, Haworth in West Yorkshire held a powerhouse of novel writing: the home of the Brontë family. Anne, Charlotte and Emily Brontë had time in their short lives to produce masterpieces of fiction although these were not immediately appreciated by Victorian critics. *Wuthering Heights*, Emily's only work, in particular has violence, passion, the supernatural, heightened emotion and emotional distance, an unusual mix for any novel but particularly at this time. It is a prime example of Gothic Romanticism from a woman's point of view during this period of time, examining class, myth, and gender. Another important writer of the period was George Eliot, a pseudonym which concealed a woman, Mary Ann Evans, who wished to write novels which would be taken seriously rather than the romances which women of the time were supposed to write.

Style

Victorian novels, influenced as they were by the large sprawling novels of sensibility of the preceding age, tended to be idealized portraits of difficult lives in which hard work, perseverance, love and luck win out in the end; virtue would be rewarded and wrongdoers are suitably punished. They tended to be of an improving nature with a central moral lesson at heart. While this formula was the basis for much of earlier Victorian fiction, the situation became more complex as the century progressed.

George Eliot in particular strove for realism in her fiction and tried to banish the picturesque and the burlesque from her work. Another woman writer, Elizabeth Gaskell, wrote even grimmer, grittier books about the poor in the north of England, but even these usually had happy endings. After the death of Dickens in 1870 happy endings became less common. Such a major literary figure as Charles Dickens tended to dictate the direction of all literature of the era, not least because he edited *All the Year Round,* a literary journal of the time. His fondness for a happy ending with all the loose ends neatly tied up is clear and although he is well known for writing about the lives of the poor, they are sentimentalized portraits made acceptable for people of character to read, to be shocked but not disgusted. The more unpleasant underworld of Victorian city life was revealed by Henry Mayhew in his articles and book *London Labour and the London Poor.*

This change in style in Victorian fiction was slowly becoming clear; by the 1880s and 90s, books were more realistic and often grimmer. Even writers of the high Victorian age were censured for their plots attacking the conventions of the day, with *Adam Bede* being called "the vile outpourings of a lewd woman's mind" and *The Tenant of Wildfell Hall* "utterly unfit to be put into the hands of girls". The disgust of the reading audience perhaps reached a peak with Thomas Hardy's *Jude the Obscure,* which was reportedly burnt by an outraged bishop of Wakefield. The cause of such fury was Hardy's frank treatment of sex, religion, and his disregard for the subject of marriage (a subject close to the Victorians' heart, with the prevailing plot of the Victorian novel sometimes being described as a search for a correct marriage).

Hardy had started his career as seemingly a rather safe novelist writing on bucolic scenes, but his disaffection with some of the institutions of Victorian Britain was present as well as an underlying sorrow for the changing nature of the English countryside. The hostile reception to *Jude* in 1895 meant that it was his last novel, but he continued writing poetry into the mid 1920s. Other authors such as Samuel Butler and George Gissing confronted their antipathies to certain aspects of marriage, religion or Victorian morality and peppered their fiction with controversial antiheroes. Butler's *Erewhon,* for one, is a utopian novel satirising many aspects of Victorian society with Butler's particular dislike of the religious hypocrisy attracting scorn and being depicted as "Musical Banks".

Whilst many great writers were at work at the time, the large numbers of voracious but uncritical readers meant that poor writers, producing salacious and lurid novels or accounts, found eager audiences. Many of the faults common to much better writers were used abundantly by writers now mostly forgotten: over-sentimentality, unrealistic plots and moralising obscuring the story. Although immensely popular in his day, Edward Bulwer-Lytton is now held up as an example of the very worst of Victorian literature with his sensationalist story-lines and his over-boiled style of prose. Other writers popular at the time but largely forgotten now include Mary Elizabeth Braddon, Charlotte Mary Yonge, Charles Kingsley, and R. D. Blackmore.

Children's Literature

The Victorians are sometimes credited with 'inventing childhood', partly via their efforts to stop child labour and the introduction of compulsory education. As children began to be able to read, literature for young people became a growth industry, with not only established writers producing works for children (such as Dickens' *A Child's History of England*) but also a new group of dedicated children's authors. Writers like Lewis Carroll, R. M. Ballantyne and Anna Sewell wrote mainly for children, although they had an adult following. Other authors such as Anthony Hope and Robert Louis Stevenson wrote mainly for adults, but their adventure novels are now generally classified as for children. Other genres include nonsense verse, poetry which required a child-like interest (e.g. Lewis Carroll). School stories flourished: Thomas Hughes' *Tom Brown's Schooldays* and Kipling's *Stalky & Co.* are classics.

Poetry and Drama

Poetry in a sense settled down from the upheavals of the romantic era and much of the work of the time is seen as a bridge between this earlier era and the modernist poetry of the next century. Alfred Lord Tennyson held the poet laureateship for over forty years and his verse became rather stale by the end but his early work is rightly praised.

Some Victorian poetry highly regarded at the time such as *Invictus* is now seen as jingoistic and bombastic but Tennyson's Charge of the Light Brigade was a fierce criticism of a famous military blunder; a pillar of the establishment not failing to attack the establishment. Comic verse abounded in the Victorian era. Magazines such as *Punch magazine* and *Fun magazine* teemed with humorous invention and were aimed at a well-educated readership. The most famous collection of Victorian comic verse is the Bab Ballads.

The husband and wife poetry team of Elizabeth Barrett Browning and Robert Browning conducted their love affair through verse and produced many tender and passionate poems. Both Matthew Arnold and Gerard Manley Hopkins wrote poems which sit somewhere in between the exultation of nature of the romantic Poetry and the Georgian Poetry of the early 20th century. Arnold's works hearken forward to some of the themes of these later poets while Hopkins drew for inspiration on verse forms from Old English poetry such as *Beowulf*.

The reclaiming of the past was a major part of Victorian literature with an interest in both classical literature but also the medieval literature of England. The Victorians loved the heroic, chivalrous stories of knights of old and they hoped to regain some of that noble, courtly behaviour and impress it upon the people both at home and in the wider empire. The best example of this is Alfred Tennyson's *Idylls of the King* which blended the stories of King Arthur, particularly those by Thomas Malory, with contemporary concerns and ideas. The Pre-Raphaelite Brotherhood also drew on myth and folklore for their art with Dante Gabriel Rossetti contemporaneously regarded as the chief poet amongst them, although his sister Christina is now held by scholars to be a stronger poet.

In drama, farces, musical burlesques, extravaganzas and comic operas competed with Shakespeare productions and serious drama by the likes of James Planché and Thomas William Robertson. In 1855, the German Reed Entertainments began a process of elevating the level of (formerly risqué) musical theatre in Britain that culminated in the famous series of comic operas by Gilbert and Sullivan and were followed by the 1890s with the first Edwardian musical comedies. The first play to achieve 500 consecutive performances was the London comedy *Our Boys* by H. J. Byron, opening in 1875. Its astonishing new record of 1,362 performances was bested in 1892 by *Charley's Aunt* by Brandon Thomas. After W. S. Gilbert, Oscar Wilde became the leading poet and dramatist of the late Victorian period. Wilde's plays, in particular, stand apart from the many now forgotten plays of Victorian times and have a much closer relationship to those of the Edwardian dramatists such as George Bernard Shaw, many of whose most important works were written in the 20th century. Wilde's 1895 comic masterpiece, *The Importance of Being Earnest,* was the greatest of the plays in which he held an ironic mirror to the aristocracy while displaying virtuosic mastery of wit and paradoxical wisdom. It has remained extremely popular.

The interest in older works of literature led the Victorians much further afield to find new old works with a great interest in translating of literature from the farthest flung corners of their new empire and beyond. Arabic and Sanskrit literature were some of the richest bodies of work to be discovered and translated for popular consumption. The Rubaiyat of Omar Khayyam is one of the best of these works, translated by Edward Fitzgerald who introduced much of his own poetic skill into a rather free adaptation of the 11th century work. The explorer Richard Francis Burton also translated many exotic works from Science, philosophy and discovery

The Victorian era was an important time for the development of science and the Victorians had a mission to describe and classify the entire natural world. Much of this writing does not rise to the level of being regarded as literature but one book in particular, Charles Darwin's *On the Origin of Species,* remains famous. The theory of evolution contained within the work shook many of the ideas the Victorians had about themselves and their place in the world. Although it took a long time to be widely accepted, it would dramatically change subsequent thought and literature.

Other important non-fiction works of the time are the philosophical writings of John Stuart Mill covering logic, economics, liberty and utilitarianism. The large and influential histories of Thomas Carlyle: *The French Revolution, A History, On Heroes and Hero Worship* and Thomas Babington Macaulay: *The History of England from the Accession of James II*. The greater number of novels that contained overt criticism of religion did not stifle a vigorous list of publications on the subject of religion.

Two of the most important of these are John Henry Newman and Henry Edward Cardinal Manning who both wished to revitalise Anglicanism with a return to the Roman Catholic Church. In a somewhat opposite direction, the ideas of socialism were permeating political thought at the time with Friedrich Engels writing his *Condition of the Working Classes in England* and William Morris writing the early socialist utopian novel *News from Nowhere*. One other important and monumental work begun in this era was the *Oxford English Dictionary* which would eventually become the most important historical dictionary of the English language.

Nature Writing

In the U.S.A., Henry David Thoreau's works and Susan Fenimore Cooper's *Rural Hours* (1850) were canonical influences on Victorian nature writing. In the U.K., Philip Gosse and Sarah Bowdich Lee were two of the most popular nature writers in the early part of the Victorian era. The Illustrated London News, founded in 1842, was the world's first illustrated weekly newspaper and often published articles and illustrations dealing with nature; in the second half of the nineteenth century, books, articles, and illustrations on nature became widespread and popular among an increasingly urbanized reading public.

Supernatural and Fantastic Literature

The old Gothic tales that came out of the late nineteenth century are the first examples of the genre of fantastic fiction. These tales often centered on larger-than-life characters such as Sherlock Holmes, famous detective of the times, Barry Lee, big time gang leader, Sexton Blake, Phileas Fogg, and other fictional characters of the era, such as Dracula, Edward Hyde, The Invisible Man, and many other fictional characters who often had exotic enemies to foil. Spanning the eighteenth and nineteenth centuries, there was a particular type of story-writing known as gothic. Gothic literature combines romance and horror in attempt to thrill and terrify the reader. Possible features in a gothic novel are foreign monsters, ghosts, curses, hidden rooms and witchcraft. Gothic tales usually take place in locations such as castles, monasteries, and cemeteries, although the gothic monsters sometimes cross over into the real world, making appearances in cities such as London and Paris.

Influence of Victorian Literature

Writers from the United States and the British colonies of Australia, New Zealand and Canada were influenced by the literature of Britain and are often classed as a part of Victorian literature, although they were gradually developing their own distinctive voices. Victorian writers of Canadian literature include Grant Allen, Susanna Moodie and Catherine Parr Traill. Australian literature has the poets Adam Lindsay Gordon and Banjo Paterson, who wrote *Waltzing Matilda* and New Zealand literature includes Thomas Bracken and Frederick Edward Maning.

The problem with the classification of Victorian literature is great difference between the early works of the period and the later works which had more in common with the writers of the Edwardian period and many writers straddle this divide. People such as Arthur Conan Doyle, Rudyard Kipling, H. G. Wells, Bram Stoker, H. Rider Haggard, Jerome K. Jerome and Joseph Conrad all wrote some of their important works during Victoria's reign but the sensibility of their writing is frequently regarded as Edwardian.

The persistent popular embrace of Victorian literature has had a profound influence on modern literature and media. Writers such as Dickens and the Brontë sisters still sell robustly on most book resellers' lists and are frequently adapted into films and television productions, both directly and in modernized retellings. In addition, many modern novels such as *A Great and Terrible Beauty* demonstrate that the intricate cultural mores of the Victorian era finds a home in the modern cultural psyche.

11

Modernist Literature

Modernism as a literary movement reached its height in Europe between 1900 and the middle 1920s. Modernist literature addressed aesthetic problems similar to those examined in non-literary forms of contemporaneous Modernist art, such as Modernist painting. Gertrude Stein's abstract writings, for example, have often been compared to the fragmentary and multi-perspectival Cubism of her friend Pablo Picasso.

The general thematic concerns of Modernist literature are well-summarized by the sociologist Georg Simmel:

> "The deepest problems of modern life derive from the claim of the individual to preserve the autonomy and individuality of his existence in the face of overwhelming social forces, of historical heritage, of external culture, and of the technique of life."

The Modernist emphasis on a radical individualism can be seen in the many literary manifestos issued by various groups within the movement. The concerns expressed by Simmel above are echoed in Richard Huelsenbeck's "First German Dada Manifesto" of 1918:

> "Art in its execution and direction is dependent on the time in which it lives, and artists are creatures of their epoch. The highest art will be that which in its conscious content presents the thousandfold problems of the day, the art which has been visibly shattered by the explosions of last week. The best and most extraordinary artists will be those who every hour snatch the tatters of their bodies out of the frenzied cataract of life, who, with bleeding hands and hearts, hold fast to the intelligence of their time."

The cultural history of humanity creates a unique common history that connects previous generations with the current generation of humans. The Modernist re-contextualization of the individual within the fabric of this received social heritage can be seen in the "mythic method" which T.S. Eliot expounded in his discussion of James Joyce's *Ulysses*:

> "In using the myth, in manipulating a continuous parallel between contemporaneity and antiquity, Mr. Joyce is pursuing a method which others must pursue after him ... It is simply a way of controlling, of ordering, of giving a shape and a significance to the immense panorama of futility and anarchy which is contemporary history."

Modernist literature attempted to move from the bonds of Realist literature and to introduce concepts such as disjointed timelines. In the wake of Modernism, and post-enlightenment, metanarratives tended to be emancipatory, whereas beforehand this was not a consistent characteristic. Contemporary metanarratives were becoming less relevant in light of the events of World War I, the rise of trade unionism, a general social discontent, and the emergence of psychoanalysis. The consequent need for a unifying function brought about a growth in the political importance of culture.

Modernist literature can be viewed largely in terms of its formal, stylistic and semantic movement away from Romanticism, examining subject matter that is traditionally mundane—a prime example being *The Love Song of J. Alfred Prufrock* by T. S. Eliot. Modernist literature often features a marked pessimism, a clear rejection of the optimism apparent in Victorian literature. But the questioning spirit of modernism could also be seen, less elegiacally, as part of a necessary search for ways to make sense of a broken world. An example is *A Drunk Man Looks at the Thistle* by Hugh MacDiarmid, in which the individual artist applies Eliot's techniques to respond (in this case) to a historically fractured nationalism, using a more comic, parodic and "optimistic" (though no less "hopeless") modernist expression in which the artist as "hero" seeks to embrace complexity and locate new meanings.

However, many Modernist works like T. S. Eliot's *The Waste Land* are marked by the absence of a central, unifying figure. In rejecting the solipsism of Romantics like Shelley and Byron, such works also reject the association of the subject with Cartesian dualism, collapsing narrative and narrator into a collection of disjointed fragments and overlapping voices.

Modernist literature often moves beyond the limitations of the Realist novel with a concern for larger factors such as social or historical change. These themes are prominent in "stream of consciousness" writing. Examples can be seen in Virginia Woolf's *Kew Gardens* and *Mrs Dalloway*, James Joyce's *Ulysses*, Katherine Porter's *Flowering Judas*, Jean Toomer's *Cane*, William Faulkner's *The Sound and the Fury*, and others.

Modernism as a literary movement is seen, in large part, as a reaction to the emergence of city life as a central force in society. Furthermore, an early attention to the object as freestanding became in later Modernism a preoccupation with form. The dyadic collapse of the distance between subject and object represented a movement from *means* to *is*. Where Romanticism stressed the subjectivity of experience, Modernist writers were more acutely conscious of the objectivity of their surroundings. In Modernism the object *is*; the language doesn't mean it *is*. This is a shift from an epistemological aesthetic to an ontological aesthetic or, in simpler terms, a shift from a knowledge-based aesthetic to a *being*-based aesthetic. This shift is central to Modernism. Archibald MacLeish, for instance, said, "A poem should not mean / But be."

Characteristics of Modernism

Formal/Stylistic Characteristics

- Free indirect speech
- Stream of consciousness
- Juxtaposition of characters
- Wide use of classical allusions
- Figure of speech
- Intertextuality
- Personification
- Hyperbole
- Parataxis
- Comparison
- Quotation
- Pun
- Satire
- Irony

- Antiphrasis
- Unconventional use of metaphor
- Symbolic representation
- Psychoanalysis
- Discontinuous narrative
- Metanarrative
- Multiple narrative points of view

Thematic Characteristics

- Breakdown of social norms
- Realistic embodiment of social meanings
- Separation of meanings and senses from the context
- Despairing individual behaviours in the face of an unmanageable future
- Spiritual loneliness
- Alienation
- Frustration
- Disillusionment
- Rejection of history
- Rejection of outdated social systems
- Objection to traditional thoughts and traditional moralities
- Objection to religious thoughts
- Substitution of a mythical past
- Two World Wars' effects on Humanity

12

Postmodern Literature

The term Postmodern literature is used to describe certain tendencies in post-World War II literature. It is both a continuation of the experimentation championed by writers of the modernist period and a reaction against Enlightenment ideas implicit in Modernist literature.

Postmodern literature, like postmodernism as a whole, is hard to define and there is little agreement on the exact characteristics, scope, and importance of postmodern literature. However, unifying features often coincide with Jean-François Lyotard's concept of the "meta-narrative" and "little narrative," Jacques Derrida's concept of "play," and Jean Baudrillard's "simulacra." For example, instead of the modernist quest for meaning in a chaotic world, the postmodern author eschews, often playfully, the possibility of meaning, and the postmodern novel is often a parody of this quest. This distrust of totalizing mechanisms extends even to the author; thus postmodern writers often celebrate chance over craft and employ metafiction to undermine the author's "univocal" control (the control of only one voice). The distinction between high and low culture is also attacked with the employment of pastiche, the combination of multiple cultural elements including subjects and genres not previously deemed fit for literature. A list of postmodern authors often varies; the following are some names of authors often so classified, most of them belonging to the generation born in the interwar period:

> William Burroughs (1914-1997), Alexander Trocchi (1925-1984), Kurt Vonnegut (1922-2007), John Barth (b. 1930), Donald Barthelme (1931-1989), E. L. Doctorow (b. 1931), Robert Coover (1932), Jerzy Kosinski (1933-1991) Don DeLillo (b. 1936), Thomas Pynchon (b. 1937), Ishmael Reed (1938), Kathy Acker (1947-1997), Paul Auster (b. 1947), Orhan Pamuk (b. 1952).

Postmodernist writers often point to early novels and story collections as inspiration for their experiments with narrative and structure: *Don Quixote, 1001 Arabian Nights, The Decameron,* and *Candide,* among many others. In the English language, Laurence Sterne's 1759 novel *The Life and Opinions of Tristram Shandy, Gentleman,* with its heavy emphasis on parody and narrative experimentation, is often cited as an early influence on postmodernism.

There were many 19th century examples of attacks on Enlightenment concepts, parody, and playfulness in literature, including Lord Byron's satire, especially *Don Juan;* Thomas Carlyle's *Sartor Resartus;* Alfred Jarry's ribald *Ubu* parodies and his invention of 'Pataphysics; Lewis Carrol's playful experiments with signification; the work of Isidore Ducasse, Arthur Rimbaud, Oscar Wilde. Playwrights who worked in the late 19th and early 20th century whose thought and work would serve as an influence on the aesthetic of postmodernism include Swedish dramatist August

Strindberg, the Italian author Luigi Pirandello, and the German playwright and theorist Bertolt Brecht. In the 1910s, artists associated with Dadaism celebrated chance, parody, playfulness, and attacked the central role of the artist. Tristan Tzara claimed in "How to Make a Dadaist Poem" that to create a Dadaist poem one had only to put random words in a hat and pull them out one by one.

Another way Dadaism influenced postmodern literature was in the development of collage, specifically collages using elements from advertisement or illustrations from popular novels. Artists associated with Surrealism, which developed from Dadaism, continued experimentations with chance and parody while celebrating the flow of the subconscious. André Breton, the founder of Surrealism, suggested that automatism and the description of dreams should play a greater role in the creation of literature.

He used automatism to create his novel *Nadja* and used photographs to replace description as a parody of the overly-descriptive novelists he often criticized. Surrealist René Magritte's experiments with signification are used as examples by Jacques Derrida and Michel Foucault. Foucault also uses examples from Jorge Luis Borges, an important direct influence on many postmodernist fiction writers. He is occasionally listed as a postmodernist, although he started writing in the 1920s. The influence of his experiments with metafiction and magical realism was not fully realized in the Anglo-American world until the postmodern period.

Comparisons with Modernist Literature

Both modern and postmodern literature represent a

break from 19th century realism, in which a story was told from an objective or omniscient point of view. In character development, both modern and postmodern literature explore subjectivism, turning from external reality to examine inner states of consciousness, in many cases drawing on modernist examples in the *stream of consciousness* styles of Virginia Woolf and James Joyce, or explorative poems like The Waste Land by T. S. Eliot. In addition, both modern and postmodern literature explore fragmentariness in narrative- and character-construction.

The Waste Land is often cited as a means of distinguishing modern and postmodern literature. The poem is fragmentary and employs pastiche like much postmodern literature, but the speaker in *The Waste Land* says, "these fragments I have shored against my ruins". Modernist literature sees fragmentation and extreme subjectivity as an existential crisis, or Freudian internal conflict, a problem that must be solved, and the artist is often cited as the one to solve it. Postmodernists, however, often demonstrate that this chaos is insurmountable; the artist is impotent, and the only recourse against "ruin" is to play within the chaos. Playfulness is present in many modernist works (Joyce's *Finnegans Wake* or Virginia Woolf's *Orlando*, for example) and they may seem very similar to postmodern works, but with postmodernism playfulness becomes central and the actual

Shift to Postmodernism

As with all stylistic eras, no definite dates exist for the rise and fall of postmodernism's popularity. 1941, the year in which Irish novelist James Joyce and English novelist Virginia Woolf both died, is sometimes used as a rough boundary for postmodernism's start.

The prefix "post," however, does not necessarily imply a new era. Rather, it could also indicate a reaction against modernism in the wake of the Second World War (with its disrespect for human rights, just confirmed in the Geneva Convention, through the atomic bombings of Hiroshima and Nagasaki, the Holocaust, the bombing of Dresden, the fire-bombing of Tokyo, and Japanese American internment). It could also imply a reaction to significant post-war events: the beginning of the Cold War, the civil rights movement in the United States, postcolonialism (Postcolonial literature), and the rise of the personal computer (Cyberpunk fiction and Hypertext fiction).

Some further argue that the beginning of postmodern literature could be marked by significant publications or literary events. For example, some mark the beginning of postmodernism with the first performance of *Waiting for Godot* in 1953, the first publication of *Howl* in 1956 or of *Naked Lunch* in 1959. For others the beginning is marked by moments in critical theory: Jacques Derrida's "Structure, Sign, and Play" lecture in 1966 or as late as Ihab Hassan's usage in *The Dismemberment of Orpheus* in 1971. Brian McHale details his main thesis on this shift, although many postmodern works have developed out of modernism, modernism is characterised by an epistemological dominant while postmodernism works are primarily concerned

Post-war Developments

Though postmodernist literature does not refer to everything written in the postmodern period, several post-war developments in literature (such as the Theatre of the Absurd, the Beat Generation, and

Magical Realism) have significant similarities. These developments are occasionally collectively labeled "postmodern"; more commonly, some key figures (Samuel Beckett, William S. Burroughs, Jorge Luis Borges, Julio Cortázar and Gabriel Garcia Marquez) are cited as significant contributors to the postmodern aesthetic.

The work of Jarry, the Surrealists, Antonin Artaud, Luigi Pirandello and so on also influenced the work of playwrights from the Theatre of the Absurd. The term "Theatre of the Absurd" was coined by Martin Esslin to describe a tendency in theatre in the 1950s; he related it to Albert Camus's concept of the absurd. The plays of the Theatre of the Absurd parallel postmodern fiction in many ways. For example, *The Bald Soprano* by Eugène Ionesco is essentially a series of clichés taken from a language textbook. One of the most important figures to be categorized as both Absurdist and Postmodern is Samuel Beckett.

The work of Samuel Beckett is often seen as marking the shift from modernism to postmodernism in literature. He had close ties with modernism because of his friendship with James Joyce; however, his work helped shape the development of literature away from modernism. Joyce, one of the exemplars of modernism, celebrated the possibility of language; Beckett had a revelation in 1945 that, in order to escape the shadow of Joyce, he must focus on the poverty of language and man as a failure. His later work, likewise, featured characters stuck in inescapable situations attempting impotently to communicate whose only recourse is to play, to make the best of what they have. As Hans-Peter Wagner says, "Mostly concerned with what he saw as impossibilities in fiction (identity of characters; reliable consciousness; the reliability of language itself; and the rubrication of literature in genres) Beckett's experiments with narrative form and with the disintegration of narration and character in fiction and drama won him the Nobel Prize for Literature in 1969. His works published after 1969 are mostly meta-literary attempts that must be read in light of his own theories and previous works and the attempt to deconstruct literary forms and genres. Beckett's last text published during his lifetime, *Stirrings Still* (1988), breaks down the barriers between drama, fiction, and poetry, with texts of the collection being almost entirely composed of echoes and reiterations of his previous work. He was definitely one of the fathers of the postmodern movement in fiction which has continued undermining the ideas of logical coherence in narration, formal plot, regular time sequence, and psychologically explained characters."

"The Beat Generation" is a name coined by Jack Kerouac for the disaffected youth of America during the materialistic 1950s; Kerouac developed ideas of automatism into what he called "spontaneous prose" to create a maximalistic, multi-novel epic called the Duluoz Legend in the mold of Marcel Proust's *In Search of Lost Time.* "Beat Generation" is often used more broadly to refer to several groups of post-war American writers from the Black Mountain poets, the New York School, the San Francisco Renaissance, and so on. These writers have occasionally also been referred to as the "Postmoderns". Though this is now a less common usage of "postmodern", references to these writers as "postmodernists" still appear and many writers associated with this group (John Ashbery, Richard Brautigan, Gilbert Sorrentino, and so on) appear often on lists of postmodern writers. One writer associated with the Beat Generation who appears most often on lists of postmodern writers is William S. Burroughs. Burroughs published *Naked Lunch* in Paris in 1959 and in America in 1961; this is considered by some the first truly postmodern novel because it is fragmentary, with no central narrative arc; it employs pastiche to fold in elements from popular genres such as detective fiction and science fiction; it's full of parody, paradox, and playfulness; and, according to some accounts, friends Kerouac and Allen Ginsberg edited the book guided by chance. He is also noted, along with Brion Gysin, for the creation of the "cut-up" technique, a technique (similar to Tzara's "Dadaist Poem") in which words and phrases are cut from a newspaper or other publication and rearranged to form a new message. This is the technique he used to create novels such as *Nova Express* and *The Ticket That Exploded*.

Magical Realism is a technique popular among Latin American writers (and can also be considered its own genre) in which supernatural elements are treated as mundane (a famous example being the practical-minded and ultimately dismissive treatment of an apparently angelic figure in Gabriel Garcia Marquez's "A Very Old Man with Enormous Wings"). Though the technique has its roots in traditional storytelling, it was a center piece of the Latin American "boom", a movement coterminous with postmodernism. Some of the major figures of the "Boom" and practitioners of Magical Realism (Gabriel Garcia Marquez, Julio Cortázar etc.) are sometimes listed as postmodernists. This labeling, however, is not without its problems. In Spanish-speaking Latin America, *modernismo* and *posmodernismo* refer to early twentieth-century literary movements that have no direct relationship to *modernism* and *postmodernism* in English. Finding it anachronistic, Octavio Paz has argued that postmodernism is an imported grand récit that is incompatible with the cultural production of Latin America.

Along with Beckett and Borges, a commonly cited transitional figure is Vladimir Nabokov; like Beckett and Borges, Nabokov started publishing before the beginning of postmodernity (1926 in Russian, 1941 in English). Though his most famous novel, *Lolita* (1955), could be considered a modernist or a postmodernist novel, his later work (specifically *Pale Fire* in 1962 and *Ada or Ardor: A Family Chronicle* in 1969) are more clearly postmodern.

Scope of Postmodernist Literature

Postmodernism in literature is not an organized movement with leaders or central figures; therefore, it is more difficult to say if it has ended or when it will end (compared to, say, declaring the end of modernism with the death of Joyce or Woolf). Arguably postmodernism peaked in the 60s and 70s with the publication of *Catch-22* in 1961, *Lost in the Funhouse* in 1968, *Slaughterhouse Five* in 1969, *Gravity's Rainbow* in 1973, and many others.

Some declared the death of postmodernism in the 80's with a new surge of realism represented and inspired by Raymond Carver. Tom Wolfe in his 1989 article "Stalking the Billion-Footed Beast" called for a new emphasis on realism in fiction to replace postmodernism. With this new emphasis on realism in mind, some declared *White Noise* in 1985 or *The Satanic Verses* in 1988 to be the last great novels of the postmodern era.

A new generation of writers—such as David Foster Wallace, Dave Eggers, Michael Chabon, Zadie Smith, Chuck Palahniuk, Neil Gaiman, Jonathan Lethem—and publications such as *McSweeney's*, *The Believer*, and the fiction pages of *The New Yorker*, herald either a new chapter of postmodernism or something else entirely—post-postmodernism. Amazon.com described the Mark Z. Danielewski 2000 novel *House of Leaves* as "post-postmodern."

Common Themes and Techniques

All of these themes and techniques are often used together. For example, metafiction and pastiche are often used for irony. These are not used by all postmodernists, nor is this an exclusive list of features.

Irony, Playfulness, Black Humor

Linda Hutcheon claimed postmodern fiction as a whole could be characterized by the ironic quote marks, that much of it can be taken as tongue-in-cheek. This irony, along with black humor and the general concept of "play" (related to Derrida's concept or the ideas advocated by Roland Barthes in *The Pleasure of the Text*) are among the most recognizable aspects of postmodernism. Though the idea of employing these in literature did not start with the postmodernists (the modernists were often playful and ironic), they became central features in many postmodern works. In fact, several novelists later to be labeled postmodern were first collectively labeled black humorists: John Barth, Joseph Heller, William Gaddis, Kurt Vonnegut, Bruce Jay Friedman, etc. It's common for postmodernists to treat serious subjects in a playful and humorous way: for example, the way Heller, Vonnegut, and Pynchon address the events of World War II. A good example of postmodern irony and black humor is found in the stories of Donald Barthelme; "The School", for example, is about the ironic death of plants, animals, and people connected to the children in one class, but the inexplicable repetition of death is treated only as a joke and the narrator remains emotionally distant throughout. The central concept of Joseph Heller's *Catch-22* is the irony of the now-idiomatic "catch 22", and the narrative is structured around a long series of similar ironies. Thomas Pynchon in particular provides prime examples of playfulness, often including silly wordplay, within a serious context. *The Crying of Lot 49*, for example, contains characters named Mike Fallopian and Stanley Koteks and a radio station called KCUF, while the novel as a whole has a serious subject and a complex structure.

Intertextuality

Since postmodernism represents a decentered concept of the universe in which individual works are not isolated creations, much of the focus in the study of postmodern literature is on intertextuality: the relationship between one text (a novel for example) and another or one text within the interwoven fabric of literary history. Critics point to this as an indication of postmodernism's lack of originality and reliance on clichés. Intertextuality in postmodern literature can a reference or parallel to another literary work, an extended discussion of a work, or the adoption of a style. In postmodern literature this commonly manifests as references to fairy tales – as in works by Margaret Atwood, Donald Barthelme, and many other – or in references to popular genres such as sci-fi and detective fiction. An early 20th century example of intertextuality which influenced later postmodernists is "Pierre Menard, Author of the Quixote" by Jorge Luis Borges, a story with significant references to *Don Quixote* which is also a good example of intertextuality with its references to Medieval romances. *Don Quixote* is a common reference with postmodernists, for example Kathy Acker's novel *Don Quixote: Which Was a Dream*. Another example of intertextuality in postmodernism is John Barth's *The Sot-Weed Factor* which deals with Ebenezer Cooke's poem of the same name. Often intertextuality is more complicated than a single reference to another text. Robert Coover's *Pinocchio in Venice,* for example, links Pinocchio to Thomas Mann's *Death in Venice.* Also, Umberto Eco's *The Name of the Rose* takes on the form of a detective novel and makes references to authors such as Aristotle, Arthur Conan Doyle, and Borges .

Pastiche

Related to postmodern intertextuality, pastiche means to combine, or "paste" together, multiple elements. In Postmodernist literature this can be an homage to or a parody of past styles. It can be seen as a representation of the chaotic, pluralistic, or information-drenched aspects of postmodern society. It can be a combination of multiple genres to create a unique narrative or to comment on situations in postmodernity: for example, William S. Burroughs uses science fiction, detective fiction, westerns; Margaret Atwood uses science fiction and fairy tales; Umberto Eco uses detective fiction, fairy tales, and science fiction, Derek Pell relies on collage and noir detective, erotica, travel guides, and how-to manuals, and so on. Though pastiche commonly refers to the mixing of genres, many other elements are also included (metafiction and temporal distortion are common in the broader pastiche of the postmodern novel). For example, Thomas Pynchon includes in his novels elements from detective fiction, science fiction, and war fiction; songs; pop culture references; well-known, obscure, and fictional history mixed together; real contemporary and historical figures; a wide variety of well-known, obscure and fictional cultures and concepts. In Robert Coover's 1977 novel *The Public Burning*, Coover mixes historically inaccurate accounts of Richard Nixon interacting with historical figures and fictional characters such as Uncle Sam and Betty Crocker. Pastiche can also refer to compositional technique, for example the cut-up technique employed by Burroughs. Another example is B. S. Johnson's 1969 novel *The Unfortunates*; it was released in a box with no binding so that readers could assemble it however they chose.

Metafiction

Metafiction is essentially writing about writing or "foregrounding the apparatus", making the artificiality of art or the fictionality of fiction apparent to the reader and generally disregards the necessity for "willful suspension of disbelief". It is often employed to undermine the authority of the author, for unexpected narrative shifts, to advance a story in a unique way, for emotional distance, or to comment on the act of storytelling. For example, Italo Calvino's 1979 novel *If on a winter's night a traveler* is about a reader attempting to read a novel of the same name. Kurt Vonnegut also commonly used this technique: the first chapter of his 1969 novel *Slaughterhouse Five* is about the process of writing the novel and calls attention to his own presence throughout the novel. Though much of the novel has to do with Vonnegut's own experiences during the firebombing of Dresden, Vonnegut continually points out the artificiality of the central narrative arc which contains obviously fictional elements such as aliens and time travel. Similarly, Tim O'Brien's 1990 novel/story collection *The Things They Carried,* about one platoon's experiences during the Vietnam War, features a character named Tim O'Brien; though O'Brien was a Vietnam veteran, the book is a work of fiction and O'Brien calls into question the fictionality of the characters and incidents through out the book. One story in the book, "How to Tell a True War Story", questions the nature of telling stories. Factual retellings of war stories, the narrator says, would be unbelievable and heroic, moral war stories don't capture the truth.

Poioumena

Poioumenon (plural, "poioumena") is a term coined by Alastair Fowler to refer to a specific type of metafiction in which the story is about the process of creation. In many cases, the book will be about the process of creating the book or includes a central metaphor for this process. A common example of this is Laurence Sterne's *Tristram Shandy* which is about the narrator's frustrated attempt to tell his own story. A significant postmodern example is Vladimir Nabokov's *Pale Fire,* in which the narrator, Kinbote, claims he is writing an analysis of John Shade's long poem "Pale Fire", but the narrative of the relationship between Shade and Kinbote is presented in what is ostensibly the footnotes to the poem. Similarly, the self-conscious narrator in Salman Rushdie's *Midnight's Children* parallels the creation of his book to the creation of chutney and the creation of independent India. Other postmodern examples of poioumea include Doris Lessing's *The*

Golden Notebook, John Fowles's *Mantissa,* and William Golding's *Paper Men,* and Gilbert Sorrentino's *Mulligan Stew.*

Historiographic metafiction

Linda Hutcheon coined the term "historiographic metafiction" to refer to works that fictionalize actual historical events or figures; notable examples include *The General in His Labyrinth* by Gabriel Garcia Marquez (about Simón Bolívar), *Flaubert's Parrot* by Julian Barnes (about Gustave Flaubert), *Ragtime* by E. L. Doctorow (which features such historical figures as Harry Houdini, Henry Ford, Archduke Franz Ferdinand of Austria, Booker T. Washington, Sigmund Freud, Carl Jung), and Rabih Alameddine's Koolaids: The Art of War which makes references to the Lebanese Civil War and various real life political figures. Thomas Pynchon's *Mason and Dixon* also employs this concept; for example, a scene featuring George Washington smoking marijuana is included. John Fowles deals similarly with the Victorian Period in *The French Lieutenant's Woman.* In regards to critical theory, this technique can be related to *The Death of the Author* by Roland Barthes.

Temporal Distortion

This is a common technique in modernist fiction: fragmentation and non-linear narratives are central features in both modern and postmodern literature. Temporal distortion in postmodern fiction is used in a variety of ways, often for the sake of irony. Historiographic metafiction is an example of this. Distortions in time are central features in many of Kurt Vonnegut's non-linear novels, the most famous of which is perhaps Billy Pilgrim in *Slaughterhouse Five* becoming "unstuck in time". In *Flight to Canada,* Ishmael Reed deals playfully with anachronisms, Abraham Lincoln using a telephone for example. Time may also overlap, repeat, or bifurcate into multiple possibilities. For example, in Robert Coover's "The Babysitter" from *Pricksongs & Descants,* the author presents multiple possible events occurring simultaneously—in one section the babysitter is murdered while in another section nothing happens and so on—yet no version of the story is favored as the correct version.

Magic Realism

Literary work marked by the use of still, sharply defined, smoothly painted images of figures and objects depicted in a surrealistic manner. The themes and subjects are often imaginary, somewhat outlandish and fantastic and with a certain dream-like quality. Some of the characteristic features of this kind of fiction are the mingling and juxtaposition of the realistic and the fantastic or bizarre, skillful time shifts, convoluted and even labyrinthine narratives and plots, miscellaneous use of dreams, myths and fairy stories, expressionistic and even surrealistic description, arcane erudition, the element of surprise or abrupt shock, the horrific and the inexplicable. It has been applied, for instance, to the work of Jorge Luis Borges, the Argentinian who in 1935 published his *Historia universal de la infamia,* regarded by many as the first work of magic realism. Colombian novelist Gabriel García Marquez is also regarded as a notable exponent of this kind of fiction – especially his novel *One Hundred Years of Solitude.* The Cuban Alejo Carpentier is another described as a "magic realist". Postmodernists such as Salman Rushdie, Italo Calvino, and Gunter Grass commonly use Magical Realism in their work. A fusion of fabulism with magical realism is apparent in such early 21st century American short stories as Kevin Brockmeier's "The Ceiling," Dan Chaon's "Big Me," Jacob M. Appel's "Exposure," and Elizabeth Graver's "The Mourning Door".

Technoculture and Hyperreality

Fredric Jameson called postmodernism the "cultural logic of late capitalism". "Late capitalism" implies that society has moved past the industrial age and into the information age. Likewise, Jean Baudrillard claimed postmodernity was defined by a shift into hyperreality in which simulations have replaced the real. In postmodernity people are inundated with information, technology has become a central focus in many lives, and our understanding of the real is mediated by simulations of the real. Many works of fiction have dealt with this aspect of postmodernity with characteristic irony and pastiche. For example, Don DeLillo's *White Noise* presents characters who are bombarded with a "white noise" of television, product brand names, and clichés. The cyberpunk fiction of William Gibson, Neal Stephenson, and many others use science fiction techniques to address this postmodern, hyperreal information bombardment.

Paranoia

Perhaps demonstrated most famously and effectively in Joseph Heller's *Catch-22* and the work of Thomas Pynchon, the sense of paranoia, the belief that there's an ordering system behind the chaos of the world is another recurring postmodern theme. For the postmodernist, no ordering system exists, so a search for order is fruitless and absurd. *The Crying of Lot 49* by Thomas Pynchon has many possible interpretations. If one reads the book with a particular bias, then he or she is going to be frustrated. This often coincides with the theme of technoculture and hyperreality. For example, in *Breakfast of Champions* by Kurt Vonnegut, the character Dwayne Hoover becomes violent when he's convinced that everyone else in the world is a robot and he is the only human.

Maximalism

Dubbed maximalism by some critics, the sprawling canvas and fragmented narrative of such writers as Dave Eggers has generated controversy on the "purpose" of a novel as narrative and the standards by which it should be judged. The postmodern position is that the style of a novel must be appropriate to what it depicts and represents, and points back to such examples in previous ages as *Gargantua* by François Rabelais and the *Odyssey* of Homer, which Nancy Felson hails as the exemplar of the polytropic audience and its engagement with a work.

Many modernist critics, notably B.R. Myers in his polemic *A Reader's Manifesto*, attack the maximalist novel as being disorganized, sterile and filled with language play for its own sake, empty of emotional commitment—and therefore empty of value as a novel. Yet there are counter-examples, such as Pynchon's *Mason & Dixon*, James Chapman's *Stet*, and David Foster Wallace's *Infinite Jest* where postmodern narrative coexists with emotional commitment.

Minimalism

Literary minimalism can be characterized as a focus on

a surface description where readers are expected to take an active role in the creation of a story. The characters in minimalist stories and novels tend to be unexceptional. Generally, the short stories are "slice of life" stories. Minimalism, the opposite of maximalism, is a representation of only the most basic and necessary pieces, specific by economy with words. Minimalist authors hesitate to use adjectives, adverbs, or meaningless details. Instead of providing every minute detail, the author provides a general context and then allows the reader's imagination to shape the story. Among those categorized as postmodernist, literary minimalism is most commonly associated with Samuel Beckett.

Perspectives

John Barth, the postmodernist novelist who talks often about the label "postmodern", wrote an influential essay in 1967 called "Literature of Exhaustion" and in 1979 wrote "Literature of Replenishment" in order to clarify the earlier essay. "Literature of Exhaustion" was about the need for a new era in literature after modernism had exhausted itself. In "Literature of Replenishment" Barth says,

> My ideal Postmodernist author neither merely repudiates nor merely imitates either his twentieth-century Modernist parents or his nineteenth-century premodernist grandparents. He has the first half of our century under his belt, but not on his back. Without lapsing into moral or artistic simplism, shoddy craftsmanship, Madison Avenue venality, or either false or real naiveté, he nevertheless aspires to a fiction more democratic in its appeal than such late-Modernist marvels as Beckett's *Texts for Nothing*. The ideal Postmodernist novel will somehow rise

> above the quarrel between realism and irrealism, formalism and 'contentism,' pure and committed literature, coterie fiction and junk fiction.

Many of the well-known postmodern novels deal with World War II, one of the most famous of which being Joseph Heller's *Catch-22*. Heller claimed his novel and many of the other American novels of the time had more to do with the state of the country after the war:

> The antiwar and anti government feelings in the book belong to the period following World War II: the Korean War, the cold war of the Fifties. A general disintegration of belief took place then, and it affected *Catch-22* in that the form of the novel became almost disintegrated. *Catch-22* was a collage; if not in structure, then in the ideology of the novel itself ... Without being aware of it, I was part of a near-movement in fiction. While I was writing *Catch-22*, J. P. Donleavy was writing *The Ginger Man*, Jack Kerouac was writing *On the Road*, Ken Kesey was writing *One Flew Over the Cuckoo's Nest*, Thomas Pynchon was writing *V.*, and Kurt Vonnegut was writing *Cat's Cradle*. I don't think any one of us even knew any of the others. Certainly I didn't know them. Whatever forces were at work shaping a trend in art were affecting not just me, but all of us. The feelings of helplessness and persecution in *Catch-22* are very strong in Pynchon and in *Cat's Cradle*.

Novelist and theorist Umberto Eco explains his idea of postmodernism as a kind of double-coding:

> I think of the postmodern attitude as that of a man who loves a very cultivated woman and knows that he cannot say to her "I love you madly", because he knows that she knows (and that she knows he knows) that these words have already been written by Barbara Cartland. Still there is a solution. He can say "As Barbara Cartland would put it, I love you

> madly". At this point, having avoided false innocence, having said clearly it is no longer possible to talk innocently, he will nevertheless say what he wanted to say to the woman: that he loves her in an age of lost innocence.

Novelist David Foster Wallace in his 1990 essay "E Unibus Pluram" makes the connection between the rise of postmodernism and the rise of television with its tendency toward self-reference and the ironic juxtaposition of what's seen and what's said.

Bibliography

Allen, Walter Ernst. *The English novel: a short critical history.* London: Phoenix House, 1954.

Altick, Richard Daniel. *The art of literary research.* 3rd ed. New York: Norton, 1981.

Baer, Florence E. *Folklore and literature of the British Isles: an annotated bibliography.* New York: Garland Pub., 1986.

Baker, Ernest Albert. *The history of the English novel.* London: H. F. & G. Witherby, [1934-39]. 10 v.

Bateson, Frederick Wilse. *The Cambridge bibliography of English literature.* New York: Macmillan, 1941. 5 v.

Baugh, Albert Croll. *A literary history of England.* 2nd ed. New York: Appleton-Century-Crofts, 1967.

Case, Arthur Ellicott. *A bibliography of English poetical miscellanies, 1521-1750.* Oxford: University Press, 1935.

Carpenter, Charles A. *Modern British drama.* Arlington Heights, IL: AHM Pub. Corp., c1979.

Chambers, Edmund Kerchever. *English literature at the close of the Middle Ages.* New York: Oxford University Press, 1947.

Courthope, William John. *A history of English poetry.* London: Macmillan and Co., 1903-35.

Drabble, Margaret. *The Oxford companion to English literature.* 5th ed. rev. and updated. Oxford; New York: Oxford University Press, 1995.

Dyson, A. E. *English poetry; select bibliographical guides.* London; New York: Oxford University Press, 1971.

English Association. *The year's work in English studies.* London: Published for the English Association by John Murray, etc., 1919.

English drama, excluding Shakespeare: select bibliographical guides. London; New York: Oxford University Press, 1975.

Greenfield, Stanley B. *A bibliography of publications on Old English literature, to the end of 1972: using the collections of E. E. Ericson.* Toronto; Buffalo: University of Toronto Press, 1980.

Grimes, Janet. *Novels in English by women, 1891-1920: a preliminary checklist.* New York, NY: Garland Publishing, 1981.

Harmon, Willliam; Holman, C. Hugh. *A handbook to literature.* 7th ed. Upper Saddle River, NJ: Prentice-Hall, 1996.

Harner, James L. *Literary research guide: a guide to reference sources for the study of literatures in English and related topics.* New York: Modern Language Association of America, 1993.

Ian Ousby (ed.). *The Cambridge guide to literature in English.* Revised Edition. Cambridge; New York: Cambridge University Press, 1993.

Messerli, Douglas. *Index to periodical fiction in English, 1965-1969.* Metuchen, NJ: Scarecrow Press, 1977.

Nicoll, Allardyce. *English drama, 1900-1930; the beginnings of the modern period.* New York: Cambridge University Press, 1973.

Perkins, David. *A history of modern poetry.* Cambridge, MA: Belknap Press of Harvard University Press, 1976-1987.

Rosa, Alfred F. *Contemporary fiction in America and England, 1950-1970: a guide to information sources.* Detroit, MI: Gale Research Co., 1976.

Stevenson, Lionel. *The history of the English novel: volume XI: yesterday and after.* New York: Barnes & Noble, 1967.

Wearing, J. P. *The London stage, 1890-1899: a calendar of plays and players.* Metuchen, NJ: Scarecrow Press, 1976. 2 v.

Index